The Silencing of Ruby McCollum

UNIVERSITY PRESS OF FLORIDA

Florida A&M University, Tallahassee
Florida Atlantic University, Boca Raton
Florida Gulf Coast University, Ft. Myers
Florida International University, Miami
Florida State University, Tallahassee
University of Central Florida, Orlando
University of Florida, Gainesville
University of North Florida, Jacksonville
University of South Florida, Tampa
University of West Florida, Pensacola

The Silencing of Ruby McCollum

Race, Class, and Gender in the South

Tammy Evans

Foreword by Jacqueline Jones Royster
Afterword by Lynn Worsham

University Press of Florida
Gainesville · Tallahassee · Tampa · Boca Raton
Pensacola · Orlando · Miami · Jacksonville · Ft. Myers

Copyright 2006 by Tammy Evans
Printed in the United States of America on recycled, acid-free paper
All rights reserved

11 10 09 08 07 06   6 5 4 3 2 1

A record of cataloging-in-publication data is available from
the Library of Congress.

ISBN 0-8130-2973-2

Photos are reproduced by permission of the author unless
otherwise noted.

The University Press of Florida is the scholarly publishing agency
for the State University System of Florida, comprising Florida
A&M University, Florida Atlantic University, Florida Gulf
Coast University, Florida International University, Florida State
University, University of Central Florida, University of Florida,
University of North Florida, University of South Florida, and
University of West Florida.

University Press of Florida
15 Northwest 15th Street
Gainesville, FL 32611-2079
http://www.upf.com

For my family and friends
for believing in me,
and for the people and places of my hometown
for giving me something to believe in.

We will have to repent in this generation not merely for the vitriolic words and actions of the bad people, but for the appalling silence of the good people.

—Dr. Martin Luther King Jr.
Letter from Birmingham Jail
April 16, 1963

Contents

. . . .

Tammy Evans is a daughter of the South, and in *The Silencing of Ruby McCollum: Race, Class, and Gender in the South*, she has researched and written a very southern story. She chronicles the 1952 murder trial of Ruby McCollum, an African-American woman in the small southern community of Live Oak, Florida. On the surface, the narrative is fairly ordinary rather than remarkable. A "crazy" forty-two-year-old African-American woman shoots and kills a prominent forty-four-year-old white doctor and state senate nominee, Dr. C. LeRoy Adams, for "no good reason." "Justice" is served. McCollum is convicted and sentenced to prison. The "no good reason," however, is Evans's story, and she tells it well, as only a good southern daughter—who has gathered some very special analytical tools, who has developed a perspective enriched by a knowledge of the intersecting axes of social, political, and economic power, and who has a deep love and respect for her home—might carefully, critically, and lovingly do.

In the introduction, Evans makes her ambitious intentions clear: "I aim to exemplify how dominant power and capital structures in the early

1950s South worked to protect southern myths regarding race, class, and gender, and, more specifically, how these longtime myths contributed to the fate of one woman." Her purpose is not to elevate McCollum to heroism, or to render in miscast twenty-first-century nostalgia the violence of McCollum's "dis-orderly" action, or even to expose the historical misdoings of a quiet southern town. I find that the most significant framework for understanding Evans's intentions is to see in this well-told tale that she defines the research/writing task in a way that permits the localized focus on the McCollum story to reach out in compelling and instructive ways beyond itself.

The Silencing of Ruby McCollum serves as an instrument for enlightenment and sociohistorical recovery, offering those of us who live now a more fully textured understanding of how critical resources can be brought to bear to gain knowledge of a self, a community, and a region that can ultimately be revelatory for a nation. In other words, this analysis not only meaningfully applies some pretty important terms of engagement—race, class, gender, and culture—to a 1950s story that took place in Live Oak, Florida, but also illustrates how this story speaks to a persistently troubled nation. *The Silencing of Ruby McCollum* becomes a parable for interrogating complex personal, social, and political relationships. As this statement suggests, seeing Evans's ambitious rhetorical intentions to render more vibrantly, and thereby to preserve more meaningfully, the historical importance of the McCollum case pushes readers to see larger implications. The core narrative of this analysis serves as a springboard by which Evans encourages readers to see more clearly the rhetorical nature of silence and to see how understanding its performative nature helps us to gain a better sense of the truths, shadows, and consequences of what it has meant in Live Oak, and by extension elsewhere, to turn the eyes, ears, mind, soul, and voice away from the sociopolitical hierarchies that surround us in sense making, history making, and knowledge building. Evans writes: "I am in dialogue with both McCollum's silent past and my own, and in the process I am becoming what Adrienne Rich describes as '*consciously* historical—that is, a person who tries for memory and connectedness against amnesia and nostalgia' (145). Here I aim to challenge silences that for far too long have gone unbroken."

By this approach, *The Silencing of Ruby McCollum* becomes more than simply a curious narrative of things left unsaid in the legal case of one African-American woman and, in turn, a generous effort on Evans's part to re-instantiate the fullness of McCollum's life and times. The account also becomes a display of values added to this storytelling/history-telling event through the mediation of theoretically well-grounded rhetorical analysis. It is, in fact, this scholarly dimension of *The Silencing of Ruby McCollum* that, in my view, is particularly instructive to those of us in rhetorical studies and cultural studies. Evans uses John Searle's theory of first and second speech acts and the work of other scholars who are interrogating the notion of silence as a performative speech act to suggest that silence is a "discursive, and consequently cultural, act." Positioning silence in the McCollum case as a performance that is vibrantly yoked to the spoken (the court records) and the written (earlier publications and the personal records of major parties in the case) performance draws critical attention to the constituent features of the processes and circumstances in McCollum's case that create the silence and make it work with such compelling force. Evans takes this approach not so much to just indict systems of oppression as to help readers see the dynamic intersections and interactions of power in American lives—even in her own.

Another important dimension of *The Silencing of Ruby McCollum*, especially with regard to its placement not just in rhetorical studies but in cultural studies as well, is the particular voice and body through which this analysis is rendered. Evans is a native of the South and indeed of Live Oak, Florida, itself. She is a white, post-1960s woman who grew up among the economic elite of this town. In this case, she has researched and written about an African-American woman in her own hometown, a story that she could have ignored. In not ignoring it, she accepts the obligation of engagement across social boundaries and the obligation of not letting herself—her race, gender, and culture—off the analytical hook. With this approach, Evans participates actively in the important work of raising a mirror to her own face, to the face of her home community, as well as to the face of our nation to enrich the critical, or perhaps more accurately, the noncritical perspectives that we have habitually held on such noble concepts as truth, justice, equality, and freedom.

What becomes evident via this particular narrative is the power of beliefs, the power of social hierarchies, the power of silence, and the critical roles of public narrative in the making and sustaining of institutionalized memory. Readers see that there was another Ruby McCollum that had more to her than the one historically encoded in the public narratives of U.S. law and literature. In all likelihood, there was a "truer" McCollum, a person who was not permitted to emerge in 1952. Having a mechanism for debarking the context, circumstances, and conditions of McCollum's life and actions helps a more fully textured view to emerge, such that we have, by contrast to the 1952 story, "good reason" to conclude that McCollum was neither poor nor uneducated, as stereotypes might lead one to presume, and that there also was a pretty good chance that she was neither mentally ill nor even out of control. Quite likely, as Evans's analysis claims, she was instead an unprivileged and highly constrained African-American woman whose voice got muted and whose circumstances got overwritten by the institutionalized silences that so thoroughly and completely surrounded her and rendered both the particular realities in her life and their social and political implications unsayable—by either McCollum or anyone else.

The most important point that I'd like to underscore about *The Silencing of Ruby McCollum* comes not from the Evans text itself but from the fact that, by coincidence, I am writing in the midst of the horrific accounts of Hurricane Katrina and its devastating effects on the Gulf Coast region. This 2005 drama that continues to unfold is also a story of the South. It is yet another case in which the nation's deeply ingrained dynamics of race, class, and gender give rise to public interpretations of events that fall in line with well-established patterns (for example, the focus on the "craziness" of Mother Nature as opposed to analysis that meaningfully engages with issues of race, class, and gender).

In 1952, the contours of the Ruby McCollum case were enveloped by silencing mechanisms of that era that contemporary theoretical frameworks make all too familiar to us today. However, in 2005, we are operating within our own, sometimes more subtle, versions of these very same mechanisms. The tragic stories of neglect and unresponsiveness that are emerging almost hourly from the Gulf Coast region demonstrate that so much in our contemporary lives and relationships remains just as deeply embedded within hierarchies of power as McCollum's case was over fifty years ago. In the Gulf Coast, we see the overwhelming evidence that the tragedies are about African-Americans rather than whites, and when they are about whites, they are overwhelmingly about ordinary and lower-class whites rather than affluent ones. We see that the impact of the devastation is keenly felt by women, children, and the elderly. The suffering, in fact, is inescapably heart-wrenching. We see the unmistakable consequence of not having the resources to evacuate an endangered area, and we see the equally unmistakable result of an affluent nation that has been interestingly slow (taking several days instead of what could have been hours) to respond to its own people—poor, black, infirm, and without status by various measures though they were.

Indeed, there is much resonance between the case of Ruby McCollum and the case of the Gulf Coast tragedies. While divided by a half century, they are nevertheless part of the whole cloth of race, class, and gender experiences that has been the story of many, many generations now in the United States. There is no question about whether the embedding of hierarchies of power around these issues continues. Clearly, it does. The only real question is whether we have learned enough to do anything that is substantially different with regard to the fates of the people who are caught in such webs.

Without a doubt, Evans and other scholars are giving more critical attention to our past and the residual forces of these histories. We understand more than we ever have about how past worlds were made and how the impacts and consequences of those composition processes have had and continue to have such compelling force. The excellence of this work, not only in rhetorical studies and cultural studies but in other fields as well, has given us something that was not available in 1952—an opportunity to break amazingly resounding silences. Just as Evans helps readers to see that *The Silencing of Ruby McCollum* is more than a sad and mysterious story, we now have the opportunity to see that recent Gulf Coast scenarios are more than unanticipated tragedies caused by unpredictable twists and turns of nature. With this moment of convergence between ongoing hierarchies and instructive theoretical frameworks, we have an occasion, and even an imperative, not to look away from material conditions and not to engulf the truths and consequences of those conditions in iron-clad silences but, alas, to face these challenges head-on, eye to eye, in order to take into account both the spoken and the powerfully unspoken, the said and the interestingly unsayable of our social, political, and cultural practices. With *The Silencing of Ruby McCollum,* and other works of this type (with Kevin Boyle's *Arc of Justice* being an excellent example), there is opportunity that we should not misuse.

Jacqueline Jones Royster
Professor of English
Ohio State University
September 1, 2005

Acknowledgments

· ·

This book would never have come to fruition without some very important people. First, I wish to thank my husband, Jack, and my son, Brian, for their patience and understanding during the many secluded hours I spent researching and writing this text. My sister, Jamie Hankinson, Esq., and her husband, Barry, deserve recognition for their tireless involvement at every step of this work and, most especially, I would like to thank Jamie for her invaluable input regarding the legal aspects of McCollum's case. Lynn Worsham, a scholar to whose caliber and character I aspire, was involved in this project since its inception, and it is entirely due to her that the end result is a book of which I am very proud. Jacqueline Jones Royster also provided valuable input regarding this project during its preliminary stages, and for that she has both my respect and gratitude. I would also like to thank Patty Stephens and Brant Helvenston IV, two dear, lifelong friends who provided humor, perspective, and a tireless listening ear. Thank you, Patty and Brant, for your involvement and enthusiasm, but most of all, thank you for your friendship. Special thanks also go to the Special Collections Department of the Ohio State University, specifically Geoffrey

Smith, Ph.D., Elva Griffith, and James Smith. Their care of the William Bradford Huie Papers and their willingness to assist me during every stage of this project led to both an immeasurably better book and a professional partnership that exemplifies the true nature of archival research. Special thanks also go to Martha Hunt Huie, a remarkable southern woman and kindred spirit who generously donated both her time and energy in the interest of me and this project. Excerpts from *Ruby McCollum: Woman in the Suwannee Jail* and the photograph of William Bradford Huie appear courtesy of M. H. Huie. The photograph of Ruby McCollum and the many excerpts I include in this text from the *Pittsburgh Courier* are reprinted by permission of GRM ASSOCIATES, INC., agents for the *Pittsburgh Courier*, from various issues of 1952 and 1953, ©1952, 1953, by the *Pittsburgh Courier*. I also especially appreciate the willingness of Arthur Ellis Jr. to share excerpts from a series of e-mails that passed between the two of us. His research into McCollum contributes to a long overdue body of scholarship that I hope will continue to grow. Like Dr. Ellis, Mr. Alvis Summers was very generous with his time, and I wish to thank him for sharing information about McCollum with me.

Finally, I wish to extend my gratitude to the Estate of Zora Neale Hurston, who extended its permission for me to quote extensively from her personal correspondence and to print Hurston's previously unpublished essay "My Impressions of the Trial." This material is used with the permission of the Estate of Zora Neale Hurston, and it is my fondest hope that in some small measure my book celebrates the remarkable voice of Hurston, a truly gifted woman writer. The NAACP, too, generously extended permission for me to quote excerpts from four letters connected with Harry T. Moore and the Willie James Howard case. The author wishes to thank the National Association for the Advancement of Colored People for authorizing the use of this material.

The epigraph for chapter 1 is from AS I LAY DYING by William Faulkner, copyright 1930 and renewed 1958 by William Faulkner. Used by permission of Random House, Inc. The epigraphs for both the introduction and the conclusion are from "Unsaid" and "Chaos Staggered Up the Hill" from COLLECTED POEMS 1951–1971 by A. R. Ammons. Copyright © 1972 by A. R. Ammons. Used by permission of W. W. Norton & Company, Inc.

Introduction

. . . .

Have you listened for the things I have left out?
I am nowhere near the end yet and already
>   *hear*
>   *the hum of omissions,*
the chant of vacancies, din of
silences

A. R. Ammons, "Unsaid," lines 1–6

On August 3, 1952, in the small community of Live Oak, Florida, a thirty-seven-year-old African-American housewife named Ruby McCollum shot and killed Dr. C. LeRoy Adams, a forty-seven-year-old white physician recently elected to the state senate and rumored to be a strong contender for the governorship.

Like most other small towns in the Deep South at the time of the murder, Live Oak was conservative in its politics and deeply committed in its faith. It was also strictly segregated, with black and white citizens alike knowing exactly what behavior was accepted and, more important, what behavior would not be tolerated. Of course, Adams's murder (a crime to which McCollum readily confessed) was heinous by any measure. According to firsthand accounts, the shooting was unprovoked, and since Adams was revered in Live Oak by both black and white citizens for his generosity and friendly nature, his murder caused an unprecedented backlash against McCollum. So intense was Live Oak's revulsion that immediately after the murder McCollum was transported for her own safety under armed guard to the state prison nearly fifty miles away in Raiford. Her subsequent trial was deliberate and swift; when the jury convened for the last time, she was found guilty of murder in the first degree and sentenced to death by electrocution. Two years later, however, McCollum was declared insane and spent many of the remainder of her years in Florida's state mental institution in Chattahoochee.

These are the widely publicized facts of the story of Ruby McCollum. They are well documented in newspaper and magazine accounts of the murder and in a best-selling book published in 1956 by William Bradford Huie, *Ruby McCollum: Woman in the Suwannee Jail*. More than fifty years after Adams's murder, the story is still an immovable touchstone in Live Oak. The town remains much as it was in 1952; elderly citizens who recall that hot August morning when McCollum killed one of Live Oak's most prominent and promising individuals are reluctant to discuss it. "Damn shame," most respond when questioned about the murder. "Ruby had no call to do what she done. But all that was a long time ago. Folks here have moved on." Such reticence is common, and considering the unwanted media spotlight trained on Live Oak immediately after Adams's murder and during McCollum's trial, perhaps it is to be expected. In 1952, outsiders were regarded with suspicion in Live Oak, and today they still are. To talk of Ruby McCollum is somehow vaguely impolite. The whole business was unseemly, and according to most people, "that McCollum mess" is best forgotten. It was an unpleasant event that resulted in unpleasant allegations, and in Live Oak some things are best left unsaid.

Because McCollum was allowed neither to fully tell her story in court nor to be interviewed during her long incarceration, exactly what happened in the days and hours prior to the murder will never be known. Notes and letters written by McCollum, however, allege years of mental and physical abuse she suffered at Adams's hand. For example, McCollum contends that on the day of the shooting she was pregnant with Adams's child and had previously given birth to another child fathered by him. Yet if McCollum was never allowed to tell her story, ample evidence attests to the fact that she desperately *wanted* to tell it: "I am praying that you will come in to see me so that I can tell you the whole story," she wrote to Huie in 1954 (McCollum, Notes). At that time, powerful legal and cultural codes in Live Oak prevented anyone from breaking McCollum's silence and—more important—sullying the "good name" of Adams, a white man.

Today more than fifty years of silence in Live Oak have dictated a sanitized "public" version of why McCollum murdered Adams—that is, if one can even find members of the community willing speak of the murder at all. Few will talk of McCollum, and if they do it is to denounce her. Racial tensions in the early 1950s taught individuals in Live Oak hard lessons about what happens to folks either black or white who speak out of turn. McCollum tried to do it, and she was committed to a mental institution. Huie tried to do it, and he was jailed for contempt of court. Zora Neale Hurston, then a reporter for the *Pittsburgh Courier*, tried to do it, and she fled the community in fear for her life. The national media tried to do it, and citizens closed their ranks with the unanimous refrain "no comment." Fear was the common denominator in all of these instances. Dredging up ugly accusations in 1952 about a white man murdered by a black woman was not only futile, it was dangerous.

This book examines the silencing of Ruby McCollum and the role of acts of silence in the preservation of a specific public memory in Live Oak and the South at large. By couching archival and other discursive formations in the context of this particular public memory, I aim to exemplify how dominant power and capital structures in the early 1950s South worked to protect southern myths regarding race, class, and gender, and, more specifically, how these longtime myths contributed to the fate of one woman. As is evident at every turn in the McCollum case, these myths were infinitely more precious than dollars, and as such they were protected and enforced at any price. They were the South's cultural capital—its raison d'être—and they were first and foremost defended by acts of silence.

Frank interrogation into the silencing of Ruby McCollum is particularly important because acts of silence are not exclusive to her, the early 1950s, or the southern United States. Cheryl Glenn, for example, writes in *Unspoken: A Rhetoric of Silence* that "current explorations into silence thus work to remind us of how much more we have to learn about women's and men's delivery of silence, especially when history, rhetoric, linguistics, politics, and culture offer us so many silent passages, some eventually (some never) spoken or heard" (xii). The case of Ruby McCollum is one such "silent passage." Long buried as a painful chapter in the South's history, her trial and conviction are particularly compelling reminders of both the dynamics of acts of silence and the high cost of failing to recognize the rhetorical power inherent in them. "Like speech," Glenn continues, "the meaning of silence depends on a power differential that exists in every rhetorical situation: who can speak, who must remain silent, who listens, and what those listeners can do" (9). For me to somehow manage to "forget" Ruby McCollum (as so many others before me have done) or to ignore acts of silence that occurred during her trial and conviction would consequently mean a surrender of my hard-won agency both as a woman and as a rhetorical scholar. Like it or not, *convenient* or not, the voice of Ruby McCollum resonates through my past, and this book is the result of my listening closely to acts of silence present in texts either written by or about her—texts that previously have been either ignored or radically undertheorized. The silencing of Ruby McCollum, then, is much more than an isolated moment in the South's history, and to view it as such is to miss the scope of important work already begun by Glenn and others. This book is presented, then, both as a long-overdue historical analysis of the silencing of Ruby McCollum and as a modern-day cautionary tale regarding the often underestimated power of acts of silence, whenever and wherever they may occur.

Cultural studies scholar Cary Nelson calls for "a return to rhetoric of a special historicized and politicized sort, rhetorical analysis that focuses on historically delineated struggles over meaning and form. Various sorts of texts and discourses would be studied in relation to one another within temporal frames" (224), and it is precisely Nelson's relational approach to history, politics, and language that I adopt in this book. Specific documents written either by or about McCollum exemplify race, class, and gender constructions that in the 1950s South worked to perpetuate longtime southern myths and preserve cultural capital. Taking into account both the "meaning" of these silences (their influence on McCollum, Live Oak, and the South) and their "form" (the manifestation of these silences by and in discursive formations) is my primary aim. Yet texts written about McCollum—whether newspaper articles, letters, or Huie's monograph—vary wildly in their representation of both her and the murder itself, and so it is often difficult to determine precisely where fact ends and fiction begins. J. Hillis Miller, however, reminds us that fiction "presupposes that the world may not be ordered in itself or, at any rate, that the social and psychological function of fictions is what speech-act theorists call 'performative.' A story is a way of doing things with words. It makes something happen in the real world" (69). By taking into account the *created* nature of texts generated by and about McCollum, I argue that acts of silence in the South have the dynamics of a linguistic speech act in three contexts: the town in which McCollum lived; her trial and imprisonment; and William Bradford Huie's 1956 text *Ruby McCollum: Woman in the Suwannee Jail*, which describes both Adams's murder and Live Oak's reaction to it. John Searle writes that "the task of a theory of performatives is to explain how the speaker can intend and the hearer can understand a second speech act from the making of the first speech act, the statement" (85). Acts of silence in the South, then, function much like Searle's performatives. The "second speech act" inherent in them—the power of silence's "statement" in various discourse communities to filter that which is determined to be true from that which is determined to be false and, consequently, censured—is, I argue, the force from which silence derives both its power and its stealth.

One way of conceptualizing this notion of silence as a performative speech act is through Kenneth Burke's theory of "dramatism," a five-part organizational strategy that "treats language and thought primarily as modes of action" (xxii). Burke argues that the elements of his pentad function in relation to one another; the positioning of any term, therefore, influences other terms relevant to the particular "scene" under discussion. In other words, as Burke writes, "What is involved when we say what people are doing and why they are doing it?" (xv). By identifying acts of silence as performative speech acts operating in specific contexts relating to McCollum, I aim to complicate Burke's question by asking, How do *acts of silence as modes of action* affect "what people are doing and why they are doing it?" Not even the most minor characters in the drama of Ruby McCollum are exempt from the ripple effect of silence. Patricia Yaeger, for example, writes that in the South "political power not only penetrates local bodies, it seeps through people who seem inconsequential and suggests the public logic behind their disarray" (240–41). An examination of local discourses informed by what happened in Live Oak on August 3, 1952, goes a long way toward answering the question of how acts of silence as modes of action function in texts informed by the case of Ruby McCollum. More important, however, these local silence-filled discourses can help us understand the "public logic" behind a much larger rhetorical politics of silence in the American South.

If acts of silence in the McCollum case perform "like a language," it is due in part to the fact that these silences are couched in rhetorical constructs that by their very nature are contingent and fluid. "The catchphrases 'like a language' and 'like a text,'" Nelson cautions, "need to be combined and historicized" (224). An analysis of archival texts both informing and informed by McCollum, then, is at once particularly necessary and difficult. "For our perceptions to become known to us," Nelson writes, "for us to be able to represent them to ourselves and others, they must be given linguistic form or its equivalent. . . . At the very least . . . cultural studies can take such linguistic representations *as* cultural artifacts rather than as reflections of the real" (216). In the case of McCollum, acts of silence manifest themselves in linguistic representations such as newspaper articles, letters, court documents, interviews, magazine articles, notes, and a monograph. But in spite of the diversity of these discursive formations, acts of silence evident in them are together indicative of cultural practices that—although in the case of Ruby McCollum are exemplified by specific acts of silence couched in specific historical texts—are not temporally exclusive to them. Consequently, this book aims to discuss texts surrounding the McCollum affair both as cultural artifacts within a specific historical framework *and* as linguistic acts that transcend time and contribute to a political, interested rhetoric of silence in the South and elsewhere.

In a letter dated January 31, 1955, the editor of Live Oak's weekly newspaper condemned the galley proofs that Huie sent to him of *Ruby McCollum*: "Throughout the book I note a desire to belittle the country I love. Naturally I resent this and to see untrue facts used to do this, irksome. There is no fear here as you picture; rather a calmness to be admired. . . . It is well to remember that Live Oak and Suwannee County will endure when Bill Huie . . . *The Woman in the Suwannee Jail* and every character therein have long been forgotten." At the time, this sense of righteous indignation regarding Huie's highly controversial book was typical of the reaction of other citizens in Live Oak as well, and an awareness of the complex subject-positioning of these individuals is necessary before attempting to interrogate acts of silence in which many were complicit. But of equal importance is my own interested position as a white woman, scholar, writer, archival researcher, and former resident of Live Oak.

I lived in Live Oak from my birth in 1959 until I moved away for good in 1982. My childhood resonates with the ghost of Ruby McCollum, and when I was a child, speaking of either her or Huie's book was strictly forbidden. My father was a physician in Live Oak from 1958 until his death in

1974, so perhaps it was fear for his professional standing in the community that made him and my mother so cautious. Or, just as likely, perhaps my parents chose to believe what they were told when they moved to Live Oak as newlyweds: Adams's murder was an unfortunate, isolated incident out of keeping with the town's usual monotony. A native southerner from Tennessee, my mother, I'm sure, knew differently. I'm equally sure that my father, born and raised in Indiana (at the time, a state with a burgeoning Ku Klux Klan membership), did too. Yet the fact remains that neither they nor anyone else I knew ever raised questions about the McCollum case. So thoroughly was inquiry concerning McCollum discouraged that only recently did I acquire Huie's text. Most of the people and places mentioned in the book I know well, but in contrast to Huie's emphasis on the *masculinity* of Live Oak, it is the women I most vividly recall when I think of the town. I remember the brush of their white-gloved hands on the top of my head as I clung to my mother's skirts after church services on Sunday mornings; the lull of their voices as my sister and I napped in beds tall and stately as wedding cakes in their spare rooms; the lemon scent of their heavy, coiled hair; the cheerful glint of diamonds on their ears, throats, and fingers; and, most of all, their effortless grace. Of course, there were men, too. Tall, booming men who fussed over me and called me "Sugar," who smoked cigars, killed rattlesnakes, and went to Jaycee meetings. But my recollections of these men come not without effort, and I am struck by the contrast. Huie's book describes my hometown as a place ruled by unscrupulous men and riddled with racism, violence, and hypocrisy. And I don't quarrel with his description; even as a child I sensed powerful enforced dichotomies among black and white, male and female, rich and poor. What compels me to write about McCollum, however, is the lack of attention southern studies scholars have paid to the influence of these dichotomies on her and the fact that today they continue to perpetuate acts of silence on local, national, and international levels.

Acts of silence are not accidental or arbitrary; they are carefully taught. For example, women in Live Oak taught me everything I know of loveliness, and for most of my childhood, loveliness was all I knew. Only now, afforded time and distance, do I begin to understand the complex dynamics of race, class, and gender in the construction of this loveliness and, more important, the silences that worked to prevent exposure of its ugly underside. In her foreword to *Killers of the Dream*, a recollection and analysis of her southern upbringing, Lillian Smith contends that, for her, the act of writing the book was generative as well as reflexive: "I was in dialogue with myself as I wrote," she writes, "as well as with my hometown and my childhood and history and the future, and the past. Writing is both horizontal and vertical exploration. It has to true itself with facts but also with feelings and symbols, and memories that are never quite facts but sometimes closer to the 'truth' than is any fact" (13). Smith's text details acts of silence that dominated her childhood in Jasper, Florida, a town adjacent to Live Oak and virtually identical to it in terms of population, race, and economics. Like Smith's *Killers of the Dream*, my own text is also necessarily overwritten by the temporal framework of the many years I lived in Live Oak and my day-to-day existence as a white woman. This book, then, is a dialectic both with and against memory—a dialectic that takes place in the complex, overlapping temporal space of the past and the present.

The same silences that shaped my childhood were particularly acute for Ruby McCollum. In the early 1950s, both Ruby's gender and her race dictated that she observe specific rules of silence. But by the same token, McCollum was different from other African-Americans who lived in Live Oak and, for that matter, most of the whites. McCollum and her husband, Sam, were wealthy. Together they managed a highly profitable bolita gambling ring that was rumored to net thousands of dollars in cash each week. Her home was arguably one of the finest in Suwannee County, and she consistently dressed in stylish clothes purchased during her frequent shopping trips to nearby Jacksonville. Her son, Sam Jr., attended college, and her three daughters lacked for nothing. It was not, however, Sam and Ruby's wealth that threatened the code of southern silence. After all, since many citizens in Live Oak speculated that Sam and Ruby were careful to pay off Live Oak's key law enforcement officials, silence worked to everyone's advantage. What, then, *did* threaten the citizens of Live Oak to the extent that the community created a virtual vacuum around McCollum after her arrest and during her trial? If she were truly, according to public opinion, a deranged woman who shot Adams in an inexplicable fit of anger, why was it necessary to so thoroughly sequester her? Didn't the facts speak plainly enough for themselves? What more could McCollum possibly have said to justify the elaborate ruse of her repeatedly touted "fair trial"? Why so much trouble and expense to keep one so-called crazy nigger woman quiet? These are important questions, and they beg to be answered. I'm sure McCollum well understood her expected function as scenic backdrop in a southern drama dominated by men. More than anything else, the fact that she chose to challenge this role led to her demise.

In similar fashion, I now recognize that my own lack of memories about men during my years in Live Oak is not, as I once supposed, due to the power women had over the shaping of my life. Instead, it is due entirely to the power men had over the shaping of women. Perhaps this unspoken masculine authority is one reason why women in the South cling so tightly to one another. We recognize our mutual invisibility. Such recognition is silent by decree, or, more accurately, it materializes in a unique form of *verbal* silence: a complex tapestry of polite conversation tightly woven around topics of church, home, and children. To publicly speak of other less pleasant things is to step out of character, and to step out of character in Live Oak in 1952 risked jeopardizing the validity of an entire community's performance.

Even the cool objectivity supposedly afforded me by scholastic discourse and authoritative secondary sources does not entirely quiet the admonitions I hear as I write this page. "Oh, honey, don't say *that*," my long-dead mother murmurs just over my shoulder. "What will people think? Remember, pretty is as pretty does." The phrase was the mantra of my childhood, and today it haunts me still. When I was a girl, I thought it meant that if my actions were "pretty" and conformed to the rules of Christianity and society, then, in turn, I would be "pretty," an upright individual with an established sense of place. However, in light of my study of acts of silence surrounding the McCollum affair, I now realize that the phrase actually exemplifies pervasive fictionalizing processes at work in my upbringing. In other words, if I choose to ignore ugly inequities in southern culture and the silences they generate, then the reality I *fictionalize for myself* will remain uncluttered with voices I am not prepared to hear or understand. The fact, for example, that McCollum and I are both women is where our similarities end. As an African-American, McCollum lived a segregated existence with which I cannot possibly claim to identify. For me to do so would be the ultimate act of reductionism and self-importance. My choice to engage in this project, therefore, could be construed as motivated by racial arrogance. My presumption to construct yet *another* coherent textual narrative about McCollum—one that is, at best, three times removed from McCollum herself, could be viewed as a careful paring away of McCollum's complicated existence as a black woman to fit the confines of what I understand: life within a white skin. Like Huie's book, Hurston's newspaper articles, and transcripts of McCollum's trial, my position in this book is by necessity one of "storyteller of stories told about Ruby McCollum," and like all storytellers, what I choose to include and what I choose to silence in my narrative radically complicates the finished tale.

It is no small irony that in spite of what I contend to be an undertow of silence in the South, the region has long been steeped in narrative, what Fred Hobson in *Tell about the South* describes as "the southern rage to explain" (3). Similarly, much of the text produced about the McCollum affair is testimony to a desperate need for the community to explain Adams's murder and to rationalize why the act (and acceptance) of the explanation itself were so important. This need to account for the actions of Ruby McCollum is indicative of Hobson's contention that "the Southerner, more than other Americans, has felt he *had* something to explain, to justify, to defend, or to affirm." If Hobson's assertion holds true of the citizens of Live Oak involved in the McCollum case, what exactly *did* the community so desperately want "to explain, to justify, to defend, or to affirm" (3)? And why, in spite of the flurry of texts written about the case, do so many questions remain? Contemporaneous accounts of McCollum's actions relayed in newspaper articles, transcripts of McCollum's two trials, and Huie's monograph are, therefore, of much less importance than what is discarded, or silenced, within them. In addition, private texts written by McCollum to family members, friends, and her attorneys; letters and anonymous notes written by citizens of Live Oak to Huie; and notes taken by Hurston during McCollum's trial reveal multiple competing discourses informing accounts of the McCollum affair. Most of these competing discourse communities are grounded in Live Oak—a place publicly united in its condemnation of McCollum, yet one I argue to be privately fragmented by fear, divided by race, and silenced by enforcement. An analysis of the process of "telling" about McCollum—the construction of meaning about her through text—is an important step toward understanding how silence influences discourse and culture. Moreover, such analysis moves forward discussions concerning the South's mysterious autonomy, a unity that remains undeniable in spite of the region's long history of internal racial difference and economic inequities.

Celeste Condit writes that historical narratives "should be treated by critical scholars as meaning-full. . . . Because the past is materially present in the languages and institutions in which we live, and which we seek to alter, and because history is our language about that past's presence, history must be struggled over" (178). Therefore, if I cannot ever fully identify with McCollum, I *can* examine the process of my own textual construction of her and argue that acts of silence in my text and others are both the site of struggle and symptomatic of it. By way of contextualizing McCollum and the community in which she lived, chapter 1 thus establishes the racial climate of Live Oak, Florida, in 1952 and locates this specific southern community in the larger context of the American South. In addition, this chapter addresses issues that I as a scholar and archival researcher have grappled with during the course of my writing and research. At the onset of this project, my aim was to somehow "objectively" discuss Ruby McCollum, yet my interested position as a white southern woman and native of Live Oak made such "objectivity" elusive. And even if it *were* possible to learn the definitive "truth" about McCollum through an examination of texts written by and about her, the contingency of history and language placed me in double jeopardy if I attempted to convey it. As a result, my first chapter argues the *textual* nature of the South by historicizing the role of silence in the region and locating Live Oak and the South in what I argue to be a long tradition of southern storytelling and myth-making practices perpetuated by discourse. Moreover, acts of violence committed in Live Oak before, during, and after Adams's murder are indicative of strong efforts by members of specific discourse communities to enforce and protect these myths. Gender and class formations in place in Live Oak in 1952 particularly worked to justify violence against individuals not inclined to adopt a specific "public" memory of McCollum and Adams. Because McCollum's actions threaten multiple southern myths and the cultural capital they protect, chapter 1 complicates the publicized "facts" of Adams's murder and the community's desperate struggle to avoid publicity and outside interference immediately after McCollum's arrest. More important, however, this chapter identifies silence as a vital force in broad southern myth-making and capital systems that inform the actions of Ruby McCollum, the community of Live Oak, and the South as a whole in the early 1950s.

Chapter 2 grounds the South in what I view to be two dominant discursive formations—religion (the word of God) and law (the word of man). Although many southern studies scholars acknowledge these primary discourses, most fail to address the dynamics of silence within them. In the context of these discursive formations, I provide a discussion of the trials of Ruby McCollum and introduce William Bradford Huie's and Zora Neale Hurston's involvement in her case. Court transcripts, notes written by McCollum, newspaper accounts of her trial, and letters written by McCollum's family and attorneys provide evidence that events informing McCollum's arrest and imprisonment are dominated by acts of silence fueled by specific power structures and southern myths. These acts of silence, first, ensured that McCollum's murder of Adams (and its explicit challenge to white authority) was loudly and publicly condemned and, second, conceal profound traumas McCollum may have privately suffered during her term in the Suwannee County Jail. I argue that during the process of McCollum's trial, legal machinery in place in Live Oak constructed contradictory "public" and "private" versions of the law. In other words, while the judicial system in Live Oak publicly asserted that McCollum deserved (and got) an impartial, scrupulously fair trial, this chapter aims to show that legal proceedings surrounding McCollum were often carefully scripted. Such scripting includes, but is not limited to, McCollum's alleged "miscarriage" during her incarceration, the refusal of the court to admit Loretta (the eighteen-month-old child that McCollum contended was fathered by Adams) into evidence, and multiple objections (sustained by the judge) to attempts by McCollum's attorneys to disclose what Mc-Collum described as Adams's abusive tendencies toward her in the years prior to his murder. Live Oak's black population was particularly mindful of silences tacitly sanctioned and enforced through legal channels, yet the predominately white media and judicial system in Live Oak loudly protested otherwise. Zora Neale Hurston's coverage of McCollum's trial for the *Pittsburgh Courier*, for example, stresses Hurston's awareness of her own precarious positioning as an African-American woman during her stay in segregated Live Oak, and although (or because) he was white, Huie encountered particular difficulties of his own with the town's legal system. Text is the common weapon McCollum, Hurston, and Huie used to combat these silences, yet for all three individuals—McCollum in particular—the fight in most cases proved futile, and in all cases, dangerous.

Chapter 3 furthers the discussion of Huie's involvement in the McCollum affair and his complicated partnership with Zora Neale Hurston. By referencing letters Huie received from residents of Live Oak concerning *Ruby McCollum* and newspaper accounts of his arrest for contempt of court while he was writing the book, I argue that Huie's text—the only inclusive account of the McCollum affair—is perhaps necessarily shaped by acts of silence. This chapter also provides an extensive discussion of Hurston's *Pittsburgh Courier* articles concerning McCollum and how Hurston's positioning as a black woman in 1950s Live Oak proved particularly complex. Letters Hurston wrote to Huie offer perhaps the best examples of Hurston's precarious stance in terms of both Live Oak's black community and her professional relationship with Huie. In spite of her best efforts, Hurston was largely unsuccessful in persuading African-Americans in Live Oak to break their silence concerning McCollum. As a white man, Huie had more luck. However, as I discovered many times during the course of my research, any text claiming to provide "the truth" about Ruby McCollum, her relationship with Dr. Adams, and the community of Live Oak at large is by necessity highly fictionalized. Questions regarding authorial "intent" permeate discourses informed by the McCollum affair, and as this chapter illustrates, Huie's and Hurston's texts are especially problematic.

Since the purpose of this book is not to "solve" the McCollum murder mystery (although I admit the prospect is intriguing), the conclusion emphasizes the value of theorizing present-day acts of silence and the implications of such intellectual work for cultural, political, feminist, and rhetorical scholars. Using the groundwork previously set forth regarding the power of silence to both initiate and withhold personal agency, this portion of the book presents several more recent high-profile instances in which acts of silence either continue to perpetuate race, class, and gender inequities (such as the Margaret Mitchell Trust suit and the École Polytechnique massacre) or instances in which longtime, suppressive silences are, at last, in the process of being broken (such as the reopening of investigations into the murders of Harry T. Moore and Emmett Till and the recent conviction of Edgar Ray Killen for the murders of three civil-rights workers in 1964). Moreover, the conclusion discusses the silence-filled death and burial of Ruby McCollum, a woman who left this world in much the same way that she lived in it: surrounded by unanswered questions and cloaked in impermeable silence.

Smith contends that the act of writing is transformative: "The writer transcends her material in the act of looking at it, and since part of that material is herself, a metamorphosis takes place. *Something happens within*: a new chaos, and then slowly, a new being" (14). Throughout this book I argue that acts of silences in the South similarly *transform acts of writing about McCollum*. Because silence functions as a speech act in the South, it is dynamic, recursive, and infinitely contingent; in texts informed by Adams's murder, these acts of silence—like words—attempt to create order out of chaos, at once imposing certainty and raising doubt about McCollum and the community in which she lived. Over fifty years have passed since that quiet Sunday morning when, for whatever reason, McCollum found the silence in Live Oak deafening and decided to break it. Perhaps she shot Adams because she could no longer endure what she alleged had become a relentless cycle of physical and mental abuse. Or perhaps she was, as Huie writes in *Ruby McCollum*, merely "an irate Negress enraged over a bill for medical charges" (45). In any event, Smith is correct: the act of writing about her has caused a transformation in me of sorts. I am in dialogue with both McCollum's silent past and my own, and in the process I am becoming what Adrienne Rich describes as "*consciously* historical—that is, a person who tries for memory and connectedness against amnesia and nostalgia" (145). Here I aim to challenge silences that for far too long have gone unbroken, and somehow I know that Ruby McCollum—and all of us—deserve at least that much.

one　"words and doing"

. . . .

The Politics of Silence in Southern Rhetoric

I would think how words go straight up in a thin line, quick
and harmless, and how terribly doing goes along the earth,
clinging to it, so that after a while the two lines are too far apart
for the same person to straddle from one to the other.

William Faulkner, *As I Lay Dying*

MOST ACCOUNTS OF the day Ruby McCollum shot Dr. C. LeRoy Adams invariably mention two Live Oak landmarks: the First Methodist Church and the Suwannee County Courthouse. In 1956, for example, William Bradford Huie described the shooting in *Ruby McCollum: Woman in the Suwannee Jail*: "The shots were fired in the doctor's office across the street from the Suwannee County courthouse and jail," he wrote. "They were fired within eighty yards of the white Methodist church, and the first shot came at the instant the white Methodists began taking communion" (21). Jack Harper, a reporter for the *Tallahassee Democrat*, also noted the murder's close proximity to the church and the courthouse. In his 1973 retrospective "News of Famous Killing First Heard from Pulpit," he wrote that the shooting "was announced from the pulpits of the town's churches," and that after the murder "a crowd of towns people and farmers were milling about the courthouse grounds" (39). Even today, over fifty years after McCollum catapulted Live Oak into the national media spotlight, the church and the courthouse continue to figure prominently in recollections of August 3, 1952. "We were in church," one Live Oak resident said when I asked him and his wife to recall the day of the shooting, "the Methodist church, right across the street from the courthouse."

If the Methodist church and the Suwannee County Courthouse are included in most descriptions of what happened in Live Oak on August 3, 1952, it is perhaps because religion and law have traditionally bolstered not only the community of Live Oak but also its larger framework: the American South. In 1952, Live Oak was a small, rather picturesque town, and today it retains many of the same characteristics described by Stephen Trumbull, staff writer for the *Miami Herald*. "Live Oak, Suwannee County," he wrote in 1954, "is more small-town-South than anything ever dreamed up for *Gone With the Wind* or *The Birth of a Nation*. It's picture book stuff, with long, grey beards of Spanish moss draping the trees, plus magnolias in the background." Trumbull's choice of words is telling. His headline reads, "Live Oak Drama Like Fiction," and indeed what happened that memorable August morning does seem incongruous to its setting—an act of unprecedented evil completely out of place in the snug confines of a law-abiding, Christian community like Live Oak. Yet the story *is* real, and it is made all the more so by McCollum defiantly choosing to pull the trigger that ended Adams's life in the shadow of the Methodist church and the Suwannee County Courthouse, both symbols of Live Oak's permanence and order that seldom, if ever, had been publicly challenged prior to August 3.

The setting of the murder, a quiet southern town, and the fact that a black woman had shot and killed a prominent white man made Live Oak and McCollum famous overnight. McCollum's arrest and conviction created a media frenzy comparable only to that generated by the trials of O. J. Simpson and Michael Jackson, and accounts of it covered the front pages of newspapers nationwide. Reporters from around the United States crowded into tiny Live Oak, and with them came decidedly un-Christian allegations that Adams had fathered McCollum's youngest child. With all the media attention, residents of Live Oak were nervous. Their little town, formerly a quiet sanctuary characterized by good Christian living and southern civility, was increasingly being depicted in the press as a stranger to both.

There is no denying that McCollum broke the law that Sunday morning she murdered Adams, but she did not act without a sense of justice; it was justice by her own definition. And if she was not physically in church that day, I am convinced that when she methodically pulled the trigger she looked—on her own terms—full on the face of God. There is, then, more than one story line informing the events of August 3, 1952, and McCollum herself is actually only part of a much larger drama, a longtime southern mythology dominated by acts of silence and often enforced by fear. Of course, McCollum's actions in the summer of 1952 were wildly out of character for a black woman in a small southern town. The fact that she shot Adams, in effect, turned on the houselights in Live Oak in midperformance and left the community scrambling to regain its composure in the unexpected glare of intense media scrutiny. For her error, McCollum was summarily tossed out of the production, placed in isolation, and all but forgotten. From the very beginning, however, McCollum realized that the murder of white man by a black woman did not fit into what she knew to be her reality. Huie writes in *Ruby* that when McCollum was asked why she killed Adams, she didn't answer directly. Instead she replied, "I don't know whether I did right or not" (26). Like most citizens of Live Oak in 1952, McCollum undoubtedly knew the importance of "doing right"; laws both written and unwritten made certain that what was "right" was clearly scripted for both blacks and whites in Live Oak.

If the story of Ruby McCollum seems like fiction, then perhaps it is because the process of "doing right" in the South is itself the product of larger fictionalizing practices. McCollum broke two cardinal rules the day she ended Adams's life, one public and one private. First, she committed murder, a legal and religious taboo, for which she was swiftly and with much fanfare brought to justice. Second, and in many ways more threatening to the community than the murder itself, she exposed to the rest of the world the complex and often contradictory process of "doing right" in the South. Silence is a crucial part of this process, especially in terms of Live Oak's delicately balanced race relations that, although on the surface they appeared calm in 1952, were the result of strict and often violent enforcement. McCollum is exceptional because as a black woman she acted against the rules of "doing right" when she murdered a prominent white physician. But—and this is the point—the *reaction* of the community of Live Oak to the murder is as revealing as the murder itself. After the shooting, city officials and ordinary citizens alike rallied to justify their handling of the McCollum case. McCollum, however, was actually of secondary concern to Live Oak. Much more pressing to the townspeople was the justification and protection of the myth of white supremacy, a regional fiction so revered that when the actions of one black woman threatened to challenge its validity, an entire community became mute and perhaps has not yet regained its voice.

In *Ruby*, Huie describes McCollum's arrest by members of the police force, sheriff's office, and highway patrol. "And here the irony begins," he writes. "These men represented the state of Florida, the county of Suwannee, the city of Live Oak. They were guardians of the society of Suwannee County. Ruby had broken the law, defied the society. Yet these men were afraid, not of Ruby but of consequences of her act. They were afraid of what might 'come out' at a trial. They feared collective 'embarrassment'" (26). More than anything else, these men and the greater population of Live Oak resented possible outside intervention in the white-based autonomy of their community—and an entire region—governed by silence and enforced by fear. So the question remains: Did Ruby McCollum "do right" when she took the law into her own hands and murdered a white man whom she asserted had repeatedly raped and beaten her over a period of six years? If to "do right" means to remain silent about practices that are wrong, then the answer is no, she did not. But a much more compelling question is, Did McCollum have *the right to do* what she did, and if so, why was the community of Live Oak so terrified at the possibility of publicly admitting so?

This chapter aims to present the story (or, rather, several different versions of the same story, depending on who is doing the telling) of Ruby McCollum and the events of August 3, 1952. Central to this act of telling is a discussion of Live Oak—a tightly knit community heavily influenced by the larger framework of the American South. Therefore, in order to begin to understand McCollum, one must also understand her positioning in both the small community of Live Oak and the larger community of the southern states as a whole. Or more precisely, one must appreciate how in 1952 McCollum did *not* fit the expectations set forth for an African-American woman in a segregated, deeply conservative southern town. Discourses written about McCollum reveal much about the definition and enforcement of what was "right" in Live Oak and the South at large in the early 1950s. Yet as important as these discourses are, they are actually indicative of a larger cultural language: the all-encompassing rhetoric of southern silence.

Silence in the South is like a shimmering mirage that hovers in the distance over a blacktop country road; it is always there, yet at the same time it is impervious to close inspection. As a child in Live Oak, I thought that if only I could run fast enough, I could reach that place where the road met the horizon. Many times I picked a marker immersed in the magical waves—a fence post, a tall pine, a weathered tobacco barn—and ran toward it. But always when I reached my landmark, it would have lost its bewitching shimmer and stand solid and impermeable against the blue summer sky. The dynamics of southern silence, and particularly acts of silence informing the McCollum affair, work in much the same way. Time has worked its magic, and August 3, 1952, has largely faded from memory. Citizens of Live Oak are now over fifty years down the road from the infamous day McCollum killed Adams. The journalists have long since gone, and her trial, accounts of which were once front-page news from coast to coast, has for the most part been forgotten. The site of the murder no longer stands; Adams's office was torn down long ago to make way for a neat row of shops. Even the Suwannee County Hospital where Adams practiced is gone, recently replaced by a more modern facility of which the residents of Live Oak are especially proud. The Methodist church and the Suwannee County Courthouse, however, remain today much as they were in 1952. They are solid reminders of what is important in this small town and testimony to the convictions of its citizens. But also still standing is the former home of Ruby McCollum. It is difficult to find; tall stands of bamboo and vines weave a nearly impermeable wall around the perimeter, as if the house itself is attempting to discourage prying eyes. Once described as one of the finest homes in the county, it is now wildly overgrown. Thick ropes of wisteria drape its tightly shuttered windows, and its once regal yellow stucco has faded to ochre. Sam Jr., McCollum's son, still owns the house. He is now in his seventies and never speaks of his mother or what happened that August morning when he was nineteen years old. And while most days the Methodist church and the Suwannee County Courthouse are teeming with activity, the McCollum home is always silent.

In 1952, according to Zora Neale Hurston, silence characterized Live Oak. She writes of "a smothering blanket of silence" she found typical during her stay in the community while covering the McCollum trial for the *Pittsburgh Courier*:

> Some conformed by a murmuration of evasions, some by a frontal attack that this was something which it would not be decent to allow the outside world to know about, and others by wary wordlessness.
>
> It amounted to a mass delusion of mass illusion. A point of approach to the motive for the slaying of the popular medico and politician had been agreed upon, and however bizarre and unlikely it might appear to the outside public, it was going to be maintained and fought for. Anything which might tend to destroy this illusion must be done away with. Presto! It just did not exist. ("My Impressions")

Acts of silence surrounding McCollum surface again in the January 14, 1980, follow-up piece that journalist Al Lee wrote for Florida's *Ocala Star-Banner*. When Lee questioned Suwannee County sheriff Robert Leonard about the murder, Leonard responded, "To tell you the truth, it's a thing of the past," and Live Oak police chief Elwood Howard answered in kind: "Why it's all but forgotten. You don't hardly hear anything about it around here now. I never hear it mentioned any more." Even McCollum herself had little to say: "Ruby McCollum is unable to remember the shooting incident, the trial, or her term in jail," Lee wrote. "She does not deny that one of her three daughters—Loretta—was fathered by the doctor. She will not confirm it, either. To that question, she rests her chin on folded hands, stares ahead through a pair of shades, and remains stoically silent. The question goes unanswered" ("Animosity"). Since Lee's interview, little has been written about McCollum to break these kinds of silences, and my several visits to Live Oak during the course of this project only confirmed what I already knew: Live Oak continues to downplay or outright ignore Ruby McCollum. She is no longer, for the most part, an anomaly, or, as many asserted in 1952, a monster. Instead, she is becoming something much worse. For most people she is now not even a memory.

The story of McCollum has always vacillated between fact and fiction, and since the events of August 3, 1952, have never been clear, the lack of certainty regarding exactly what happened that hot summer day seems somehow apt. But, as Harry Crews writes, the South is a place where fantasy and reality often overlap in practices of narration: "Nothing is allowed to die in a society of storytelling people," he writes. "It is all—the good and the bad—carted up and brought along from one generation to the next. And everything that is brought along is colored and shaped by those who bring it" (21). If stories of Ruby McCollum are shaped by those who tell them, one point of reference remains unaltered from one story to the next: all are, in the end, stories of silence. These silences may serve to distort, conceal, or even outright repudiate McCollum, but the one thing they cannot do is eradicate the fact that Live Oak and Ruby McCollum are inextricably linked. As much as the community of Live Oak would like to believe otherwise, McCollum remains a significant point of reference on the complex road of both the town and the South's history. The Methodist church and the Suwannee County Courthouse may stand as public testament to Live Oak's ability to endure, but McCollum's home, although cloaked in vines and its edges softened by years of rain and neglect, also stands. It may be more difficult to find than either the church or the courthouse, but it is there—one has only to know where to look.

"So Much Wrong, and It Seemed Right"

Live Oak is located midway between Tallahassee and Jacksonville, Florida, along Interstate 10, a major artery that cuts a wide swath through the state. Live Oak benefits from Interstate 10's proximity; like most other exits in Florida, the one in Live Oak boasts an obligatory McDonald's restaurant, popular with locals after Suwannee High School football games and weary travelers making the trek to Disney World. In 1952, however, the area where McDonald's now stands was populated only by pine, scrub oak, and a few scattered cattle. Interstate 10 did not exist, and even if it had, few residents of Suwannee County traveled far from home. Among the four thousand citizens who lived in and around Live Oak in 1952, cash was scarce and needed for items that could not be scratched out of backyard gardens or made by hand, such as children's shoes and coffee. What little money there was to be made in Live Oak came almost exclusively from agriculture: watermelons, corn, and especially tobacco. Suwannee County's porous, sandy soil and abundant sunshine and generous summer rains resulted in tobacco known throughout the South for its high quality and distinctive color. But nature is fickle. Too much (or too little) rain, an infestation of cutworms, or an unseasonably cool spell could, and often did, spell disaster for the farmer who relied on tobacco for his livelihood. Some years prices paid on the open market were high; other years they were precariously low. In August 1952, the height of tobacco season in Live Oak, growers were optimistic. The long warehouses teemed with buyers who walked the rows of tobacco laid out for inspection. Auctioneers rattled off bids, and money changed hands. As always, it was an important, busy time. It was a time, Huie writes in *Ruby*, "when most everybody has some money and therefore might be expected to feel less frustrated, less inclined toward mutilation" (19).

When Sam McCollum, a handsome black man with distinctive grey eyes, moved his family to segregated Live Oak in 1937, he had few legitimate options. Jobs were scarce, and he wanted better odds than those of a hand-to-mouth tobacco farmer. Born in Zuber, Florida, near Ocala, he was poor when he, his wife, Ruby, and their four-year-old son, Sam Jr., settled in Live Oak. But by August 1952, Sam was rich by the standards of most everyone in Live Oak. He had the reputation of a man ambitious by nature and necessity. Both he and Ruby liked expensive things; they also had a son in college, three young daughters, and a new baby on the way. But Sam's wealth was no accident. He was a cautious man not given to taking chances, and when he came to Live Oak he knew that the farming game was far too precarious to ever be really profitable. What he needed was a sure-fire win, and he found it in bolita.

Although illegal, bolita rings were common in many Florida communities in the early 1950s, and Live Oak was no exception. Similar to today's lottery, the game originated in Cuba, with players paying for the chance to "hit" a particular number on a wheel or a combination drawn from a bag filled with numbered balls. "Bolita Sam," as McCollum was known in Live Oak, did not play the game himself—a much too risky venture. Instead, he established and controlled it, and by 1952 he was averaging thousands of dollars each week in profits. That year not only was Sam rich, he was becoming famous. The *Tampa Tribune*, for example, ran the following piece on January 16, 1952:

> This land of Stephen Foster and the storied Suwannee River is in the grips of a bold and flourishing numbers racket and the good people of the county are becoming alarmed. . . . [This is] one of the "gamblingest" counties in Florida. . . .

8

. . .

The
Silencing
of Ruby
McCollum

The kingpin of Bolita operations in Live Oak's Negro district is Samuel C. McCollum of 328 Wood Street.

McCollum, who resembles Amos of the Amos and Andy radio team, lives in a big, two-story house surrounded by a trim brick fence. A two-car garage houses his new sedans. Unlike some other gamblers he does not maintain a respectable business as a "front." There is no other visible means of support.

Two of his chief lieutenants, however, do operate legitimate businesses. William Manker . . . owns a fleet of taxicabs, while Charles Hall . . . is a Negro undertaker. . . . Peddlers maintain regular routes through both white and Negro districts.

Why, then, if bolita was illegal in Suwannee County and clearly frowned upon, was McCollum not arrested and his business shut down? One answer lies in an April 18, 1952, editorial published in Live Oak's weekly newspaper, the *Suwannee Democrat*, which states that not only was bolita still being played, but that "the amount played has increased considerably," and, as a result, so had the number of lucrative kickbacks to individuals in positions of power who allegedly funded the operation. "Law enforcement officers are given new cars, weekly payoffs or other compensation to close their eyes," the editorial contends. If the *Democrat* is correct, powerful individuals in Live Oak looked the other way because Sam made it extremely profitable to do so. As a racketeer, and in particular a *Negro* racketeer, McCollum could not afford to lose the goodwill of these powerful white men. Both groups, in short, needed the other. McCollum's bolita ring generated a great deal of easy money; shutting down Sam's operation not only would hurt him and his "writers," it would also dry up a significant source of revenue for powerful city officials who, like Sam, had families to support.

Ruby, Sam's wife, enjoyed the material goods and social status that bolita profits provided. She shopped often in Jacksonville and always at the best stores. Her home was well appointed, and her children lacked for nothing. Ruby was a smart and ambitious woman, and before marrying Sam she had graduated from the Fessenden Academy north of Ocala, one of the best high schools in the state, where she trained to become a teacher. She was not, however, a beautiful woman, and in the few photographs of her available, her face is broad and plain. Yet her eyes, her best feature, are alert and inquisitive. If, as one Live Oak resident remembers, "Ruby was certainly no Lena Horne," what McCollum lacked in striking beauty she more than made up for in intelligence. She was Sam's confidant after their marriage, and, more important, she was his business partner; she kept his books and looked after the details of his many interests.

In addition to bolita, Sam owned and operated several "jukes" (small bars), tobacco allotments, and rental properties. Ruby was responsible for keeping track of the money and keeping Sam's life tidy and free from distractions. She was by all accounts a "good wife." Her house was neat, and her children were clean and well fed. But in spite of Ruby's money and keen intelligence, or perhaps because of them, she was especially sensitive to her limitations as a woman and a Negro. In August 1952, she was also three months pregnant, and her marriage had been deteriorating for some time. Compounding Ruby's frustration was the fact that one of Sam's bolita "writers" had gotten drunk and vomited on her new rug during a party at her home. Sam ordered her to clean up the mess, and when she refused, he beat her (Huie, Research). In the four months prior to August 1952, she had been hospitalized three times and diagnosed with depression and a tendency toward hypochondria. To anyone on the outside looking in, Ruby seemed to be slowly unraveling.

Dr. C. LeRoy Adams was familiar with Ruby's alleged physical ills, as she was frequently to be found at his office in downtown Live Oak. Adams had also delivered Ruby's middle daughter, Sonja, in 1945 and cared for Ruby after the birth. Like Sam and Ruby, Adams and his wife, Florrie Lee, were poor when they came to Live Oak with their two young children in 1944. Adams had previously tried his hand at pharmacy (the business failed), run for sheriff of Hamilton County (he lost), and struggled academically before finally graduating last in his class from the University of Arkansas medical school. But by 1952 Adams's luck had turned. At the age of forty-seven, he had a successful practice, and his boundless energy enabled him to treat literally hundreds of patients—both blacks and whites—in his segregated office each week. He worked long hours and also made frequent house calls. He was highly charismatic and could, according to Huie, "talk you out of being sick" (Huie, Research). Edith Park, a registered nurse who worked closely with Adams in his office for two years, knew him well. In an undated letter she wrote to Huie, Park describes Adams as a "shot doctor":

> No patient left his office without a shot. Anyway, with most of those natives getting acquainted with medicine and a new hospital, of which most of them were afraid, it was as good a way as any to get

them used to the idea that medicine wasn't just herb tea. Most of the shots were inexpensive, injectable vitamin compounds, which wouldn't hurt the best of us, and penicillin. Lots of the pain those natives had was the pain of lost hope and despondency; and believe me, I'd hear them later say, "Doc, you don't know how that medicine helped me. I'll drop by for some more sometime." In other words, when they felt down again, they'd drop by and see the "Doc," get a shot of that there magic stuff, and feel like new again for awhile. (Park, Letters to Huie)

Park remembers Adams as a huge man, six feet two inches tall and weighing nearly three hundred pounds—"all belly and no hips"—who was wildly popular among the locals, especially the poor. His segregated waiting rooms were almost always filled with patients, but his aspirations were by no means limited to those of a country doctor; he also had political ambitions.

Adams won the Florida state senate district 17 seat, and it was rumored in Suwannee County that he was a frontrunner in the upcoming governor's race. He had built his senate campaign on the premise that he was a common man, as exemplified in the following excerpts taken from several letters to the public Adams ran in the *Suwannee Democrat.* "I understand your needs because I was raised with many of you," Adams wrote on April 25, 1952. "I went to school with many of you. I dug ditches on the W.P.A. with many of you. I rode turpentine woods and worked with timber around many of your homes" (16). On April 18, 1952, Adams condemned the rich: "If it were left to me," he wrote, "I would have taxes only on liquor, racing, cabarets, and places where the wealthy squander their money, with no taxation on the farmer, laborer, and low income groups" (7). On April 11, 1952, he stated that a seat on the state senate "is a position of service and trust, and not one of financial gain" (7). The fact that Adams often reduced or outright forgave payment for medical services was legendary in Suwannee County and perhaps more than anything else contributed to his status as a "big man," a man who truly cared about the common folk. For example, Adams usually sat and visited with his patients and their families during house calls. He ate whatever he was offered with his feet propped up and his collar loosened. This sense of easy familiarity, combined with the fact that he spoke to everyone, no matter how low their station, made Adams in some circles larger than life—a man devoted wholly to the needs of others. The fact that Adams had lost his only son, twenty-two-year-old Sonny, in a February 1952 traffic accident rendered him an even more sympathetic figure in the public eye. Sonny's death resonated with the poor; like them, they reasoned, Adams knew firsthand the pain of arbitrary deprivation.

Park, however, recalls in a letter to Huie another side of Adams far different from this public façade—a little-known, much more sinister side:

> He despised weak-livered men. And he used them, and they didn't even know it. He'd put his arm around some yellow-livered SOB and call him "Pal," and as soon as his back was turned would spit on the ground. "Help that sonofabitch? I wouldn't help him dig his own grave, even if I thought it would help him get in it sooner!" They never knew. . . . They never guessed. . . .
>
> I never knew an unhappier man. Really unhappy down underneath. No, he didn't care. He laughed, he hurt people, he'd kill an animal on purpose, hitting it with his car. He'd curse a person out, laying them so low—never apologize—hit or miss . . . really not caring about a solitary thing because he was a pathological liar and he knew he could lie his way out of it. (Park, Letters to Huie)

According to Park, even Adams's reaction to his son's death was, in part, carefully scripted: "Dr. Adams felt the depth of Sonny's death," Park wrote to Huie, "but he also used it as a way to get people's sympathy to get votes. . . . They'd come in and start sympathizing, and he would shed honest tears. Then they would say, 'Well, Doc, it ain't much, but the least I can do, is vote for you.' He would thank them, and say, 'Well, I was a-countin' on you anyway. You've always been a friend of mine, you know.'" Few knew this side of the beloved doctor; he was careful to keep it hidden. Park argues, however, that it was always there. She contends Adams was fueled by an unquenchable desire for power, so he was careful to cultivate a public face that masked his capability for cruelty. Adams's true nature would have perhaps escaped detection forever if not for his untimely death, but, according to Park, Live Oak was a strange place full of secrets. "I wasn't surprised at anything that ever happened," Park wrote to Huie, "because I knew the unusual and rare was always happening. . . . So much bad, so often that it almost seemed right. Where did one draw the line anyway between right and wrong? When there was so much wrong, and it seemed right?"

Park wasn't the only woman in Live Oak struggling with questions of right and wrong in the summer of 1952. Ruby McCollum spent a long, sleepless night the first Saturday in August of that year preoccupied with where right ended and wrong began. Finally she grew tired of wondering, McCollum's actions the following morning shook the community to its core, raised countless questions, and created a multilevel, unprecedented scandal. Citizens were, in fact, sure of only two things in Live Oak after August 3, 1952: LeRoy Adams was dead, and Ruby McCollum—at long last—had definitively drawn the line.

Silent Stories and the Construction of Ruby McCollum

In 1983, Adrienne Rich described herself as "pursued by questions of historical process, of historical responsibility, questions of historical consciousness and ignorance and what these have to do with power" (137). Before anything more can be said of McCollum—before attempting to relay the murder itself, her trial, or her long incarceration—I must address questions similar to Rich's in the context of the Ruby McCollum saga, or at the very least acknowledge their existence.

It is all too easy to construct a coherent narrative about McCollum that ignores or downplays concerns such as those raised by Rich. Lust, greed, and murder have always made for fascinating reading, and it is tempting, like several who have written about McCollum before me, to spackle words seamlessly over cracks in the McCollum story left by time and distance. The temptation to fill in these gaps—to narratize McCollum in a way that makes sense—is tremendous. My intrusion here (at the peak of the "action" so to speak in the story of Ruby McCollum) is, consequently, both deliberate and necessary. Did McCollum, in fact, spend a "long, sleepless night" before she shot Adams? I have no way of knowing. Huie, however, contends that she did: "During the sleepless Saturday night, walking back and forth through her upstairs hallway in the darkness," Huie writes in *Ruby*, "she had decided to kill the doctor" (24). Huie, however, never spoke with Ruby McCollum regarding the night before the murder (or anything else for that matter). Perhaps McCollum instead slept peacefully, content in the knowledge that she was fully prepared to finally end her own suffering. Or just as likely, perhaps it was only after she awoke that she decided to murder Adams. Or McCollum may never have "decided" to shoot Adams at all prior to Sunday morning; the murder may have occurred in self-defense. Or, as McCollum testified, it may have been an accident. There are even those individuals in Live Oak who swear Ruby herself didn't pull the trigger; someone else did, and she only served as an unlucky scapegoat.

Certainly the issue of whether or not McCollum slept well the night before Adams's murder is trivial and hardly matters. What does matter, however, is the fact that Huie's text is not alone in "writing over" or "writing away" this and other moments in McCollum's life. More important, this practice of gap filling says a great deal about narrative power in reference to McCollum—who has it, who wants it, and why. After all, how McCollum spent her last night of freedom is inconsequential—the issue has always been *why* she shot Adams, not what she did immediately beforehand. But if Huie's act of narrative gap filling is not important in terms of the murder itself, it is profoundly relevant in the larger context of stories told about McCollum. Over the years, these various stories have worked to construct McCollum's public memory, a memory created without the contribution of McCollum's own voice. Ruby McCollum is—and has always been—what the words of others have made her. Rarely allowed to speak for herself, she has been described in print as everything from an enraged Negress to a stubborn old lady, but she has never been characterized as what I believe she wanted first and foremost to be—a woman with a voice.

Rich stresses connections among history, responsibility, and power, and these connections are particularly relevant to discourses like Huie's written about the McCollum affair. Often overlooked in these texts is the arbitrary nature of their content, or more precisely, the *seemingly* arbitrary choices writers make regarding what they emphasize or downplay—and what these choices say about power and privilege. Stories about McCollum are doubly complex because they are stories told almost entirely by peripheral characters, with hearsay, innuendo, speculation, and gossip serving as their hallmarks. The fact that in 1952 Live Oak was a racially divided, extremely conservative community contributed to what individuals in the town were willing to have committed to print. Fear of retribution shaped the words of Live Oak citizens, and a desire for large circulation numbers shaped the words of out-of-town reporters; the more scandalous the story, the more newspapers were sold. Accounts of the murder and McCollum's trial reported in the *Suwannee Democrat* were also highly constructed but toward a very different end. These articles seem to be motivated almost exclusively by a desire to show the town in its best light and to prove to "outsiders" reading (and writing) about the case that rumors of rampant racism in Live Oak were strictly that—unsubstantiated hearsay. It is important, then, to remember that there are always several discourse communities at work in any text written about Ruby McCollum and that these texts resonate most loudly with what is left *unsaid*; for every voice that speaks, there are others—either by choice or force—that keep still.

If various stories written about McCollum reveal more about the *tellers* of these stories than about McCollum herself, and if, as I argue, the most significant voices in them are silenced, how do I justify (much less construct) another story about McCollum? More important, how do I examine texts written about her—texts that I argue are contingent and interested—both within and against the inescapably political confines of the written word? How do I achieve the delicate balance between positive storytelling that, as Jacqueline Jones Royster argues, "engage[s] in a process of using multidimensional viewpoints as a heuristic for historical reconstruction" and "keep[s] the eyes and the mind open for the imaginable, that is, for opportunities to make connections and draw out likely possibilities" (83), and storytelling that, instead, dictates the "likely possibilities" themselves? At what point does Royster's fluid concept of storytelling become, like Huie's text, so filled with peripheral voices that the voice of McCollum herself cannot be heard? In short, what does one *do* with a story like McCollum's that because of its pervasive silences does not easily yield to clear distinctions between fact and fiction?

Royster writes that the ability to envision possibilities is a generative act particularly useful in terms of African-American histories. Royster advocates a "long view" of history that utilizes what she terms *critical imagination*: "With a long view," Royster writes, "the historical narrative does not reference individual experience. It references instead institutional, collective patterns in broad scope. These patterns form a cultural landscape, the contextual backdrop against which to render a meaningful and perhaps even a representative story" (83). The collective texts of the McCollum affair lend themselves to Royster's long view of history; taken together, they form a representative story—in fact, several representative stories—of power dynamics at work in Live Oak and the American South in the early 1950s. Royster, however, is careful to note that the use of critical imagination does not "negate the need to do the hard work of engaging systematically in theoretically grounded processes of discovery, analysis, and interpretation." This "hard work" of historical discovery, Royster argues, should be tempered by responsibility; writers should be "particularly careful about 'claims' to truth by clarifying the contexts and conditions of our interpretations and by making sure that we do not overreach the bounds of either reason or possibility" (83–84). My concern, like Royster's, is that all too frequently archival research begins as an act of critical imagination that, over time, transforms itself into an act of critical *invention* when the researcher compiles his or her findings and translates them into a single representative text. Such is the case with Huie's and others' accounts of McCollum. And when acts of imagining make the shift to acts of invention, the result is a profound imbalance of power between the scholarly historical writer and his or her subject of inquiry.

Scholars are, after all, storytellers. We tell our stories for different reasons than fiction writers, and our stories take different forms, but scholarship, particularly scholarship involving archival research, remains by necessity a specific kind of storytelling. Hayden White, for example, argues that the practices of writers who produce fiction and the practices of writers who produce historical discourse overlap in several important ways. His metahistorical view, like Royster's "long view" of history, encourages a broad, self-conscious approach to history and a critical awareness that so-called factual accounts are not exempt from acts of emplotment on the part of the "objective" historian. White writes: "It is sometimes said that the aim of the historian is to explain the past by 'finding,' 'identifying,' or 'uncovering' the 'stories' that lie buried in chronicles; and that the difference between 'history' and 'fiction' resides in the fact that the historian 'finds' his stories, whereas the fiction writer 'invents' his. This conception of the historian's task, however, obscures the extent to which 'invention' also plays a part in the historian's operations" (6–7). Like White, Carlo Ginzburg acknowledges the constructed nature of textual histories. Unlike White, however, Ginzburg takes a microhistorical view of the past. In his *The Cheese and the Worms*, Ginzburg reconstructs the life of an obscure miller who lived during the Inquisition and was ultimately tried and sentenced to death. Ginzburg contends that his microhistorical (or short-view) approach to history's minutiae also proved problematic, and he writes, reminiscent of the metahistorical approaches of Royster and White, that he could not ignore gaps he encountered during the construction of his text:

The obstacles interfering with the research were constituent elements of the documentation and thus had to become part of the account; the same for the hesitations and silences of the protagonist in the face of his persecutors' questions—or mine. Thus, the hypotheses, the doubts, the uncertainties became part of the narration; the search for truth became part of the exposition of the (necessarily incomplete) truth attained. Could the result still be defined as "narrative history"? For a reader with the slightest familiarity with twentieth-century fiction, the reply was obviously yes. (23–24)

My purpose here is not to express a preference for either macro or micro approaches to narrative histories. Both have their merits and their short-comings. Instead, my purpose is to point out that scholars writing both long and short views of history find themselves faced with the same problem: How does the historical writer distinguish between prose that accurately describes past events (as if this were possible) and prose that creates those events through practices of "writing over" moments that cannot be known firsthand? Moreover, to what extent does the interested position of the writer shape the ways he or she chooses to bridge these textual fissures? Where, in fact, does "factual writing" end and "storytelling" begin? In terms of texts written about McCollum, these are important questions that have never before been considered, much less answered.

Resisting what she calls "historical amnesia" is, for Rich, to ask, "What is missing, *who* is missing, in the versions of history, the canons of literature, we are being taught?" (153). Characterizing McCollum as a victim, a murderess, an adulteress, or a maniac, as other writers before me have done, negates the issue of how the various *tellers* of her story figure into the warp and woof of discourses written about her. McCollum, then, is not mine to characterize; she is not mine to assimilate; and she is most certainly not mine to "explain." The fact that I write from the position of a woman does not go nearly far enough for me to claim that my text functions as an objective lens through which to view her. My point is that there is no objective textual history of McCollum, and there never will be. There are, instead, *histories*—multiple and often competing texts that due to the subjective nature of experience and the written word simultaneously both embrace and exclude her.

In the final analysis, if language is contingent, the writer is interested, and history is unknowable, how do we account for the powerful and contradictory urge to (re)construct the past through text? More specifically, why do I feel compelled to contribute yet *another* story to the many already written about McCollum? J. Hillis Miller writes, "Nothing seems more natural and universal to human beings than telling stories" (66). He adds, however, that "the fact that narrative is so universal, so 'natural,' may hide what is strange and problematic about it" (67). Miller argues, like Royster, White, and Ginzburg, that fiction writing and historical writing are similar. "The two forms of narration," Miller writes, "are closely related forms of 'order-giving' or 'order-finding,' in spite of the fact that fictional narratives are subject to referential restraints in a way very different from the way histories submit themselves to history and claim to represent things that really happened *exactly as* they really happened" (68). I would add, however, that even though fiction and historical narratives share similarities, it is perhaps the historical narrative that is more tightly bound to conventional methods of storytelling. Most people who read histories expect these texts to have a clear beginning, middle, and end. They also expect the narrators to be reliable and for the text to "thematize" moments in history—to make these moments function as cogent pages in a larger contemporary story in which the reader of the text also plays a part. The story of Ruby McCollum, however, is problematic not only because of its gaps and silences but also because in 1952 McCollum's behavior did not neatly conform to expected social convention. Miller writes that a central function of narrative—and one of the reasons we desire it so strongly—is that it functions as a kind of social tutorial, one that helps us "learn to take our places in the real world, to play our parts there" (69). Narrative histories—particularly in the South—are closely related to fiction in this respect. "Fictions may be said to have a tremendous importance," Miller continues, "not as the accurate reflectors of a culture but as the makers of that culture and as the unostentatious, but therefore all the more effective, policemen of that culture. Fictions keep us in line and tend to make us more like our neighbors" (69). In the early 1950s, the South in general and Live Oak in particular highly valued this process of assimilation, and silences surrounding the case of Ruby McCollum find their roots here. In other words, Live Oak's primary struggle was not so much with McCollum's actions on August 3, 1952; it was, instead, with where to locate them in the confines of a highly scripted—and revered—southern narrative history. Considering the plethora of myths that inform southern ideology—for example, the myth of the black seductress, the myth of the sanctified southern woman, the myth of southern manhood, and, of course, the myth of white supremacy—it should come as no surprise that it is difficult to separate fact and fiction in texts written about McCollum. One thing, however, is certain: McCollum's actions on August 3, 1952, could not be assimilated into any "accepted" story told in the South. And because the citizens of Live Oak could not assimilate McCollum, they did the next best thing. They vilified her as an *exception* to the norm, and in doing so even more strongly inscribed for Live Oak's body politic what it believed to be the *correct* history of their community.

It is important to realize that texts written about Ruby McCollum are contingent and interested on four overlapping levels. First, information that found its way into texts written about her and the events of August 3, 1952, frequently originated from members of a segregated, conservative community ruled by powerful social conventions that were often enforced by fear. Second, individuals writing about McCollum frequently wove this (mis)information into texts that fictionalize, "write over," or "write away" significant gaps and silences. Third, because McCollum's actions did not conform to the larger publicly acknowledged historical narratives existing in the South in the early 1950s, the texts these writers produced, no matter what their respective stance regarding McCollum, are by necessity infused with *silent* stories. In other words, stories written about Ruby McCollum are actually stories written more about regional and local silences than about McCollum herself. Finally, my own role as yet another writer constructing stories about McCollum is informed by silences generated by the passage of time and my positioning as a woman, a scholar, and perhaps most significant, a native southerner. In the final analysis, then, at the heart of any text written about McCollum is not McCollum at all. At issue instead is the larger context of her story: narrative practices of southern myth inscription and the particular regional rhetoric with which these myths were—and often still are—constructed.

James Berlin writes that rhetoric, ideology, and history are inextricably linked. "Rhetoric," Berlin argues, "thus explicitly reinforces the subject's notion of what exists, what is good, and what is possible, and does so . . . through indicating who may engage in discourse, to whom discourse is to be addressed, and what may be the permissible contents of the message" (143). What I argue to be an overall rhetoric of silence in the South conforms to Berlin's notion that discourse links the material, social, political, and cultural realms. Acts of silence in texts about Ruby McCollum "write" reality; silence determines by default who is permitted voice, whose words are given merit, whose words are denounced, who may listen, and—above all—who must remain mute within the confines of a regional ideology dominated by myths and often enforced by intimidation.

What, then, are the specific stories that constitute these southern myths and how do these myths inform McCollum's story (and vice versa)? More important, in what ways were citizens of Live Oak in the early 1950s complicit in the perpetuation of these longtime southern myths, and how do we know? Answering these questions requires analysis on two levels: first, a discussion of the South's regional history in terms of myth-making

The Politics
of Silence
in Southern
Rhetoric

practices and the discourses used to perpetuate them and, second, examination of the particular language used to construct and enforce these southern fictions. Illustrative texts written about McCollum are where to begin these two kinds of analysis, and to find them we must return to the summer of 1952, when Live Oak's private rhetoric of silence was all too publicly broken.

Myths, Gods, and Monsters

Sunday mornings in Live Oak were, according to Huie, "a time to repair the damages of Saturday night: to sew up the cuts, set the broken jaws and limbs, and cauterize the holes of the night's traffic and conflict" (*Ruby* 20). So although August 3 was a Sunday—a day when most citizens in Live Oak were settling into pews in the town's several churches—Dr. LeRoy Adams had already treated many patients by midmorning.

Adams's office was located directly next to the Suwannee Hotel and adjacent to Dale and Radford's Building Supply Company on Ohio Avenue, the main street running through downtown Live Oak. According to several witnesses who were present in Dr. Adams's waiting room on the day of the shooting, the building had two entrances that opened into two separate waiting areas—one for white patients and another for blacks—and both waiting rooms held several patients when seventeen-year-old Harold Musgrove arrived at 10:30 a.m. with his mother, father, and infant sister. According to Musgrove's testimony, his father parked the pickup truck in the alley next to Dale and Radford's, approximately fifty-one feet from the "colored" entrance to Adams's office, and Harold waited outside while his mother and father took his sister to be treated. According to Huie's research and transcripts of Musgrove's testimony during the trial, Harold observed Ruby McCollum standing by a two-toned blue Chrysler parked on the west side of the alley: "Ruby was standing close to the steering wheel by the car, two small children in back—three times she went to office and looked in, bobbed her head, then came back. She got in several times, started car, backed it out, then pulled back into same place . . . went on for 30–45 minutes . . . never left." Carrie Daily, a black woman who had taken her sixteen-year-old daughter to Adams's office that morning, also observed McCollum prior to the shooting. "[Daily and her daughter, Carrie] saw Elwood Howard, constable, arrive with two cut coloreds. Doc drove up, parked, opened door and came in. . . . The cut ones were handled first . . . cut girl and boy. . . . Carrie had seen Ruby come to door and bob her head. . . . Ruby came in and stayed a few minutes then went back out" (Huie, Research).

While McCollum paced back and forth in front of Dr. Adams's office, seven-year-old Sonja and ten-month-old Loretta, two of Ruby's three daughters, watched from the car. Their sister, eleven-year-old Kay, was attending services at the "colored" Baptist church with her father. None of the McCollum children suspected that in fewer than twenty-four hours their mother would be incarcerated and two men would be dead: their father—who would die of a "bad heart," according to official reports—and Adams, who would die clutching a one-hundred-dollar bill in his fist. Finally their mother stopped pacing and entered Adams's office.

There were three patients in the black waiting room, and witnesses testified that the doctor whistled cheerfully in the white treatment area. By McCollum's own admission, in her purse was a gun—a worn .32 Smith & Wesson—and nineteen one-hundred-dollar bills. According to Huie's notes and Carrie Daily's testimony during the trial, witnesses seated in the Negro waiting room described what happened next in similar ways:

> "Ruby went right on in there where he [Adams] was and she says . . . "I want that," and he said, "This?" and she said "No," and he said, "This?" and she said "Yes," and he said "Make up your mind." She [McCollum] came on out and stood crossways in the door and opened her pocketbook and got a bill out, and he went into the colored room whistling, and she went to him and said, "Give me a receipt for this," and he said "What?" and she said "Give me a receipt for this," and he said "I don't keep no books." He said "Come down here tomorrow and Thelma [Adams's secretary] will run over the books and tell you what is owing. . . . Furthermore, that ain't half the money what you owe me," and she said, "How much do I owe?" and he said, "You owe more than a hundred dollars," and she says, "Well, I ain't going to pay no hundred dollars. I'm gonna pay my part, and the other fellow is going to pay his." I could hear her, but I couldn't see her then, and he said, "Well, it matters a damn with me. I'm gonna get mine if I have to carry it to the judge's office." She said, "I know you will. You can get yours." He puts up his hand and says, "Woman, I'm tired of fooling with you," and he made one step toward the waiting room. The gun fired, and he hollered, "Oh, oh, police, police," and I looked down and said, "Dr. Adams is shot.

Let's go." And we ran out, and as soon as we got out on the ground another pistol fired, and we took off then. We ran down to the filling station and told them. (Huie, Research)

Ruby testified that after the shooting she drove home, changed her dress, and heated formula for her youngest child, Loretta. A few minutes later, several police officers arrived. One of the men went upstairs with Ruby. At first she denied that she was Ruby McCollum (even though she was well known to all of the officers) and said: "Is something wrong? Has somebody done something?" (Huie, Research). Then she admitted to the shooting and showed the officer where she had thrown the gun into the bamboo hedge below the bathroom window. Fearing for her life, the officers loaded McCollum into a patrol car and drove her to Raiford State Penitentiary under armed guard.

When McCollum arrived at the penitentiary, the remaining eighteen one-hundred-dollar bills in her purse had somehow vanished, but no mention of the money's mysterious disappearance is made in the *Suwannee Democrat*'s account of the shooting. The front page on Friday, August 8, is riddled with the McCollum affair. The most prominent column is prefaced by the bold headline "Dr. Adams Slain by Negress: State Senate Nominee Shot in His Office Sunday Morning. Ruby McCollum Confesses to Killing: Is Rushed to Raiford State Prison." The subsequent article describes Ruby as "a 32-year-old negro woman, wife of Sam McCollum, well-to-do farmer here formerly known as 'Bolita Sam' for alleged activities in the numbers racket." The shooting, the *Democrat* stated, took place "apparently in an argument over a medical bill" and states that McCollum first denied knowledge of the murder "but then confessed to the shooting and told officers where she had thrown the murder weapon. It was found in the hedge at her home."

A description of Adams's funeral, "the largest and most sincerely attended funeral ever witnessed in Suwannee County," also appears on page 1 of the *Suwannee Democrat*, and adjacent to it is an account of Sam McCollum's sudden death in Ocala at the age of forty-five "of a heart attack," stating that he had "been considered one of the major numbers operators in Suwannee County." Of particular note is the *Democrat*'s assertion that Sheriff Howell "emphasized that McCollum's death was from natural causes."

Two additional items appearing in the *Suwannee Democrat* that day are of special consequence: an editorial written by the editor of the *Democrat*, and a cautionary note to the citizens of Live Oak. Both are important because they clearly illustrate what would become the public face of the McCollum affair. The editorial deifies Adams, describing him as "always ready and willing to answer a call, no matter the day or hour" and asserting that "the good work he did will live as a monument to his busy and active life while among us." Yet perhaps the most intriguing column appearing on page 1 of the *Suwannee Democrat* on August 8, 1952, is strategically located to the right of the column describing Sam McCollum's mysterious death. It cautions Live Oak residents to ignore "some vicious rumors . . . being circulated in Live Oak concerning the recent tragedy which struck here in the form of Dr. C. L. Adams' death" and advises citizens "to believe only what you know to be true. Doubt everything that can't be checked." Separating rumor from fact in the McCollum case, however, would prove difficult. Checking information was simply not possible; Adams was dead, and gaining access to McCollum was problematic at best. What was possible, however, was damage control, which the *Suwannee Democrat* began with a vengeance immediately after Adams's murder.

The community of Live Oak knew that outside inquiry into the McCollum affair could be disastrous to the community. Already there had been talk that only powerful white men could provide the protection and financing that Sam's popular bolita games demanded. "There is strong feeling," Emmett Peter Jr. of the *Tampa Morning Tribune* wrote, "that the colored men and women are only the front or salesmen for a syndicate headed by white people in this county" and that "McCollum is only a lieutenant for a white gambling overlord or maybe a syndicate." Seeming proof of Peter's speculations came on June 22, 1954—well after Ruby McCollum had been tried and convicted—when Edith Park gave the following sworn statement directly implicating Adams in bolita activities:

> For approximately two years immediately prior to his death on August 3, 1952, I was employed by Dr. Clifford LeRoy Adams Jr., of Live Oak, Florida.
>
> On several occasions during my employment I happened to see what appeared to be considerable sums of money delivered to Dr. Adams by the Negro undertaker, Charles Hall.
>
> On each occasion I witnessed the transfer of this money by chance: in the course of my duties I would open a door and there see Hall in the process of handing over money. Each time the money seemed to be in a stack, maybe three or four inches thick, and the

bills appeared to be tens and twenties. On each occasion I appeared to take no notice; though there seemed to be some embarrassment, much shoving of money into drawers or pockets, etc. I do not know what the money was paid for. I knew of no medical or business relationship between Dr. Adams and Charles Hall. Dr. Adams never mentioned the money to me. (Park, Sworn Statement)

In addition to Park, McCollum herself alleged that Adams was involved in Sam's bolita scheme. "[Adams] let my husband run numbers for my sake," she wrote to her attorney before her trial (McCollum, Notes). Adams certainly had the community acceptance and prestige necessary to support such an extensive operation. Yet in many of the *Democrat*'s columns concerning Adams's murder, Sam McCollum is described as a "well-to-do farmer" who was "formerly" involved in bolita. If Adams's murder had suddenly made Live Oak the object of the nation's scrutiny, the *Democrat* was determined to downplay Sam's, and by implication the community of Live Oak's, involvement in bolita, even though earlier the paper had openly acknowledged the fact that Sam and others in the community had purchased gambling stamps from the state. Yet even more damning to the community was Ruby's contention (privately whispered in Live Oak and openly publicized in more liberal northern newspapers such as the *Pittsburgh Courier*) that Adams—an elected official, a respected church member, a well-liked physician, and, above all, a civic-minded white man—had raped, beaten, and otherwise abused her over a period of approximately six years. In what appears to be a frantic hand, McCollum penciled the following note to her attorney on several 4 x 6 sheets of paper during her imprisonment before the trial:

> In May he [Adams] sent me to Brewster Hospital for treatments . . . because of shots he would give me if he got mad (if I did not do as he said do). Then I asked him, "Would you kill me for something like that?" He said, "Yes, if I have it to do." After the baby came and after I got pregnant year before last in October, he didn't want me to hardly speak to a man. Oh! well he was boss. Of course I have always been afraid of him since he started with me over six years ago. When he would get mad at me, he would tear into me like a lion plus give me a big shot of medicine to almost kill me. I ask for something for it, and he says, "I know you are sick. What kind of casket do you want me to get you? I will be to your funeral. . . ." I was afraid to tell another doctor what he had given me because he would beat me up

if he found it out, especially if it was a doctor in the county. I asked him, "Why would you want to do me that way?" He said, "It takes a little of that for you sometimes."

McCollum alleged in the same note that it was common knowledge in Live Oak that Adams had fathered her youngest daughter, Loretta. Moreover, McCollum contends that others knew that Adams physically abused her:

> Dr. Adams' friends, relatives, and everybody else knew about it [Loretta]. It isn't a secret at all. Dr. Adams said, "If they want to know anything, send them to me. . . ." White and colored would just play with her, and that was all. I would do anything the doctor told me to do because I was really afraid of him. . . . He would give me needles to make me sick then give me one to get me well when he got mad at me. Beat me up, that was common. He didn't care who knew it.

During the trial, allegations that Adams repeatedly beat and otherwise terrorized McCollum were deemed "inappropriate" and inadmissible. Chapter 2 will discuss McCollum's silence-filled trial in detail, but my point here is to illustrate that the *Suwannee Democrat* early on established the more palatable public "facts" of Adams's murder. These "facts," gleaned from articles printed in the *Suwannee Democrat* and public opinion, are as follows: first, the dispute between McCollum and Adams had been over a medical bill, nothing more; second, Adams had been a man with a spotless reputation; third, if Adams *had* fathered McCollum's daughter, Loretta, it was most likely due to Ruby's relentless pursuit of Dr. Adams and not the reverse; fourth, Adams had never physically harmed Ruby in any way; and finally, the good people of Live Oak—and particularly its black citizens—were not afraid to discuss the McCollum affair. If residents had little to say to outsiders regarding the case, it was simply because there was nothing more to be said. In other words, if any stories were to be told about McCollum, the *Suwannee Democrat* would be the one to tell them. And in no way would the ramblings of one crazy black woman be allowed to disrupt the predetermined plot line.

The Ideology of Southern Silence

Stuart B. McIver argues in *Murder in the Tropics* that over the years Florida has had more than its share of sensational killings. McIver writes that Florida has "a restlessness, born of envy and jealousy, fueled by the temptations of conspicuous wealth, the lure of illicit love, the chance for a big score" (ix), so it should come as no surprise that McIver's book boasts a chapter devoted to the Ruby McCollum affair. And if, as McIver argues, there is a proliferation of sensational murders in Florida's history, his text and others like it are also testimony to the need to (re)tell these bizarre stories. The drive to "set down" and somehow make sense of crime is not exclusive to the South; one glance at recent television and film productions testifies to the nation's fascination with murder. "Murder is a mean, ugly part of life," McIver writes, "but this seems to increase rather than lessen people's interest in the ultimate breakdown in human relations. Ours is a violent society, and people still tune their sets to crime news and police dramas" (xii). The murder of LeRoy Adams is unique, however, because the most intriguing aspects of the case are found not in the murder itself but in the ripple effect the crime had on the community of Live Oak. Because the community was unable to assimilate McCollum's actions into the region's accepted public history, it cast her as an anomaly. At the time of the murder, the press described her actions as "inexplicable" and "irrational." However, when one views McCollum in the broader context of myth-making practices in the American South in the early 1950s that fostered violence, inequity, and, above all, silence, what she did on August 3, 1952—and Live Oak's reaction to it—make perfect sense.

The McCollum shooting generated a tremendous amount of text. Newspaper and magazine articles, a full-length book, and private discourses such as notes from McCollum to her attorneys and anonymous letters to Huie all constitute a rich cache of information about her case. The volume of these texts is perhaps not that unusual considering the sensational nature of the crime. What is significant, however, is that most of these texts are an intricate blend of fact and fiction. As previously discussed, Miller contends that fictions function both to construct and police reality. "The social and psychological function of fictions," he writes, "is what speech-act theorists call 'performative.' A story is a way of doing things with words. It makes something happen in the real world" (69). In much the same way, discourses about McCollum exemplify the performative power of acts of silence by constructing and enforcing what I argue to be several of the South's myth-based cultural formations. Silence, like a performative speech act, is a crucial component of southern ideology; it determines what stories are told in the South and, consequently, what stories are discarded.

Even a cursory overview of southern history confirms that the South has long had a love affair with language, so to characterize the region as "silent" perhaps seems incongruous. Acts of silence in the South, however, often work to negate the stories of minority groups, such as African-Americans and women, and by doing so, foreground stories steeped in southern myths that have historically worked to advance individuals in positions of power. Silence in the South contributes to a highly politicized regional rhetoric that, like John Searle's description of a performative speech act, is "self-referential in a special way." Acts of silence are similar to performatives because, as Searle writes, performative speech acts are "not only *about* themselves, but they also operate on themselves. They are both *self-referential* and *executive*" (101). Silence, then, is both symptomatic of the South's fictionalizing practices and the ways in which these fictions are perpetuated.

If by establishing whose words have merit and whose words do not, silence is a unique way of "doing things with words" in the South, it is also a powerful force that masks physical violence or mental trauma suffered by individuals who challenge these southern myth-fictions. The pervasiveness of silence in the South is also what makes discussion of McCollum so difficult. Writing in the context of southern fiction, Patricia Yaeger asks important questions that in the final analysis are questions concerning southern ideology and concomitant notions of white male supremacy. "*How do you write a story everyone knows but nobody hears?*" Yaeger writes. "How do you write annals for the very histories you want to annul?" (10). The lack of critical discourse written about McCollum is itself indicative of the fact that the South is steeped in ideologies. Yaeger writes that acts of silence in the South are the opposite of testimony, or speech-as-action. This lack of testimony, she argues, accounts for the stability of powerful southern ideological formations and the myths that support them. Testimony is further made difficult because it is an attempt to articulate events that are somehow beyond the power of speech. "If testimony is the essence of speech as *act*," Yaeger writes, "a site where speech reaches toward deed, it often describes experiences that erupt in *das Ding*, that seem overwhelming, unassimilable, beyond local remedy—events that are both incomprehensible and in need of a listener" (234). This act of telling is important because it publicly establishes the *reality* of traumas like McCollum's suffered in solitude. Dori Laub writes: "The emergence of the narrative which is being listened to—and heard—is, therefore, the process and the place wherein the cognizance, the 'knowing' of the event is given birth to" (Felman and Laub 57). Laub's discussion of how the "knowing" of traumatic experience occurs is valuable in terms of theorizing acts of silence surrounding Ruby McCollum. I would argue that testimony (or, more precisely, the lack of it) is particularly important in terms of southern ideology because to testify to acts of violence suffered in silence—to refuse no longer to keep these traumatic events secret—manifests them *as* traumas and important components of the South's ideological "story that nobody hears." Once these ideological formations become publicly recognized through testimony for what they are—social constructions that justify inequity—stories like McCollum's are no longer "inexplicable." Instead, they are compelling proof of both the existence of a silence-based southern ideology and a validation that testimony in the South is both necessary and dangerous.

Susan Tucker describes her childhood tutelage in southern ideology when she writes: "The rules about race were always between us. These rules did not hang over me, in a heavy way. But they were there—unspoken. . . . The rules had been made long before for reasons no one would discuss. Children learned only that discussion of the rules was not permitted" (3). Yet how can ideology—the "rules" of southern social formations—be so pervasive and, at the same time, remain undetected? And what accounts for acts of silence that prevent exposure of them? Anne Goodwyn Jones's discussion of ideology serves to explain this complex dynamic: "Ideology works," Jones writes, "because it feels like common sense; it is the mental equivalent of the air we breathe, and nearly as invisible. A typically successful strategy of ideology is to distinguish what is natural from what is unnatural. . . . Further, ideology is not arbitrary; it produces belief systems—indeed, it produces people—who are appropriate to given material conditions" (45). In terms of Live Oak in 1952, individuals in positions of power needed to somehow justify the wide gap in the "given material conditions" of blacks and whites, and in order for this justification to occur, the all-important myth of white supremacy had to be validated and enforced.

After the murder, public opinion in both the black and white communities portrayed Ruby McCollum as an iconoclast, a destroyer of the sacred image of LeRoy Adams. White citizens knew that to admit that Adams was possibly capable of illegal gambling, rape, and medical malpractice would be tantamount to admitting that white citizens in Live Oak as a whole were not above reproach. Moreover, such an admission would almost certainly have opened the community to outside scrutiny and resulted in ugly accusations of misconduct. Live Oak, then, desperately needed to shift media attention away from Adams's alleged violent mistreatment of McCollum and his (and other) powerful white men's possible involvement in illegal activities. The only way to make this shift was to keep media attention trained on McCollum and the "fact" that the motive for the shooting was *strictly an argument over a medical bill*. To do otherwise—to entertain the possibility that Adams, a white man, might be flawed—would be equivalent to challenging the myth of southern white male superiority and the legitimacy of other myths crucial to the perpetuation of power structures in Live Oak.

Members of Live Oak's African-American community publicly supported the story that McCollum shot Adams over a medical bill because they had no choice. Fear of repercussions from the white community if they did otherwise was evident to Zora Neale Hurston. "The local white people," she wrote during her coverage of the trial, "felt no such timidity about physical violence. But fear was there. It stemmed from what the outside world would say about the trial, and hence the banning of the press [from speaking with McCollum]." And further on Hurston describes the flood of words in Live Oak asserting the "irrational" and "senseless" nature of McCollum shooting Adams over something as trivial as a medical bill:

> It was like a chant. The medical bill as a motive for the slaying was ever insisted upon and stressed. It was freely admitted by all that the McCollums had always been good pay. Paid what they owed with promptness every time. Yet, there was this quick and stubborn insistence that the medical bill, and that alone, could have been the cause of the murder. It was obviously a posture, but a posture posed in granite. There existed no other, let alone extenuating circumstances. This was the story, however bizarre it might appear to outsiders, and the community was sticking to it. The press was discouraged from "confusing" the minds of the state and the nation by poking around Live Oak and coming up with some other loose and foolish notion. ("My Impressions")

Much has been made of Live Oak's unanimous and *vocal* condemnation of McCollum. However, this stream of discourse—what Hurston describes as the public's "chant"—in actuality serves as foil for pervasive silences in Live Oak. These silences were enforced through a complex surveillance system that encompassed both blacks and whites; moreover, minority citizens in particular in Live Oak knew that to publicly challenge the "sanitized" account of Adams's murder would almost certainly put them at risk.

The public story of McCollum—the murder-over-a-doctor-bill scenario—is indicative of two important aspects of her case that have never before been considered: Live Oak's construction of public fictions through the use of a specific regional rhetoric and, more important, the use of silence *in* this specific rhetoric to enforce those fictions. In 1941, W. F. Cash described the South's fondness for rhetoric and the specific social formations it advanced. "Rhetoric flourished here," he wrote, "far beyond even its American average; it early became a passion—and not only a passion but a primary standard of judgment, the *sine qua non* of leadership. The greatest man would be the man who could best wield it" (51). Further on, Cash writes, "And the shining sword of battle, the bread and wine . . . through which men became one flesh with the Logos, was, of course, rhetoric, a rhetoric that every day became less and less a form of speech strictly and more and more a direct instrument of emotion, like music (79). Not surprisingly, many accounts of the events of August 3, 1952, stress the *rational* calmness of Live Oak citizens and describe McCollum as a savage, *illogical* murderess. These same texts also seldom neglect to mention that the *Christian* community of Live Oak would ensure McCollum had a fair trial. These texts also stress that social order was natural—ordained by God—and that disorder signaled not only a disregard for the laws of man but for the laws of God as well. In Live Oak in 1952, however, this logic was fatally flawed because southern myths over time had apparently become laws in their own right. In fact, powerful individuals in Live Oak knew that if protection of these myths was necessary to preserve specific race, economic, and gender privilege, what better way to do so than to assert that these myth-based laws were "natural" and, therefore, sanctioned by God?

According to Larry Griffin, the South has a long history of constructing myths that inform a specific regional ideology:

[The South] contested the meanings America placed on slavery and freedom by rhetorically constructing slavery to be a positive good for members of both races, to be natural and ordained by God. . . . The South created its own myth of the Lost Cause to explain the Civil War as heroic sacrifice and honorific commitment to duty and family. . . . It contested America's understanding of white supremacy and condemnation of lynching by creating the myth of white southern womanhood. . . . It contested America's definition of the good and civilized and cultured life by creating its own agrarian version of such a life: a harmonious, intensely personal, and religious South grounded by and in touch with nature and the land, obviously superior to the unnatural, dehumanized, money-grubbing industrial North. (27–28)

Several of these myths inform the McCollum case, and Griffin's assertion that the South has always conceived of itself as somehow "different" from the rest of the United States partially accounts for Live Oak's aversion to "outside influence" during McCollum's trial. I contend, however, that the primary reason Live Oak discouraged questions regarding McCollum is that such questions would necessarily challenge larger ideological formations in the community regarding race and what Smith describes as the "southern tradition." Through the universal contention that McCollum's true motive for murder was an argument over a doctor bill, white citizens in Live Oak were attempting to protect something much more valuable than either bolita profits or even white supremacy—they were attempting to protect a way of viewing the world. Smith argues that ideological formations go undetected in the South, first, because they are carefully taught in childhood and, second, because individuals in the South learn by necessity to reconcile an existence dominated by contradiction:

> The mother who taught me what I know of tenderness and love and compassion taught me also the bleak rituals of keeping Negroes in their "place." The father who rebuked me for an air of superiority toward schoolmates from the mill and rounded out his rebuke by gravely reminding me that "all men are brothers," trained me in the steel-rigid decorums I must demand of every colored male. They who so gravely taught me to split my body from my mind and both from my "soul," taught me also to split my conscience from my acts and Christianity from southern tradition. (27)

Scott Romine argues that Smith's *Killers of the Dream* "explicitly correlates pathological repression and metaphoric language, the medium that allows white Southern schizophrenia to conceal itself." Discourses written about McCollum also support Romine's assertion that figurative language, or language "sustained through self-deception, repression, and displacement," is one way southern rhetoric distances itself *from* itself, and, therefore, enables it to serve as a vehicle for illogical practices of segregation and violence (99). McCollum's trial is saturated with metaphoric language and provides ample evidence of acts of silence creating one reality by denying another. There are, however, other texts informed by the McCollum affair that in much more obvious ways illustrate the "absent presence" of silence in Live Oak after Adams's murder. And not surprisingly, the most significant of these texts were generated by Live Oak's own local newspaper, the *Suwannee Democrat*.

Columns written about the McCollum murder dominate the *Suwannee Democrat* in the latter months of 1952. These columns strictly adhere to the argument-over-a-medical-bill rationale of Adams's murder and stress the "routine" nature of McCollum's arraignment, jury selection for her trial, and the trial itself. On December 12, for example, the following appeared: "Circuit court will go back into session Saturday to select the 125 name venire for the Ruby McCollum trial. . . . Sheriff Howell said it will be just a routine court session in which Judge Hal W. Adams [no relation to Dr. C. LeRoy Adams] will select the 125 names to make up the jury venire for the McCollum trial" ("McCollum Jury"). Fearing that McCollum would not receive a fair trial in Live Oak, attorneys for McCollum's defense argued for a change of venue. The request was denied when the prosecution failed to present signed affidavits from members of the community stating that McCollum could not receive a fair trial in Suwannee County. Members of the defense team argued that residents of Live Oak were afraid of repercussions if they were to sign the affidavits. Partial court transcripts from the change of venue hearing follow:

> DEFENSE: On Monday night I left some eighty affidavits, but on account of the nature of this case and the personalities involved in it, there were most of them returned to me . . . unsigned, in fact all of them, with the statement that they were afraid. . . . I wish to state to the court and into the record that diligent effort was made to obtain supporting affidavits to the defendant's motion for change of venue, and that all the colored people of this county as well as some of the reputable white people of this county which we have been able to contact are afraid to sign their names to those affidavits for fear that it would affect them materially in their business and social standing in the community. (29, 34)
>
> PROSECUTION: The state alleges that the reason they didn't or couldn't get any such affidavits was because the reputable citizens and residents of Suwannee County knew that the defendant could get a fair and impartial trial and would not sign such an affidavit. (39)

The December 12 *Suwannee Democrat* column made no mention of the uneasiness that blanketed the community of Live Oak. In fact, the *Democrat* did just the opposite. "No evidence of violence has been noted here," the paper reported on September 5. "Judge Adams said in a hearing that the trial will be conducted so that fairness and justice will be had on both sides" ("McCollum Jury").

The fact that McCollum's defense attorneys could not acquire affidavits attesting to her ability to have a fair trial in Live Oak is evidence of the magnitude of fear in Suwannee County citizens and, consequently, their unwillingness to challenge the public version of McCollum's actions on August 3, 1952. The upcoming news that McCollum would be judged by a *local* jury effectively put the community of Live Oak on notice. Powerful individuals in Suwannee County were clearly determined, organized, and very much in control.

"The Authorities Are Watching"

Why did individuals in positions of power in Live Oak object so strongly to McCollum's trial being moved to a neighboring county? This question is at the heart of the story of Ruby McCollum, but I argue that the answer is not to be found in the facts of the case alleged by the *Suwannee Democrat*.

There were profound implications of moving McCollum's trial out of Live Oak. Fear of retaliation in the community and the use of silence to perpetuate this fear are indicative of powerful forces working against Mc-Collum from the very beginning. There are, however, other reasons why the community of Live Oak resisted efforts to move McCollum's trial. Keeping McCollum's trial in Live Oak ensured that the jury would be made up of Suwannee County citizens who were virtually guaranteed to return a guilty verdict. This guilty verdict, in turn, would protect important southern myths by way of deifying the public memory of LeRoy Adams, a white man. There were other advantages to a local trial as well. Having the trial in Live Oak would give city officials control over access to McCol-lum and determine what "outsiders" could and could not know about her case and her treatment. It would also guarantee that local law enforcement officials could carefully monitor the behavior of the community at large. These same law enforcement officials were more than likely complicit in illegal activities that perhaps contributed to Adams's death, so under no circumstance could these men risk exposure. Even today speculation along these lines is strongly discouraged in Suwannee County because, as one

African-American Live Oak native told me: "Ruby McCollum is like a burning rag in this town. No matter how many times you stomp on it, it's gonna smoke for a long time after the fire's gone out. And most folks around here know that fire has got a way of flaring up again just when you think it's out for good."

Several scholars point to the seemingly schizophrenic nature of white southerners: their ability to rationalize contradictions between *words* that attest to one set of beliefs and *actions* that attest to quite another. Divided, grotesque bodies—the end result of southern contradictions—are everywhere in texts informed by McCollum. Take, for example, Hurston's description of McCollum during her trial:

> She would extend her right hand at full length and examine it in minute detail. Flex and extend the fingers and look at them very studiously; turn it and examine palm and back as if it were something new and interesting to her. Since it was the hand which had wielded the gun on Dr. Adams, I could fancy that she might be regarding it as having a separate existence, a life and will of its own and had acted without her knowledge or consent. ("My Impressions")

Hurston describes McCollum as a woman divided against herself, and the condition is characteristic not only of McCollum but also of many of the whites in Live Oak as well. Because so many bodies in the South are marked by division, many texts written about McCollum are also dualistic; they simultaneously embrace *two* realities: Live Oak's public story of the events of August 3, 1952, and the private, unspoken story of the physical and emotional trauma that McCollum alleged she endured for six years before ending Adams's life. Yaeger contends that testimony is "stretching the word beyond its expository limits and in the direction of the world" (233), and it is precisely *because* of testimony's power to initiate social change that the South so closely censures it. Felman and Laub describe the transformative power of testimony in their comparison of testimony to a speech act: "To testify—to *vow* to *tell*, to *promise* and *produce* one's own speech as material evidence for truth—is to accomplish a speech act, rather than to simply formulate a statement. As a performative *speech act*, testimony . . . addresses what in history is *action* . . . and what in happenings is *impact*" (5). Both Yaeger and Felman and Laub are correct in their assessment that testimony is transformative. I would add, however, that silence—the *lack* of testimony in the South—also functions as a transformative speech act. Silence is the catalyst by which southern myths over time come to be accepted as "facts" and, more important, why acts of violence committed in the name of protecting these myths often go unpunished.

Of course, not all acts of silence indicate oppression. Cheryl Glenn, for example, writes that acts of silence can be generative. In "Silence: A Rhetorical Art for Resisting Discipline(s)," she argues the following important point: "Silence is not in itself necessarily a sign of powerlessness or emptiness; it is not the same as absence; and silencing for that matter, is not the same as erasing. Like the zero in mathematics, silence is an absence with a function" (263). Glenn is careful to note, however, that the act of silence acquires positive force only when it is not imposed. When silence is forced, as I believe it was in the case with McCollum, the effects can be devastating. Yet even in instances when individuals in Live Oak self-select silence, it frequently functions as a kind of societal demilitarized zone—a temporarily safe haven that in no way diminishes acts of violence that break out along its borders. These skirmishes occur when the divided body, like McCollum, can no longer manage to bind the contradictory parts of itself together. Smith argues that the white southern bodies are particularly vulnerable to these kinds of ruptures; they are split between equal measures of self-discipline and fear and learn to rationalize their divided existence during childhood. "We believed," Smith writes, "certain acts were so wrong that they must never be committed and then we committed them and denied to ourselves that we had done so. It worked very well. Our minds had split: hardly more than a crack at first, but we began in those early years a two-leveled existence which we have since managed quite smoothly" (84). Silence is characteristic of southern bodies divided by denial. Yet, if silence and denial characterize life in the South, and if individuals caught in this dichotomy sense, like Smith, that they are complicit in their own destructive silencing, why do these individuals (and in the case of McCollum, an entire community) so strongly resist testimony? The answer lies in complex systems of surveillance in place in Live Oak and the South as a whole.

In 1952, Live Oak was a society dominated by surveillance. Yet the most effective of these systems were not established or monitored by Suwannee County law enforcement officials. Instead, the community of Live Oak quite effectively monitored itself. The citizens policed one another much like inmates housed in Michel Foucault's panopticon. In the panopticon, Foucault argues, inmates are constantly monitored by the invisible gaze of a powerful supervisor, and because the inmates cannot see this supervisor, they do not know precisely when they are being observed. The effect of life under the gaze of this figure—yet never knowing absolutely when one is being watched—is a community that eventually polices its members both individually and collectively, a society that, in effect, is complicit in its own oppression. In *Discipline and Punish*, Foucault writes that the panopticon, a specially constructed prison system, is effective because "the surveillance is permanent in its effects, even if it is discontinuous in its action" (201). The same theory holds true of the role of perceived retaliatory violence in the silencing of Live Oak. The community knew that individuals who challenged southern myths regarding the supremacy of the white race risked punishment. In fact, the *possibility* of violence was enough to make the citizens of Live Oak retreat into the neutral space that silence afforded. "The truth of the matter is," Smith writes regarding her southern upbringing, "the world is full of secrets and the most important are concerned with you and the feelings that roam around in you. The better part of valor is to accept these secrets and never try to find out what they are. . . . Sin hovers over all doors. Also, the Authorities are watching" (88). In the case of McCollum, if citizens in Live Oak were unsure exactly who "the Authorities" were, they could be certain of one thing: racist individuals in the community who were quick to brandish the shield afforded by their own particularly twisted interpretation of Christian doctrine. Members of the Ku Klux Klan, for example, were often quick to point out that proof of the superiority of the white race could be found no further away than the family Bible. So if actual acts of retaliatory violence were rare during McCollum's trial, the threat remained constant, and that was enough to keep the community of Live Oak united—at least publicly—against her.

Live Oak citizens had good reason to be on their guard against behavior or comments that could be construed as going against the grain of established convention. The community and surrounding area have a long history of racial intolerance, and several events that occurred in or near Live Oak prior to Adams's murder illustrate very real reasons for pervasive fear in the community. One event in particular bears discussion.

On Sunday, January 2, 1944, at approximately ten a.m., three white men in Live Oak bound a fifteen-year-old Negro boy named Willie James Howard hand and foot and forced him to jump into the Suwannee River. It seems that Willie James had given a Christmas card to a white female co-worker at Live Oak's ten-cent store, where he worked part-time. When Willie James learned that the card had offended her, he wrote a note of apology. Her father became enraged when she showed him the note. After stopping to pick up two of his closest friends, her father, a former state legislator, drove to Willie James's home. Against the objections of Willie James's mother, the men ordered the boy into the car at gunpoint. They then drove Willie James to the lumber mill where his father worked and ordered him into the car as well. The men drove to isolated Suwannee Springs, and in front of Willie James's father, put a gun to the boy's head, positioned him on the bank of the river, and ordered him to jump. The next day, a Negro undertaker pulled Willie James's body from the Suwannee River. It is rumored in Live Oak that Willie James is buried in an unmarked grave in Live Oak's Eastside Cemetery. His parents, James and Lula Howard, left Live Oak immediately after his death and never returned.

Harry T. Moore, then national president of the NAACP, learned of the murder of Willie James Howard when he returned to Suwannee County in 1944 to visit family members. Moore was born and raised in Houston, a small hamlet near Live Oak, and he had known Lula Howard, Willie James's mother, since childhood. Moore was a powerful, determined black man and a strong advocate for civil rights. The news that yet another young Negro had been lynched in Florida profoundly disturbed him. Moore wrote to Roy Wilkins, editor of the *Crisis*, and Wilkins contacted Thurgood Marshall, director and chief counsel for the NAACP defense and education fund. Marshall contacted Spessard Holland, the governor of Florida, and on February 14, 1944, the governor wrote Marshall advising him that a Live Oak grand jury had agreed to hear Mr. Howard's complaint. He cautioned, however, that it would be difficult to indict three white men strictly on the word of a Negro:

> Of course, arrangements will be made by the proper authorities to insure the safe conduct of the boy's father and we will necessarily have to abide by the action of the grand jury. I am sure you realize the particular difficulties involved where there will be testimony of three white men and probably the girl against the testimony of one Negro man. However, I invite your suggestions should you feel you have a better approach to the matter. I do not want to do anything that will in the slightest way palliate the taking of life as appears from the statement of the father. (Holland, Letter)

On March 25, 1944, Moore wrote to Wilkins and indicated he knew firsthand the profound fear that infused the black community in Live Oak. "I was born and reared in Suwannee County," Moore wrote, "and I know something about the racial situation up there. The Ku Klux Klan has been active around there during recent years. Negroes have suffered much brutality at the hands of white people. Negroes are so cowered that there is never any talk of voting or exercising any of the fundamental rights of citizenship by Negroes." In spite of Moore's efforts, however, Holland would prove to be right. On June 30, 1944, Moore wrote the following to Marshall:

> As you know, the Suwannee County, Florida, grand jury last month failed to indict the three white men accused of lynching Willie James Howard on January 2. Frankly, we expected this negative decision from a state jury, but we followed the advice of Governor Holland and your office and helped to arrange for the father to return to Live Oak for the hearing.
>
> Apparently, the local officials, especially the sheriff, were reluctant to prosecute this case. It seems that the sheriff was very much upset when he learned that Mr. Howard actually was there to testify. We are forced to wonder if the sheriff himself is not involved in this crime. It is very probable that he at least has tried to help cover up the facts in this case. (Moore, Letter to Marshall)

Ben Green's *Before His Time: The Untold Story of Harry T. Moore, America's First Civil Rights Martyr* is an excellent and well-researched account of Moore's life, and the book gives the following description of the meeting of the grand jury:

> On May 8, Willie James Howard's father testified before the Suwannee County grand jury. Since he was the only eyewitness, other than the three accused white men, no other witnesses were called. It was the word of a grieving father against the weight of a legal system that looked the other way at violence against black sons. The old man never had a chance. When he finished his sad tale of watching his son murdered before his own eyes, one grand juror inquired, "Did your boy deliver the Christmas card by hand?" and another asked, "How old was the boy?" That was it. No questions about the murder, only about the *real* crime: an impudent black boy's sending a flirtatious Christmas card to a white girl. After Howard's father was excused, the state attorney told the jurors, "The parties are guilty of murder in the first degree if they are guilty of anything." The critical word was *if*. That was the juror's way out, and they took it. After a brief huddle, they announced their decision: no indictments. (50)

In coming to its decision, the grand jury cited a lack of evidence, a decision based in part on the following sworn statement signed by the girl's father and two other men accused of forcing Willie James into the Suwannee River:

> We took Willie James in the car with us and drove to the lumber company in Live Oak, Florida, and explained the circumstances to his father who agreed to go with us and chastise the boy himself for his misdeed. We immediately drove to a place near the Suwannee River, a place just east of Suwannee Springs. When we arrived at that point, I tied the boy's feet and hands to keep him from running so that his father could whip him. James, the boy's father, took the boy and carried him some ten or twelve feet from the car where he was to whip him. But the boy, making the statement he would die before he would take punishment from his father or anyone else, made his way to the river where he jumped in and drowned himself. His father stood by and viewed the son without attempting to prevent this happening. . . . I made a dash to get ahold of him . . . but we were too late. He rolled over the bank into the river before we could reach him. (Signed Statement)

The men's statement is chilling in its lack of logic regarding what purportedly happened during the final moments of Willie James's short life. Nonetheless, the men were never indicted, and although Moore tried several more times to have the case heard, he was unsuccessful. Officials at the federal level claimed they lacked jurisdiction, and so the murder of Willie James Howard remains unpunished.

Five years later in Mims, Florida, Harry T. Moore, the man who had fought so hard to bring the killers of Willie James Howard to justice, was, like Willie James, the victim of retaliatory violence. Someone planted a bomb inside his home, and ten minutes after he, his wife, his mother, and one of Moore's two daughters retired Christmas night, it exploded. The blast destroyed the white frame house, and at the age of forty-six, Moore died on New Year's Day. His wife died nine days later. Despite several promising leads over the years, their murders remain unsolved.

In 1951, less than one year before the McCollum murder, there were twelve bombings and multiple lynchings in Florida, so many that the northern press called the spree the "Florida Terror." Green nicely captures the decorous veil of silence that insulated the rest of the nation from the reality of these horrors when he writes: "From 1921 to 1946, Florida had sixty-one lynchings—twice as many as Alabama, and topped only by Mississippi (eighty-eight). None of those killings are memorialized on the postcards that proliferate in the state's highway gift shops, but they are as much a part of Florida as bathing beauties, yawning alligators, pink flamingos, or the moss-draped Suwannee River" (45). The Ku Klux Klan was said to be a powerful force in Florida in the early 1950s, and a letter Edith Park wrote to Huie not only supports this contention but also hints at silences that inevitably accompanied any (public) speculation regarding the existence of the Klan in Live Oak:

> The Ku Klux Klan meets in an unused, white frame, clapboard church down near Branford every Monday night without fail. That was an excellent source of information for Dr. Adams. Not only that, but many things were planned there. . . .
>
> During my stay in Live Oak, there was one great, grand, and glorious parade with the Grand Dragon, and many were from North and South Carolina, and Georgia. Little old Live Oak was well shown! About a year later, there was a burning of a cross out across from old man Blue's place. It was a hideous looking sight. I asked Dr. Adams if he went (innocently, not knowing then that he was a member). "What were they burning? Who was burning it? A cross, you say? The Ku Klux Klan? Didn't know there was any." Then he immediately changed the subject. (Park, Letters to Huie)

On April 15, 1970, many years after the publication of *Ruby McCollum: Woman in the Suwannee Jail,* Huie received another letter, this time from a woman who had once lived in Lake City, a town approximately twenty miles from Live Oak. The woman wrote that she had vivid memories of the subjugation and violence that characterized the area. She had, in fact, experienced it firsthand:

> I just finished reading your book, *Ruby McCollum.* I lived in Lake City from the time I was six until I was twenty-one years old. I left in January of 1965 after losing two jobs and getting thrown out of two colleges. I was in CORE [Congress of Racial Equality] and was going to Negro dances and talking to the only Negro boy at Lake City Junior College.
>
> My mother . . . was admonished for my activities as was my sister and brother-in-law. . . . The sheriff called me into his office to warn

me that I could get *raped* at a Negro dance. Meanwhile he has two Negro mistresses and who knows how many children. . . .

I remember I was at "Chitwoods," the juke in Live Oak, once in the sixties and a man said, "There is a race riot uptown." This was about 2:00 A.M. All the men left and came back about thirty minutes later. No riot. It turned out that Mr. Chitwood just wanted to close up early. But you can see what sort of thing motivated them. If you had said Pope John or Kennedy was on Main Street, no one would have moved.

I am bitter when I think of Lake City. I had a 3.7 for the semester when I was told that they would bar me from registration the next semester if I tried to enroll. Also, I was allowed to finish the semester out on the condition that I "quit associating with colored people." I got calls at home telling me to go to Africa and other things not so pleasant.

So what does a twenty-one year old white girl do who can't go to college or get a job in a small town? She goes to New York. . . . I tell people in the city about what happened to me, and they don't believe sometimes that it could go on. (Letter from Lake City Resident)

I, too, have witnessed racial violence in Live Oak. Following a trip to the movies one night in December 1979, a friend and I rounded a curve on the outskirts of town and were startled to see a burning cross in the front yard of two sisters we had known in high school. These girls were white, but it was rumored they were friendly with Negroes. Unsure what to do, we considered contacting the police. Then we rejected the idea because, we reasoned, the police were probably complicit in the act. Since both of us had been raised in the South and were well schooled in the ways of southern silence, we decided the best course of action would be to continue on our way. I have never forgotten that night.

In 2001, PBS aired a television special dedicated to Harry T. Moore and, in part, the Willie James Howard affair. When I questioned residents in Live Oak about the program's accusation that the death of Willie James Howard was no accident, the reaction from the white community was a rather bizarre mixture of denial and anger. These individuals unanimously dismissed the program as an utter fabrication. "Nobody killed that boy," one man told me. "They scared him real good, but they didn't kill him." I fared no better in the black community. All residents I spoke to declined to discuss Willie James Howard at all. Most cited an inability to remember, but some simply said: "That was a long time ago. No good can come from talking about that stuff now."

Few people in Live Oak want to talk about Ruby McCollum anymore either. Most are simply apathetic, so perhaps the number of individuals who were residents in 1952 has dwindled to the point where there are few left who remember her. Or, on a more optimistic note, perhaps race relations are now less strained than they were in the 1950s, and citizens in Live Oak simply want to forget a dark chapter in their town's history that today no longer seems relevant. I would like to believe that either one of these speculations is possible, but I cannot. Those who remember McCollum—and after visiting the town several times, I know now that there are many—are vaguely uncomfortable discussing her. Some all too quickly dismiss allegations that Adams abused McCollum and then are overly eager to move on to another topic. Others admit that McCollum's allegations of horrific treatment at the hands of Adams are probably true, but the distinct drop in the volume of their voices betrays concern that such talk even now is inappropriate. More than one person told me to "be careful" when asking questions about McCollum, and opinion was unanimous that for me to broach the topic with law enforcement officials would be especially foolish. Yet if Live Oak residents are reluctant to discuss what happened on August 3, 1952, or are, at best, guarded in their comments, multiple texts written about McCollum thankfully still exist. These texts can teach us much about acts of silence in Live Oak in the early 1950s, but they have larger implications as well. Live Oak is, after all, a product of the larger South; so if silence continues to dominate the town, it means that—like their predecessors more than fifty years ago—residents today are well versed in the rhetoric of southern silence and the particular ideology characteristic of it. And at least in terms of Ruby McCollum, the Authorities are clearly still watching.

The
Silencing
of Ruby
McCollum

two   "it was all routine"

. . . .

The Trial(s) of Ruby McCollum

The courtroom crowd which had dwindled in size in the closing hours of the trial took the verdict without any display of emotions. It was all routine.

Suwannee Democrat, December 19, 1952

ON JANUARY 7, 1944, five days after the death of Willie James Howard and eight years before he would preside over the trial of Ruby McCollum, Judge Hal Adams (no relation to Dr. C. LeRoy Adams) was the guest speaker at a meeting of the Live Oak Woman's Club.

Adams was a popular public figure and unanimously revered in the Third Judicial Circuit, over which he had presided since 1925. The fact that he had agreed to address the Woman's Club luncheon was indeed a coup for the club's members, and the occasion was important enough to merit inclusion in the January 14, 1944, edition of the *Suwannee Democrat*. "The Bible was written in a simple, direct way," the *Democrat* quoted Adams as saying, "with so much said in so few words and it has withstood time. All other books have crumbled into dust. . . . On the material or secular side, one of the greatest of the earlier events was the wording of the Constitution of the United States by our founding fathers. In this simple declaration was given voice and expression and it became a living certainty."

The cornerstone of Adams's remarks is the use of language and two texts in particular: the Bible and the Constitution. Years later, these same two texts—the word of God and the word of man—would dominate the McCollum trial. Judge Hal Adams was a power to contend with in Suwannee County. On March 21, 1954, Stephen Trumbull, a reporter for the *Miami Herald*, described Adams as a man who "looks, talks, and acts precisely as the folks in this section of Florida think a judge should look, talk and act. No one has run against him at the polls within the memory of living man." If an indictment had been handed down in the lynching of Willie James Howard, Judge Adams would most likely have been the one to hear the case.

The story of McCollum's trial is complex. In fact, McCollum had two trials, changed defense attorneys multiple times, and was housed in two jails during the nearly five months that passed between the murder of LeRoy Adams and her conviction. From the very beginning, however, Judge Adams remained adamant that McCollum could receive a fair trial in Live Oak. He asserted as much on many occasions, and the *Suwannee Democrat* emphasized Judge Adams's strict attention to legal protocol where McCollum was concerned. "We'll take all the time we need," the August 22, 1952, *Democrat* quoted Adams as stating, "so this case can be tried calm-mindedly and with proper regards for everybody's rights. . . . That's the way it's going to be done." The article also missed no opportunity to emphasize the routine nature of the McCollum proceedings. For example, the paper described her indictment as "unheralded" and noted that Live

Oak citizens gathered in and around the Suwannee County Courthouse "showed no signs of violence whatever" ("Attorney"). Two weeks later, the *Suwannee Democrat* again noted the absence of violence in Live Oak and the steadfastness of Judge Adams. "No evidence of violence has been noted here," the paper reported. "Judge Adams said in a hearing that the trial will be conducted so that fairness and justice will be had on both sides" ("Ruby McCollum to Be Tried"). When after only three hours of deliberation the jury returned a guilty verdict on December 13, 1952, the *Suwannee Democrat* reported on December 19 that even McCollum was unaffected by the mandatory death sentence. "Ruby sat listlessly in her seat," the paper reported, "and looked vacantly at the ceiling as the verdict was rendered." Spectators present in the courtroom were also, according to the *Suwannee Democrat*, unmoved and "took the verdict without any display of emotions. It was all routine" ("Ruby Found Guilty").

The trial was in actuality anything but "routine." It was an event without precedent in Live Oak; the racial overtones of the case quickly caught the attention of the national media, and no matter how hard Judge Adams and the *Suwannee Democrat* tried to downplay the situation, every citizen knew that until McCollum's trial was over, Live Oak would be forced to conduct its business under the watchful eye of several northern newspapers. While the *Suwannee Democrat* never once mentioned either McCollum's "miscarriage" while housed in Raiford before her trial or allowed Loretta, the biracial child allegedly fathered by Adams, to be introduced into evidence, several northern newspapers reported these and other details judged too unseemly for Live Oak's local press. In the face of these revelations, however, the *Suwannee Democrat* stood firm in its assertion that McCollum shot Adams strictly due to an "argument over a medical bill." Virtually every column focusing on McCollum contended that *this* was the one and only reason for the murder. Anything else was not only untrue but also a direct attack on the good name of Dr. Adams and, by implication, the God-fearing community of Live Oak.

McCollum's assertion that she was unable to remember traumatic events—a condition described by her psychiatrists as Gasner's Syndrome (Report of Committee)—is, I argue, symptomatic of silences imposed on her by a dominant class heavily invested in the perpetuation of specific power formations in Live Oak and the South at large. Zora Neale Hurston, a reporter for the *Pittsburgh Courier*, was present during McCollum's trial, and her account of it is invaluable not only because it provides perhaps the only candid firsthand appraisal of silences surrounding McCollum, but also because Hurston wrote from the precarious position of a black woman who, momentarily displaced from the more liberal North, struggled to break, or at least account for, silences that blanketed both Live Oak's black and white communities. Hurston argued that the true story of McCollum's trial could be found only "on the other side of silence" ("My Impressions"), but during her stay in Live Oak she discovered that the silences surrounding McCollum were, for the most part, impermeable. I will not argue this point, for it is self-evident and well documented. Instead, I will address why and how these silences occurred and the specific discursive and social formations that contributed to them. In other words, if I cannot reach the other side of silences that form a veritable wall around McCollum's trial, then I can at least trace the construction of them—and in the process perhaps provide a preliminary foothold for future efforts to climb up and eventually over whatever separates us from the true story of Ruby McCollum's day in court.

"A Combination of Jesus Christ, Hippocrates, and Franklin Roosevelt"

Zora Neale Hurston's account of McCollum's trial has not previously been published in its entirety. She titles the piece "My Impressions of the Trial," and substantial portions of it appeared in William Bradford Huie's *Ruby McCollum: Woman in the Suwannee Jail*. Huie, however, extensively edited the piece. I include Hurston's original manuscript here in the appendix, and a discussion of it is important for two reasons. First, Hurston provides an excellent overview of complex race and gender formations in place in Live Oak before and during McCollum's trial, and, second, offering the reader the piece as Hurston wrote it allows her to tell what she considered to be the story of Ruby McCollum her way—without editorial silencing.

Hurston's text is structured in chronological fashion, with the first half predominately devoted to a discussion of race and gender formations in Live Oak prior to the trial, and the second half describing the trial itself. A reading of Hurston's account of the atmosphere in Live Oak immediately prior to McCollum's trial illustrates the degree of anxiety, fear, and silence that infused the town's black citizenry. Immediately after the murder, for example, McCollum was transported to the Florida state penitentiary in Raiford, and much was made of the fact that she was taken there "for her own protection." Law enforcement officials in Live Oak publicly stated they feared an outbreak of retaliatory violence. I contend, however, that McCollum's rapid removal from Live Oak was actually a concerted effort to isolate her from the general public and gain immediate and complete control over any individuals who might have contact with her. Far more than fearing for McCollum's safety, law enforcement officials in Live Oak feared leaks to the growing number of reporters in their midst concerning rumors of the *true* nature of McCollum and Adams's relationship. While housed in Raiford, McCollum was permitted visits only from her counsel and immediate members of her family. P. Guy Crews—locally known to all as "Pig Eye"—and John Cogdill, both attorneys from Jacksonville, Florida, were her first legal representatives. However, Cogdill withdrew himself from the case before the trial began, and Crews, for reasons that will be explained presently, was not permitted to represent McCollum.

Huie contends in *Ruby McCollum* that Buck McCollum, Sam's brother, retained Crews after paying his retainer from a suitcase crammed with cash, describing Crews in the process as a "cracker character" who "squinted at you through bifocals and bourbon fumes . . . could quote scripture by the yard . . . and tell the court a funny story just before the judge ordered you hanged" (61). Cogdill, Huie writes, was told by a relative who worked as a turnkey at Raiford that McCollum was headed his way and did not yet have legal representation. Therefore, along with Crews, "'Brother Cogdill' was cut in for an additional $3,000" (62). Huie relied heavily on Zora Neale Hurston's account of McCollum's trial. He also received many letters from McCollum both before and after her conviction, and during the course of writing *Ruby McCollum*, Huie became intimately acquainted with Judge Adams and other significant figures in the case. Discourses resulting from these encounters are representative of a highly complex set of rhetorical circumstances that— together with newspaper articles, transcripts of the trial itself, letters written by McCollum, and especially voices forced to keep still in Live Oak and the South at large in the early 1950s—yield a rich cache of regional and local silences that to my mind have never been adequately theorized in terms of how McCollum was (supposedly) brought to justice.

Prior to the release of *Ruby McCollum*, an article written by William Bradford Huie appeared in *Ebony* in which he charges that an editorial in the *Suwannee Democrat* after Adams's death depicted the doctor as "a combination of Jesus Christ, Hippocrates, and Franklin Roosevelt" (20). Huie's juxtaposition of religion, medicine, and politics is apt because these three forces dominated much of McCollum's trial. Adams, for example, was a member of the First United Methodist Church in Live Oak, and although he only attended sporadically, the fact that he was given to either reducing or outright forgiving payment for medical services more than made up among the faithful for his lack of Sunday morning piety. So in spite of his spotty church attendance, on August 8, 1952, the *Suwannee Democrat* alleges that the doctor's "closest acquaintances knew that his basic philosophy was Do Unto Others as You Would Have Them Do Unto You" ("Dr. Adams Slain"). If Huie's parallel between Adams and Christ is an exaggeration, it was not far off the mark in the eyes of Live Oak's body politic.

In letters she wrote to Huie, Edith Park also called up biblical imagery in recollections of Adams. Park, however, paints a very different portrait of Adams than that proffered by the *Suwannee Democrat*. She describes Adams as "completely ruthless. Nothing, absolutely nothing got in his way. It reminded me of the sea that opened in the Bible and let those tribes cross through without drowning or getting wet. Everybody just got out of his way and let him go through." Park, for example, disagrees with those who contended Adams used bribery to advance his political career. "They say he paid to get votes," she wrote to Huie. "I'll bet he didn't. He never paid to get anything. I don't know how a man could have so much power and not pay for it."

People in Live Oak had every reason to believe that Adams was well off. After all, he had a burgeoning medical practice, a house in town, and a farm complete with purebred swine. He also frequently boasted that he had large amounts of ready cash at his disposal. Park, however, disagrees with the notion that Adams was (at least in conventional terms) "sound as the American Dollar," as the *Suwannee Democrat* alleged on August 8 ("A Friend"). "His bank accounts were always overdrawn purposely," Park writes. "Many a time I waited for my paycheck, only a day or two, until he would deposit some money." If, as Park argues, Adams's shoddy banking practices were a deliberate ruse, the fate of his supposed fortune remains a mystery. "After the shooting," a Live Oak resident told me, "lots of folks around here visited every Hoboken bank for miles around looking for that money under variations of Adams's name. Nobody ever found anything." Park, however, disagrees. "I feel very sure that there was money left," she wrote to Huie, "and someone has it; neither you nor I nor the Internal Revenue will ever know who. . . . Dr. Adams used to say, 'For every ten cents I make in the office, I make ten dollars on the farm.' And I think he was right. Except I think he made a terrific amount in Bolita money. Too often I saw Charles Hall in there paying him off for him to have made only a little bit."

The fate of Ruby and Sam's bolita fortune, rumored to be an amount much greater than that of Adams's, is also murky. Huie writes in *Ruby Mc-Collum* that Sam drove home immediately after the shooting. He waited until several strange cars parked in the front yard left, and then, so the story goes, he quickly collected only a fraction of his assets—$85,000 in cash from his safe—loaded his children into the car, and drove to Ruby's mother's house in Zuber, a small community near Ocala, Florida. Sam then contacted his brother, Buck, and turned the money over to him. Buck allegedly paid Crews's and Cogdill's initial fees and then gave the remaining cash to Sam Jr., who in the meantime had returned from California, where he had been attending classes at UCLA. From there the McCollum money found its way into a Tampa bank account, but the funds were quickly seized by state attorney Keith Black, who hoped to claim the money for Adams's widow in a wrongful death civil suit. According to Huie, however, when the cash was located and transferred to Live Oak, less than $48,000 remained. What happened to the missing funds remains a mystery to this day.

In Zuber, Sam took to his bed, and in less than twenty-four hours he was dead, according to official reports, of a heart attack. Other than Sam's funeral, which was said to be an elaborate and well-attended affair, his death was largely overshadowed by the media frenzy surrounding his widow. Nonetheless, law officials in Live Oak were quickly dispatched to Chestnut Funeral Home in Ocala, where Sam's body lay before burial. The day before his death, Sam had promised officials he would return to Live Oak for questioning. When he failed to show up and state attorney Keith Black learned of his death, Black, according to Huie, ordered two deputies to Ocala to "take a look at whatever dead nigger is supposed to be Sam. Then find Sam and bring him in here" (*Ruby* 55). As ordered, the men examined the corpse and confirmed that he was, indeed, Sam McCollum.

In spite of evidence to the contrary, rumors persist in Live Oak that Sam McCollum is buried neither in Ocala nor anywhere else. Some people in Live Oak continue to believe that "Bolita Sam" somehow managed to stage his own death. One Live Oak native recalls an incident that supports the legend. The day of Ruby's arraignment, the woman told me, she and a friend were waiting as usual on a street corner in Live Oak for their rides home after working as maids in the homes of prominent white families. A black man neither woman had ever seen before approached them and pointed to a hearse parked nearby. "What would you gals say," the man asked, "if I was to tell you that the man in that coffin is alive?" Declaring him "crazy," the two women dismissed the stranger and he lumbered off, but not before he laughed and called over his shoulder: "Yeah, I'm crazy. Crazy like Sam McCollum."

"I Am Ruby McCollum"

The air in Live Oak was thick with speculation about a number of issues well before McCollum's trial even began. But while fortune hunters tore up country roads and gossips fueled rumors of Sam's possible escape from Live Oak, Ruby McCollum remained securely locked in a solitary cell in Raiford. She was permitted few visitors. Notes she wrote to her attorneys before her trial, however, attest to the fact that she was eager to speak out in her own defense. McCollum wrote to both Crews and Cogdill while she was housed in Raiford, and these texts offer an honest—if incomplete—glimpse into her state of mind prior to the trial. Ruby was clearly agitated, but I get no impression from these letters that she was not completely in control of her faculties. In what I surmise to be her first letter to Crews (the sheets are undated and written on multiple small pages), McCollum writes:

> Buck sent you to defend my case with the help of Mr. Cogdill, so please don't throw me down. Continue to use the defense relationship of six years. He [Adams] is the father of my baby. He let my husband run numbers for my sake. He wanted me to get on that table August 3rd [reference to be explained subsequently]. You read this I am sending you, and you be the judge. . . . Buck doesn't want him [Cogdill] for the main lawyer. He wants you. I told him what happened. . . . This man wants to make me to tell a lie and I am not going to do it. . . . He doesn't want this to come out on the doctor. (McCollum, Letters to Huie)

Several troubling issues surface in this note, the most obvious being McCollum's assertion that John Cogdill induced her "to tell a lie." But what lie could Cogdill have asked Ruby to tell, and why? There is evidence to support the theory that McCollum was coached regarding what to tell authorities regarding the shooting. The account she gave of it in notes written to her defense attorneys and in courtroom testimony is sketchy at best. Perhaps McCollum assumed that her husband's close connections with powerful figures in Live Oak (and her knowledge of what white men in Live Oak were possibly complicit in illegal activities) would continue to work to her advantage as it had in the past. Hurston, for example, speculated in correspondence she sent to Huie that McCollum's actions immediately after the shooting (going home, changing her dress, and calmly preparing formula for the baby) point to the fact that perhaps she "did not expect any serious consequences of her deed." Hurston writes:

> Did a double-cross throw her into her terrible mental state? Did some trouble about the numbers racket enter into the killing? It seemed to me that both Ruby and the prosecution were holding back something on this point; that Ruby was told to keep quiet and that she would receive secret help. Please consider the plot to free her that went awry. [Crews] kept winking his eye and stating confidently that she will never be executed for killing Adams. There is a lot of talk about more than one woman being driven insane by drugs administered by Dr. Adams to make them submit to him sexually. ("Impressions Gained")

In the following note written to her defense attorney, McCollum clearly recalls the conversation she had with Adams prior to the shooting and alleges that Adams pressed her to have sexual relations with him in the treatment room in his office. However, McCollum is much less confident in detailing exactly how the shooting occurred. Here, in her own words, is McCollum's account of the murder:

> That Sunday morning August 3rd, I went to him for something to get the pain out of my shoulder. . . . I told him, "I owe you for two calls. This makes me owe you how much?" He said, "nine dollars." I gave him ten dollars, and he gave me one dollar back. I said, "I want to pay one hundred dollars on the one hundred sixteen dollar bill that was sent to Sam." He said, "O.K." Then he said, "Get on the table." I said, "Wait until another time for that." He started fussing about his money. He shook me and began beating me. I begged him not to bother me. He said, "I'm gonna kill you." He grabbed a pistol and stuck it in my stomach. While tussling over it, it went off. When he turned, it went off again. He wanted me to get on that table. (McCollum, Notes)

If McCollum's account of how the shooting occurred is murky, she is crystal clear as to the reason why: "He wanted me to get on that table." Little else about the actual shooting appears to hold much significance for McCollum. In fact, she recalls the financial transaction between her and the doctor in much greater detail than the murder itself. Her description of the shooting is detached, almost as if she were an observer of Adams's death rather than an active participant in it. The gun takes on a life of its own; "it went off" independent of either her or Adams.

After an all-white jury had been selected and McCollum's sanity at the time of the murder established, her trial suffered a significant setback before it even began in earnest. On November 21, 1952, the *Suwannee Democrat* reported that "the Ruby McCollum murder trial for the shooting of Dr. C. LeRoy Adams was blown sky high here Tuesday when the State Supreme Court suspended the law license of the negress' attorney, P. Guy Crews, of Jacksonville." Crews's offense, the *Democrat* reported, had occurred over twenty years ago when he allegedly "accepted fees from a client but failed to perform legal services for him" ("Suspension").

On December 16, 1952, Odis Henderson of Jasper, Florida, became McCollum's attorney, and one week later the defense added attorney Frank Cannon, formerly of Live Oak but then a county official at Jacksonville. The second half of Zora Neale Hurston's "My Impressions of the Trial" is uncanny in its sensitivity to silences in the McCollum courtroom and the fact that these silences say so much about issues at the heart of southern ideology. Hurston references McCollum's precarious mental state during the course of her trial; she does not, however, mention a significant event that may have contributed to it. On August 23, 1952, McCollum wrote a letter to Crews. The letter is written on a full sheet of pale pink paper quite different from the small notepaper on which McCollum wrote all of her other correspondence from Raiford. An official-looking stamp reading "CENSORED R.H.C." [Raiford House of Corrections] appears in the upper left corner. "Mr. Crews," she writes, "I have not had no relations with the Dr. and no other man but my husband. The Dr. was not connected in any way with my husband in the numbers business as it is rumored. The Dr. is not my baby's father." She signs the letter "Ruby McCollum" (McCollum, Recantation). Huie contends that the letter is "obviously dictated" and points to discrepancies between this letter and McCollum's other correspondence (*Ruby* 76–77). Of course, the letter was presented as evidence during McCollum's trial. Under questioning by the State, McCollum admitted that, indeed, she had written the letter recanting her previous assertion that she had engaged in sexual relations with Dr. Adams and that he was the father of her last child. Under cross-examination by the defense, however, McCollum argued that fear drove her to write the letter. A portion of her testimony follows:

Q. Will you tell the jury now why you wrote that letter?

(State). That would be self-serving.

(The Court). Sustained. . . .

A. Well, the nurse came in and she told me that I had one baby belonging to the doctor and I am going to have another one . . .

(State). We object to that and I move to strike it as not responsive to the question; it is irrelevant and immaterial what the nurse said.

(Defense). It is certainly not irrelevant and immaterial what the nurse said and what the nurse did to her.

(The Court). There is a good deal of difference about what the nurse said along that line. The question is—was she forced to write the letter. That is relevant; the other is not. What the nurse said about babies is stricken from you.

Q. What did the nurse do to you?

A. She gave me a shot. . . .

Q. What did it do?

A. The shot made me nervous and I got where I couldn't sleep and I got real sick from it, and I asked for a piece of paper and an envelope and a three cent stamp, and it was given to me and I sat down and wrote that to Mr. Crews because I was afraid.

Q. Before you wrote that letter were there any officers or a large number of officers who were continually asking you about it or doing anything that made you afraid in reference to your pregnant condition with Dr. Adams?

(State). We object to that question because it is leading. He can let her tell what happened.

(Defense). I would like to let her tell, but he objects to that. Now, when I ask specific questions he says I lead her. . . .

Q. When you say you were afraid when you wrote that letter, what were you afraid of?

A. I don't know; most anything I guess. I was just afraid of being in such a place and didn't know exactly what they were going to do to me or anything of that sort, and I was afraid also that I would get another one of those same shots after it was stated that I would get a bigger one next time.

Q. Who told you that you would get a bigger one next time?

A. The same nurse.

Q. Some time after that did you have a miscarriage?

(State). We object to that; it is not in proper cross; it is irrelevant and immaterial.

(The Court). Sustained.

(State). That is all. (*State of Florida v. Ruby McCollum*, 470–74)

At another point during McCollum's trial, her defense attorney attempted to address the issue of her terminated pregnancy. This time, however, McCollum was not permitted to speak, and both her and Cannon's frustration is almost palpable in the following court transcript excerpt:

> Q. May I ask an additional question of the defendant, if it please the Court?
>
> (The Court). Yes, sir.
>
> Q. You testified this morning that you were pregnant on August 3rd. I ask you if you are pregnant at the present time?
>
> (State). That is irrelevant and immaterial as to the condition of the defendant at this time.
>
> (The Court). Sustained.
>
> Q. I will ask you if after some time after August 3rd of this year if you had what is known as a miscarriage?
>
> (State). We object to that as irrelevant and immaterial, and the question is too broad, vague, and remote, and it is improper and inadmissible.
>
> (The Court). Objection sustained.
>
> (Defense). The defense tenders the witness. (*State of Florida v. Ruby McCollum*, 462)

According to Huie, after McCollum was moved from Raiford in early September, she "suffered an abortion or miscarriage in the Suwannee County jail." Crews's statement to Huie is as follows: "They had needled her or done something to her to make her have that abortion. She had it there in jail alone. When I got up there at night, I thought she was a goner. I drove up the road and got some penicillin and needles and smuggled them in to her and she gave herself the shots that saved her life" (*Ruby* 78). Whether or not to believe the rather melodramatic story of how Crews single-handedly managed to save his client's life is best left to the reader. What is certain, however, is that sometime between McCollum writing the letter recanting her relationship with the doctor and the first few weeks of her incarceration in the Suwannee County Jail, she lost the child she was carrying. Precisely how this occurred may never be known. But regardless of whether McCollum lost the fetus through a natural miscarriage brought on by a combination of isolation, neglect, and fear (certainly a viable possibility) or from an imposed abortion (an equally valid proposition), the end result was the same.

On August 22, 1952, the *Suwannee Democrat* reported that during proceedings held to argue for a change of venue, McCollum "sat with her hand over her tightly closed eyes during most of the hearing" ("Attorney"). After her miscarriage it was evident that McCollum had begun to fold inward in an effort to shield herself from an increasingly horrific outside world. She was, however, judged sane by Dr. William H. McCullagh, a Jacksonville psychiatrist, who was asked to determine her fitness for trial at the request of Judge Adams. The following testimony by McCullagh taken from portions of *The State of Florida v. Ruby McCollum* details his contention that "Ruby McCollum is not psychotic (not insane) at the present time. It is my opinion that she was not psychotic (not insane) at the time of the alleged offense" (98). Interestingly enough, Dr. McCullagh was also the same psychiatrist who hospitalized McCollum twice during the early months of 1952. During McCollum's sanity hearing, McCullagh testified that he hospitalized McCollum for "a nervous disorder classified as a psychoneurosis; depressive and hypochondriacal being the predominating symptoms. . . . By depression I mean she was emotionally despondent or blue and worrying, and by hypochondria I mean that she was preoccupied with feelings she was having" (98, 99). McCullagh then stated that at the time of her hospitalization McCollum "was complaining of discomfort of her chest. . . . She was also complaining of pain in her back and lower abdomen" (99). Tests conducted on McCollum, McCullagh stated, ascertained no medical reason for her ills. However, *nothing* was mentioned during the sanity hearing regarding either a possible psychological toll on McCollum resulting from her alleged abusive six-year relationship with Adams or the trauma induced by her "miscarriage."

Hazel Carby argues that while white women were even more idealized in the South after emancipation, no such privilege extended to black women. "Black women," Carby writes, "were relegated to a place outside the ideological construction of 'womanhood.' That term included only white women; therefore the rape of black women was of no consequence outside the black community" (308–9). Violation of the black female body, then, served as an expression of white dominance. "Lynching and the rape of black women," Carby argues, "were attempts to gain control. The terrorizing of black communities was a political weapon that manipulated ideologies of sexuality" (308). It is ironic, then, that while in the process of raping the mothers, wives, and daughters of black males, some whites justified lynching in the South as an effective method of eradicating what they perceived to be the threat of sexual assault to white women by black men. Anne Goodwyn Jones echoes Carby when she contends that in the South "white women's bodies, voices, and control had long been linchpins to an elaborate ideological structure linking gender with race and class." Perpetuating myths of the white southern woman as one of "the finest productions of masculine art" worked to preserve "purity of blood and thus of white patriarchal lineage." Control of the mythologized white woman, Jones argues, "was particularly crucial since no such behavior characterized white men; on the contrary, their desiring black women and enforcing that desire was visibly producing a lighter race. Dividing women into categories—black and white, lady and woman—was one way to maintain a sense of control; enforcing these categories through the pleasures of privilege and as forms of identity guaranteed cooperation from its targets" (49–50).

Society in the early 1950s South dictated that as a white man involved with a black woman Adams was—in some circles—quietly exempt from serious censure. Concerns arose in the community, however, when the details of his murder became national news and threatened to expose the all-too-common sexual exploitation of black women by white men in the South. The problem, at least according to some Suwannee County citizens, was not that Adams and McCollum allegedly engaged in an illicit sexual relationship that produced two pregnancies. Nor was the problem that, as McCollum argued, Adams beat and otherwise abused McCollum for several years. The *real* problem stemmed from meddling interlopers in the northern press who speculated about the possible misdeeds of a prominent white man and, in the process, cast a critical eye on the white race in Live Oak and the South as a whole. This exposure was for many a far more egregious crime than Adams's alleged mistreatment of McCollum. Blacks also feared the intrusion of the media because such "trouble" brought with it the inevitable increase in white surveillance and instances of retaliatory violence against the black community. Lillian Smith describes the rationale behind attempts to reinforce this cycle of silence and efforts to protect what was commonly known as the southern tradition. "*Outside interference* became a compulsive cry to every suggestion of change," writes Smith. "Always the Outsider did the evil. . . . For everything that could not live in our mythic minds was Outside. We alienated reason; made strangers of knowledge and facts; labeled as 'intruder' all moral responsibility for our acts. Home was the mythic mind—it still is for millions" (221–22).

One consequence of what Smith calls the "mythic mind" was that regardless of McCollum's wealth, she, like other black women in the early 1950s South, could not conform to Jones's classifications of a "lady" or even a "woman"; in the final analysis, McCollum was inconsequential chattel. As such, McCollum's body was never an object of desire; it was a battlefield, and Adams's purported conquest of it signified an act of colonization and all that the term implies. Hurston writes that McCollum's initial involvement with Adams occurred in part because "Ruby was a woman who was used to getting her way about things. Sam had hurt her, so there was no longer any mingling blood." Hurston, however, contends that as the relationship between Adams and McCollum intensified, so did McCollum's sense of captivity. "There came a time," Hurston writes, "as indicated by the length of the affair and her boldness, that she no longer lived in Live Oak, nor yet the United States. Her permanent address was Dr. C. LeRoy Adams. It was a phase of life mounted on granite. The horizon of her world had no gate" ("Impressions Gained"). If in the time prior to Adams's murder McCollum had been thoroughly colonized, after the shooting it is evident that on several occasions she attempted to reclaim some sense of identity and agency. For example, on December 8, 1953, McCollum wrote to her attorneys: "To deprive me of my three month baby is murder. . . . No one knows anything about me except I am Ruby regardless to color." On March 27, 1954, McCollum again asserted her authority. "Don't send me any more envelopes addressed to no one," she wrote to Crews. "If I want to see anyone I have hands to write and address them." On March 25, 1954, however, McCollum is clearly despondent. In a note written to Huie, she pleads: "Please get me a cash bond or have me turned out of this place free. Please do that as quick as possible." Although it is evident from the note's content that McCollum was deeply troubled, her closing line belies any assumption that, although clearly under strain, she was beaten. Written in a clear, firm hand, the last sentence reads simply, "I am Ruby McCollum."

McCollum's declaration "I am Ruby McCollum," the affirmation of herself *as* herself through text, is, I argue, an attempt at what Hélène Cixous calls *écriture féminine*, or writing the body. "By writing her self," Cixous argues, "woman will return to the body which has been more than confiscated from her" through patriarchal oppression. According to Cixous, a woman "must urgently learn to speak," and in doing so will "become *at will* the taker and initiator, for her own right, in every symbolic system, in every political process" (880). Writing the body, then, is much more than the act of women freely producing discourse; it is the act—through uniquely feminine discourse—*of producing free women*. A woman's reclamation of her body *as* her body is, then, a simultaneous reclamation of her voice and her soul—both of which McCollum contended that Adams had stolen from her over a period of more than six years. There are compelling parallels between Cixous' theories regarding both the need for women to reclaim the right of expression and the subjugation that both black and white women endured in the South in the early 1950s. Attempts to silence McCollum, then, offer themselves up as representative of how regional mythologies regarding race and gender worked to enforce and perpetuate an overall rhetoric of silence in Live Oak and the South as a whole. Cixous writes: "It is by writing, from and toward women, and by taking up the challenge of speech which has been governed by the phallus, that women will confirm women to a place other than that which is reserved in and by the symbolic, that is, in a place other than silence. Women should break out of the snare of silence. They shouldn't be conned into accepting a domain which is the margin or the harem" (881). Breaking cycles of silence enforced through patriarchy, according to Cixous, is how acts of writing the body—exemplified, I argue, by McCollum's declaration "I am Ruby McCollum"—set claim to an empowered feminine space both in and against a lived experience exclusively dominated, and so colonized, by men.

Sandra Gilbert and Susan Gubar describe the either-or logic of a patriarchal world when they write, "It is debilitating to be *any* woman in a society where women are warned that if they do not behave like angels they must be monsters" (53). In the early 1950s South, this logic held particular sway for black women. It was difficult for anyone in Live Oak to admit that McCollum's actions on August 3, 1952, were anything but monstrous. Even before the murder she was not a particularly sympathetic figure, and the fact that gambling dollars funded her comfortable lifestyle made her especially suspect in the eyes of many of Live Oak's "good Christian citizens," both white and black. The point regarding Gilbert and Gubar's observation as I relate it to McCollum, however, is their emphasis on the clear division between good and evil in a patriarchy-driven society. Women who don't obey the rules are not just "bad girls," they are *monsters*—grotesque, subhuman, and asexual. The fact that McCollum was black, a woman, and wealthy made her suspect on three counts, and her alleged involvement with Adams, even if such involvement were not of her own free will, certainly did not conform to what constituted "angelic" female behavior according to dominant power structures. Many people, for example, discounted accounts that Adams abused McCollum; some argued that she in fact pursued him and that their long sexual relationship took place by mutual agreement. If that were the case, they argued, she deserved to be punished equally both for the murder itself and her bold crossing of race and class lines. Those individuals willing to consider the possibility that Adams actually raped McCollum ironically drew much the same conclusion regarding the urgency to bring her to justice. Somehow, they argued, she must have "asked for it."

As McCollum gradually moved away from what the white patriarchal society in Live Oak deemed acceptable behavior, she became—if certainly not a monster—then significantly altered. According to Gilbert and Gubar, women exhibit specific symptoms in response to oppression and "the ways in which patriarchal socialization literally makes women sick, both physically and mentally" (53). For example, well before the murder McCollum complained of mysterious aches and pains for which no medical cause could be determined. Moreover, during the course of her trial she seemed to diminish in size, folding inward as if to render herself invisible. The chair she occupied during her days in court, for example, allowed her feet to swing clear of the floor, and in a photograph snapped of her being escorted back to her cell after a day of testimony, she is hunched in a coat much too large for her, chin down, and flanked on either side by two white men who tower over her diminutive frame. By June 1954, McCollum and her family seem to have all but vanished. The child everyone clamored to see, little Loretta, was particularly inaccessible. After the murder she was taken in by Ruby's sister in New Jersey, who kept her carefully sequestered away from prying eyes. Even photographs of the McCollum family proved elusive, and photographs of Ruby were particularly difficult to come by. For example, Ruby's brother, Matt Jackson, wrote to Huie on June 29, 1954: "I do not have no photographs of the McCollum family, but I am trying on all hands to secure you some. I think my brother in Ocala has a class picture of Ruby, and Mr. Crews has one of Loretta. . . . I have written Sam Jr. for one, and as yet have not located one of Samuel Senior although I am doing my best." On July 26, 1954, Matt again contacts Huie: "I am making all effort that I possibly can to be some help to my sister and you. . . . I enclose photos of Kay and Sonja. Have not received one from Sam Jr. in service yet. I hope to soon." A picture of Ruby McCollum, however, does accompany Huie's story in *Ebony*. She appears thin, bewildered, and very much alone. The caption beneath the photograph reads, "Snapshot of Ruby McCollum was made in jail and smuggled out by friends" (20). Perhaps Matt found a creative way to accommodate Huie's request for his sister's photograph after all.

If McCollum's seeming instability resulted from the violent colonization of her body and a white patriarchal southern society that influenced and silently condoned the taking of it, then perhaps her actions on August 3, 1952, are more a commentary on the destructive force of race and class divisions in the South than an isolated instance of a madwoman's inexplicable violence. Joel Peckham writes that victims of trauma often adopt a "siege mentality" in response to regionalized race, class, and gender divisions. Over time, Peckham contends, these divisions grew increasingly difficult to justify or enforce, and, as is the case with McCollum, they take their toll in a condition akin to battle fatigue. He writes:

> By the beginning of the twentieth century southern culture had come to be based on the singular relationship between two worlds, vacillating violently at times between segregation and integration because of their inability to maintain that separation in the face of a shared culture, history, and location. The result was a culture that began to see itself in terms of transgression and taboo, borders and border crossings—inevitable passages across forbidden territories, illicit contact fraught with intense and dangerous consequences. It is understandable, given the nature of such a potentially explosive dynamic, that many members of each society began to take on a siege mentality, perceiving contact in terms of incursion and invasion. (33–34)

References to trespassing and border crossing consistent with Peckham's siege mentality also appear in Alice Bullard's discussion of the effects of colonization and her contention that "mental predispositions or states, such as trances, spirit possessions, euphoria, or phobia, take on significance within specific cultural contexts" (114). Bullard argues that French colonization played an important role in instances of madness found in North African women in the late eighteenth and early nineteenth centuries. The reactions of these North African women, whom Bullard calls "the detritus of the colonial process," are similar to those of McCollum. Bullard contends that "the 'mentally ill' in all periods are border-crossers whose transgressions reveal suppressed and hidden desires. . . . They leave rationality—in its concrete, systematic expression as 'civilization'—to dwell in madness" (115).

Like Bullard's colonized North African women, McCollum found it difficult to assimilate herself into the paradoxical confines of southern race and gender formations. Bullard cites several studies conducted by French psychiatrists who, although drawing connections between areas of dense population and an increase in instances of mental illness in women, pointedly ignored the effect of colonization on their patients and the effects of both French *and* African patriarchal practices of control. Bullard's observations regarding the perception and treatment of madness in women in colonized North Africa argues important unexplored connections among repression, femininity, and madness that I contend are particularly relevant to our understanding of McCollum. In the following excerpt, for example, Bullard advocates a new historicizing of these colonized North African women that takes into account the fact that social repression may well have contributed to instances of mental illness:

> Consider the dimensions of the evidence: the intimate link between madness and civilization; women's roles in civilization, both as prescribed and as practiced; the animosity between French and North Africans, yet their shared complicity in the patriarchal domination of women; the possibility of finding cases of "madness" that reflect prophetic or emancipatory voices (voices intent on breaking free of the rationale of the colonial order); the perennial identification of women by patriarchal cultures as irrational, unreasonable, incapable of intellectual attainments or the responsible exercise of power; the masking and limiting of female attainments through these derisive stereotypes. A gendered decolonized history would have to accommodate all of these narratives. (127)

I contend that Ruby McCollum and Bullard's North African women have compelling similarities. Both were victims of violent acts of colonization and patriarchy; both exhibited symptoms of madness; and both were closeted away without serious consideration of how the first act may have informed behavior that society viewed as symptomatic of the second. In fact, dismissing McCollum as simply "crazy" was not only the most convenient way to explain away her uncharacteristic behavior on August 3, 1952, it was also an efficient method of deflecting discussion regarding larger southern ideologies that in reality may have caused it. Certainly Bullard is correct in her assertion that a "gendered decolonized history" would advance our understanding of mental illness in colonized North African women during the late eighteenth and early nineteenth centuries. Such an approach, however, can also shed light on minority women like Ruby McCollum who in the early 1950s American South struggled to find their voices in a segregated, gendered, and profoundly silenced society.

"The Biggest Crop Raised in Dixie"

The prevalence of fundamentalist Christianity in the South and concomitant notions of "God-given" tenets regarding race and gender have direct bearing on Live Oak's reaction to McCollum and the events of August 3, 1952. Like many other small southern towns at the time, Live Oak was a deeply religious community. The prevalence of Christian ideology not only in Live Oak but also in the greater southern states during the early 1950s is important because these discourses often implicitly advanced southern myths and acts of silence they endorsed. During McCollum's trial, the law worked to the advantage of dominant power formations in Live Oak—specifically, those in place in the white community. These power structures, in turn, depended on the perpetuation of southern ideology and the silencing of marginal discourses that might challenge or refute it. I argue that versions of fundamentalist Christian doctrine were, and still are, powerful vehicles for the reinscription of many oppressive southern myths—two of the most influential in the case of McCollum being the superiority of the white race and the inferior position of women. Judge Adams, then, did not attempt to sway public opinion in his courtroom regarding the importance of silencing McCollum. He didn't have to. With most citizens of Suwannee County thoroughly indoctrinated in the stance of southern religious ideology regarding race and gender, citizens in Live Oak knew that both Judge Adams and the State of Florida had God on their side, and in the South there is no more powerful ally.

Lillian Smith writes that during each summer of her childhood an expectant air preceded the arrival of traveling evangelists and the revivals they brought to town. This sense of expectation, however, was always tempered with a healthy dose of fear. Guilt played an instrumental part in the process of keeping the faithful in line and was, Smith writes, "the biggest crop raised in Dixie, harvested each summer just before cotton is picked" (103). In the early 1950s, most southerners had been taught since birth that sinners young and old risked serious consequences, but because temptation was everywhere, staying true to the uncompromising "path of righteousness" proved no easy task. Revivals were one way of publicly calling back to the fold those individuals who had strayed from the Bible and what many believed to be the literal word of God. Childhood revivals also made a vivid impression on Harry Crews, who writes that traveling evangelists stressed the act of repentance and, hopefully, God's redemption. "Hell came right along with God, hand in hand," Crews writes. "The stink of sulfur swirled in the air of the church, fire burned in the aisles, and brimstone rained out of the rafters. From the evangelist's oven mouth spewed images of a place with pitchforks, and devils, and lakes of fire that burned forever. God had fixed a place like that because he loved us so much" (167).

Crews's description nicely captures the paradox inherent in much of early 1950s Christian doctrine in the South and what I will argue to be the guilt, shame, and fear characteristic of it. Of course, not all versions of Christianity taught in southern Baptist and Methodist churches in the early 1950s were of the fire-and-brimstone variety remembered by Crews. Many churches in the South were then, and are now, led by gentle, soft-spoken ministers who preached of God's love and forgiveness instead of His penchant for Puritanical wrath. Yet even those ministers who eschewed fear and guilt as the preferred methods for filling their pews on Sunday mornings shared with their more radical counterparts the deep-seated beliefs that blacks were inferior to whites, and that women, no matter what their race, were inferior to men. I contend that these two tenets regarding race and gender form the bedrock of McCollum's trial and conviction. Because southern Christianity often worked to endorse these myths and occupied *the* central position of power and influence in Live Oak and the South in the early 1950s, its rhetoric and ideology deserve mention here.

Judge Adams routinely addressed spectators present in the courtroom and members of the defense and prosecution teams as "brother" or "brethren." The use of these gender-specific terms served two purposes. First, it pointedly worked to exclude women, and, second, it established the role of all participants in the drama—no matter if they were part of the prosecution, the defense team, or simply curious observers—as members of a discourse community grounded in, or at the very least familiar with, southern versions of Christianity. Of course, Adams never overtly referenced biblical scripture when making decisions concerning legal protocol; to do so would have been a blatant undermining of tenets fundamental to the entire field of jurisprudence—tenets that Judge Adams consistently argued to be of the utmost importance in keeping McCollum's trial "fair" and "impartial." That being said, it is impossible to read McCollum's court transcripts without acknowledging Christian undertones at many points during the proceedings. Shivesh Thakur writes that religion and politics are inextricable, with religious organizations frequently using their power and influence to alter state policy, and politicians seeking the endorsement of religious individuals who also just happen to be voters. "Politics and religion have always had this ambivalent relationship," Thakur contends, "each fearing the other's encroachment, on the one hand, but also, from time to time, needing the other's support. . . . Religion and politics, and, therefore, religion and state, have always, in practice, been hard to keep apart" (87–88). Read in the context of the South of the early 1950s, Thakur's comments are particularly relevant because both law and religion were committed to enforcing racial segregation, and the movement has deep roots. Fred Hobson writes that Daniel Hundley's 1860 text *Social Relations in Our Southern States* provides evidence that the antebellum South saw "slavery as a positive good" in the eyes of both man and God because it "had brought the Negro out of the savagery of Africa and into the light of Christianity and, besides, had made the American South bear fruit" (71). After the Civil War, Hobson argues, white southerners chose to view even their defeat on the battlefield as evidence of superiority. "The defeat," writes Hobson, "came to be seen as *felix culpa*: the South had fallen *because* it was God's Chosen. . . . Had not God's Chosen, earlier, spent a season in captivity?" (86).

Paul van Buren argues that language lies at the heart of any religion and especially Christianity. "It makes sense to attempt to understand a religion such as Christianity, in any of its various forms," he writes, "as a linguistic enterprise. . . . In its scriptures, its many historical expressions, its cultic activity, and its dogmas and teachings from various times, it has put language in the center of the picture it presents" (67–68). Kenneth Chafin takes van Buren's concept of Christianity's linguistic foundation a step further when he argues that religious discourse in the South is primarily a political activity whose longevity and influence are directly linked to any given speaker's degree of rhetorical prowess. "It was the fundamentalists' flawless use of rhetoric, in the classical sense," Chafin writes, "and not their theology or beliefs about the Bible, that allowed them to accomplish their goals. . . . It is rhetoric that has been used to gain power and control, to manipulate people, to mask personal ambition, to cover up personal insecurities, and to hide a fear of the modern world with all its complexities" (xi). I take no issue with van Buren's argument that religion is first and foremost a linguistic activity. Also accurate is Chafin's contention that rhetoric fueled the advancement of fundamentalist religion in the South. I would add to these assertions, however, that rhetorically dynamic *acts of silence* also played an instrumental and undertheorized role in the perpetuation of southern race and gender ideologies fostered through religious discourses in the early 1950s South. During McCollum's trial, religion was part and parcel of everyday life in Live Oak, and it was common practice for fundamentalist ministers to fiercely contend that women were inferior to men (while at the same time many of these men actively idealized the vague notion of southern woman*hood*). Carl Kell and L. Raymond Camp contend that such thinking persists today, particularly among members of the Southern Baptist Convention, and reflects outdated conceptions of race and gender superiority in the South. "If Southern Baptist social practices reflect a bygone era," they write, "that seems undaunting to its presidents. Noticeably, these skilled sermonizers embrace the South of yesterday, replete with its myths of gender submissiveness and repressive fictions about sexuality. Thus, the SBC is steadfast about its adherence to antebellum Southernness, perhaps hoping that the denominational pulpit can somehow be used to return the nation to a clearer time in history" (128). If Kell and Camp's observations accurately reflect the mind-set of the Southern Baptist Convention today, Live Oak in the early 1950s had an even stronger nostalgic longing for the past and was willing to use whatever weapons it had at its disposal to speed retreat into it. McCollum's actions on August 3, 1952, threatened to challenge longtime race and gender structures that had for years been bolstered by religious rhetoric. As Kell and Camp illustrate, southern religious rhetoric advocated adherence to what the South had determined to be "God's will" while at the same time working to the advantage of white males seeking to preserve powerful positions of dominance in a community both controlled and motivated by fear. This fear, of course, came from the ever-present dread of racial violence in Live Oak against anyone willing to speak out in McCollum's defense, but it also came from religious rhetoric that emphasized God's wrath against those who chose to ignore His teachings. Since submission to church teachings in the South—and, by implication, acceptance of race and gender oppression—was the cornerstone of every good Christian, breaking the silences surrounding McCollum not only invited physical retribution but was also seen by many as showing a disregard for God's will. In other words, speculating about McCollum's motive for pulling the trigger was one thing; running the risk of *committing a sin* by doing so was quite another.

"Irrelevant and Immaterial"

The inscription of patriarchy and white supremacy through southern ideology made it possible for McCollum to admit during the course of her trial that, yes, she had engaged in sexual acts with Dr. LeRoy Adams. She was even allowed to state that Adams had fathered her last child and that she had been afraid during much of their relationship. She was not, however, permitted to describe how Dr. Adams frequently beat her. The implication of McCollum's enforced silence on this aspect of their relationship is clear. In the Deep South in 1952, many white men chose to look the other way if one of their numbers chose to have sex (consensual or otherwise) with a black woman. What was *not* acceptable, however, was to drag the "good name" of an upstanding white man through the mud by suggesting that Adams physically abused McCollum or was involved in any way in illegal gambling. For example, consider the following excerpt from McCollum's trial that occurred during McCollum's cross-examination by the defense:

> Q. Prior to the 3rd day of August had you ever had any altercation or any trouble with Dr. Adams?
>
> (State). We object on the ground that it is too broad, remote, vague and indefinite.
>
> (The Court). Sustained.
>
> Q. Now, at any time in Dr. Adams' office prior to his death did Dr. Adams ever slap you or hit you or shake you?
>
> (State). That is too broad, vague and indefinite, and it is not shown to be a part of the *res gestae* [Latin, "things done"; the events at issue], and it is irrelevant and immaterial.
>
> (The Court). Sustained.
>
> Q. I will ask you if prior to August 3rd, during the month of July, he ever struck you in his office?
>
> (The Court). Sustained.
>
> Q. I ask you if during the month of May, 1952, Dr. Adams ever struck you in his office across the street over here?
>
> (State). Same objection as to the two previous questions.
>
> (The Court). Sustained.
>
> Q. I ask you if during the month of March, 1952, if you had some altercation with Dr. Adams in his office across the street over here and he slapped you at that time?
>
> (State). We object upon the same grounds, and upon the further ground that it is leading.

(The Court). Sustained.

Q. I ask you if during the month of February, 1952, if Dr. Adams across the street in his office over here ever slapped or hit you or beat you or bruised you in any way?

(State). We object on the same grounds as to the last question.

(The Court). Sustained.

Q. I ask you if during the month of January, 1952, across the street in his office, if Dr. Adams struck and slapped you, or beat you or hit you?

(State). I object upon the same grounds stated to the last question.

(The Court). Sustained.

Q. I ask you if you ever had sexual relations with Dr. Adams during the year 1952 in his office across the street from this courthouse in Suwannee County, Florida?

(State). We object to that upon the ground it is repetition.

(The Court). It is repetition; she has already testified she did. But go ahead and answer it.

A. Yes, I did. (*State of Florida v. Ruby McCollum*, 452–53)

As the previous testimony illustrates, McCollum was permitted to state that she had sexual relations with Dr. Adams, but she was not permitted to discuss the circumstances under which the relations occurred. McCollum's notes to her attorneys, however, tell the full story of the abuse she alleged she endured during her relationship with Adams and her submission to him for fear of her life. To Judge Adams (as well as much of Suwannee County and the South at large) it was immaterial that Adams physically abused McCollum. It was of the utmost importance, however, that this abuse not be entered into testimony. To do so would possibly sway the jury's sympathies in McCollum's favor and away from what had always been described as a senseless killing "over a doctor bill." More important, to allow McCollum to testify to Dr. Adams's abuse would constitute public acknowledgment of it; this acknowledgment would, in effect, validate the *possibility* that McCollum had killed Adams as an act of self-preservation and give her a margin of sympathy with the jury that the State could simply not risk.

In similar fashion, the defense team was not permitted to introduce Loretta, the daughter McCollum contended had been fathered by Adams, into evidence. A portion of McCollum's testimony follows:

(Defense). At this time the defense has present the child that is testified about by this witness in the balcony of this courtroom, and we desire to present that child to its mother for the purpose of identifying it and for the purpose of inspection and a view of it by the jury itself.

(State). We object to the statement of counsel because the statement is improper in the presence of the jury; next, there has certainly been no proper predicate laid for the presentment of such evidence or purported evidence, and, next, it is undertaking to present here something that is entirely irrelevant and immaterial, and, next, it is undertaking to present evidence here that could constitute no defense to the charge upon which the defendant is now being tried, and, next, it is trying to admit into the record here as evidence something that is improper and not admissible.

(The Court). The objection is sustained.

(Defense). I do not wish to disobey the Court's order . . .

(The Court). The objection is sustained; go ahead with your examination.

(Defense). May I make a further comment?

(The Court). The Court has ruled. Go ahead with the witness if you have got any further questions.

Q. Ruby, will you describe the features of this last child that you have testified that Dr. Adams was the father, as to its color and as to its hair and as to its features?

(State). [Objection identical to previous].

(The Court). The objection is sustained.

Q. Is the child that you testified that Dr. Adams is its father, is it in the courtroom to your knowledge today?

A. Yes, sir.

(State). We object on the same grounds just stated to the previous question.

(The Court). Sustained.

(State). And we move to strike the answer of the witness.

(The Court). Ruby, I don't want to have to tell you any more not to answer until you see that none of the lawyers are going to raise an objection.

(Witness). O.K.

(The Court). You bear that in mind. (*State of Florida v. Ruby McCollum*, 446–48)

For those present in the courtroom who did not already know Loretta, she would not have been difficult to identify. She was a beautiful child with long, wavy hair and a ready smile. Moreover, in photographs her resemblance to Dr. Adams is startling. But in spite of her attractiveness and pleasing disposition, Loretta's birth pushed McCollum even closer to the breaking point. Before her trial, McCollum wrote to her attorneys and described Adams's reaction when she asked his help in preventing further pregnancies. The note reads, in part:

> After the baby came, I asked if he would operate on me so I wouldn't get that way again. . . . He said, "I will operate on you." He gave me a needle full of medicine. . . . I was real sick for four days before he called and asked how was I doing. He came out to my house and told me, "That was the kind of operation [you] needed." Then I told him, "Please don't let me die. I will do anything anytime if I have to. . . ." He said, "The idea of you wanting to be cut on. Lots of women wish they had the healthy ovaries or organs you have. I am not going to cut you, and you better not have one. When I get ready for you to have one, I will do it and not before." Then I said, "O.K. You are the boss."

Lillian Smith calls biracial offspring "the South's rejected children" and describes them as "little ghosts playing and laughing and weeping on the edge of the southern memory" (124–25). According to notes written by McCollum to her defense attorneys, however, Adams flaunted Loretta and considered her a prize of sorts; she was the public manifestation of his control over Ruby (and Sam) and living proof to the citizens of Live Oak that he had extensive power and was free to wield it as he pleased. As such, Loretta's role in the McCollum affair makes a compelling political statement about the complexity of southern ideology and the role of selective silence in its perpetuation. Patricia Yaeger writes that children in general occupy a complex space in the South. I would argue, however, that biracial children like Loretta are particularly relevant to discussions of silence in southern culture and the McCollum affair in particular. Yaeger writes that the southern children can carve out a "narrative space" for challenging southern ideology. Within this narrative space, Yaeger argues, the South's children function as seismologists who record tremors resulting from the collision of southern custom and logic:

Marginal to mainstream culture but caught up in its process of in-
doctrination, the child may question her society's values and provide
a narrative space for challenging its beliefs. But children also become
a tragic center for exploring the effects of race and class politics in
everyday life. As the focus of adult rules and regulations, the child is
a victim as well as a seismologist who registers the costs of a classist
or a sexist ethic; she becomes a vivid, painful pressure point, a site of
strain and unrest within an unjust social system. What the child is
busy learning, along with fractions and table manners, is an order, a
framework, a set of ideological desires and constraints. (136)

I contend that if Loretta's parents came from both the black and white
races, she is a particularly appropriate and inclusive representation of Yaeger's southern child. Yet if we turn Yaeger's paradigm on its head, Loretta
is much more than merely characteristic of children in the South; during McCollum's trial she was southern ideology made manifest. Yaeger
writes that children in the South serve as seismic recorders of regional
ideological aftershocks. I would add that biracial children like Loretta
are also the *literal result of them*. Like wreckage in the aftermath of an
earthquake, these children are the consequence of powerful frictions
produced deep within the underlying bedrock of southern ideology. Mc-
Collum's trial cleaved Live Oak's fragile landscape to reveal these pressure-
producing contradictions just under the town's decorous surface. As debris
from the all-too-public collapse of these ideology-based "rules" concerning
race and silence, both Loretta and her mother were prima facie evidence to
citizens in Live Oak that only chaos and confusion came from disturbing
the segregated foundation of their town.

Efforts during McCollum's trial to enforce specific silences concerning Adams's abusive behavior, Loretta's parentage, and McCollum's "miscarriage" were clear attempts by Live Oak's judicial system to stabilize a
southern ideological landscape severely shaken by members of the outside
press. And although damage had certainly been done, the community was
resolved in the task that lay before it: clearing the wreckage, sequestering
it away, and hoping against hope that the foundation of their town was
strong enough to withstand future aftershocks from Ruby McCollum until she could legally—and permanently—be eliminated.

Figure 1. Suwannee County Courthouse. Live Oak, Florida, 2004.

Figure 2. Former home of Dr. C. LeRoy Adams. Live Oak, Florida, 2004.

Figure 3. Former home of Ruby and Sam McCollum. Live Oak, Florida, 2004.

Figure 4. Grave site of Clifford LeRoy Adams. Live Oak, Florida, 2003.

Figure 5. Near murder site of Willie James Howard. Live Oak, Florida, 2005.

Figure 6. William Brad-
ford Huie. Live Oak,
Florida, early 1950s.
Courtesy of Martha
Hunt Huie.

Figure 7. Grave site behind Hopewell Baptist Church. Near Live Oak, Florida,
2004.

Figure 8. Road leading to rural cemetery where Jackson family members are buried. Near Ocala, Florida, 2004.

Figure 9. Rural cemetery where Jackson family members are buried. Near Ocala, Florida, 2004.

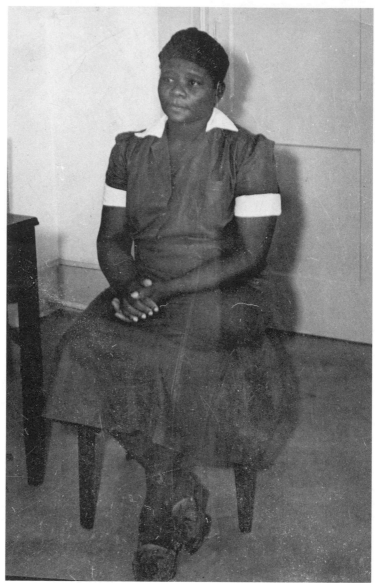

Figure 10. Ruby McCollum. Courtesy of GRM Associates, Inc., Agents for the *Pittsburgh Courier*.

three Discourses of
Contention

. . . .

Punctuating McCollum's Sentence(s) of Silence

I have been here since 1954, September 16. This is December 16,

1971. I have been up here seventeen years. I want to go back to

my own home now in Suwannee County. Please help me.

Letter from Ruby McCollum to William Bradford Huie,
State Mental Hospital, Chattahoochee, Florida

ON DECEMBER 13, 1953, Ruby McCollum was found guilty of murder in the first degree and sentenced to death by electrocution—a mandatory ruling in Florida. Attorneys for McCollum filed an appeal on April 9, 1954, that called for the case to be heard by the Florida Supreme Court. By this point, McCollum had gained another ally, a black attorney named Releford McGriff who practiced in Jacksonville. Shortly after McGriff joined her defense team, the Supreme Court found that a reversible error had occurred during McCollum's first trial when the jury visited the crime scene without her being present. As a result, McCollum was granted a new trial slated to begin in late August.

The appellate court based its decision on the following section of McCollum's appeal:

> It was imperative that counsel try to discuss the evidence with the appellant before she took the witness stand and that is the reason why a motion was made for a view of the premises by the jury. . . . The judge sent the jury out to view the premises and left the defendant in the custody of the sheriff in the courthouse and after the jury returned to the courthouse the Judge excused them for the night. Next morning, without any motion from anybody, he sent the jury back to view the premises in the presence of the defendant. . . . Even after this second unlawful view of the premises by the jury, the trial judge did not accompany the jury to the premises and another view was held without the attendance of the trial judge as required by the statute. These were the acts of an arbitrary judge who was prejudiced against the defendant in a high degree. It will be noted that the statute provides that the defendant shall be present, "unless the defendant absents himself without the permission of the Court." The defendant was in custody, without bail, and under no possibility could she absent herself anywhere except where the Court put her." (*Ruby McCollum v. State of Florida,* 42–43)

On this point, the Florida Supreme Court concurred with the appellate court. In his discussion of Supreme Court of Florida, *En Banc. McCollum v. State,* July 20, 1954, Justice Sebring writes:

> The issue is whether under the circumstances narrated the trial court committed error necessitating a new trial.
>
> Section 914.01, Florida Statutes 1951, F.S.A., provides that in all prosecutions for felony the defendant *shall be present* at arraign-

ment; when a plea is made; at the calling, examination, challenging, impaneling and swearing of the jury; at all proceedings before the court when the jury is present; when evidence is addressed to the court out of the presence of the jury for the purpose of laying the foundation for the introduction of evidence before the jury; at the rendition of the verdict; and *at a view by the jury*. (Sebring 3)

Consequently, the Florida Supreme Court ruled that "the judgment and sentence appealed from must be reversed, and a new trial had, for the reasons herein stated" (Sebring 8).

By 1954, McCollum had been housed in solitary confinement in the Suwannee County Jail for almost two years, and during that time her mental state appeared to steadily deteriorate. Along with her brother, Matt Jackson, McCollum's defense attorneys noted her decline; an insanity plea seemed inevitable and the best chance for McCollum to avoid the death penalty. Publicity generated by Zora Neale Hurston and William Bradford Huie helped keep outside interest in the McCollum case alive, an important factor if Suwannee County officials were to follow the official letter of the law and not their own localized version of it. In the months following McCollum's guilty verdict, articles printed by the *Pittsburgh Courier*, for example, raised questions regarding the legality of McCollum's conviction and her enforced state of seclusion. Hurston contributed several pieces focusing on the McCollum case, but even after her articles—including a ten-part series on McCollum's life story—ended, other *Courier* journalists continued to cover the saga. Hurston's articles in the *Courier*, however, were particularly important to efforts made in McCollum's behalf. By focusing specifically on the motivations behind McCollum's actions and not simply the sensational murder itself, Hurston emphasized the *humanness* of McCollum and her complex role as both a black woman and a resident of the Deep South. Through interviews conducted with McCollum's family and friends, Hurston's stories in the *Courier* portray McCollum as both a victim and at times a woman who contributed to her own fate through a complex tangle of pride, obsession, and fear. If, according to Hurston, McCollum was a self-admitted murderess, she was also, as Hurston writes in a letter to Huie, "a woman terribly in love, and with us females that makes strange and terrible creatures of us" (Kaplan 713). It is this level of insight that makes Hurston's columns about McCollum in the *Courier* so compelling and also accounts for Hurston's vacillation between pity and condemnation in terms of her opinion of McCollum. Clearly Hurston's unique positioning as a black woman raised not too far from Live Oak enabled her to closely identify with McCollum and the silences that bound her. Hurston herself had survived a brush with the law in the form of a 1949 unfounded morals charge, and her columns about McCollum in the *Courier* are often as revealing of Hurston's psyche as they are that of the subject she examined. These columns are valuable not only because they provide an honest assessment of McCollum and her dilemma but also because they provide a compelling and highly personal glimpse into Hurston late in her career—a time when, like McCollum, she was wracked with uncertainty.

During the course of her *Courier* series, Hurston wrote several letters to William Bradford Huie, and these letters are among the most intriguing of her prolific correspondence to personal friends and business associates. Since Hurston contributed a great deal to Huie's *Ruby McCollum: Woman in the Suwannee Jail* in terms of both research and actual text, and since both writers shared an intense concern for McCollum's safety and well-being, Hurston had close ties to Huie. However, in addition to discussing the McCollum affair, the letters also reflect Hurston's ongoing struggle to reconcile ambiguous feelings concerning the black race. For these reasons, the Hurston-Huie letters are arguably the most complete and personal account of Hurston's complex stance concerning a variety of issues including race, writing, gender, and the South. Valerie Boyd writes that during the process of composing the *Courier* articles, "Hurston found not only a responsive black audience for her work, she also found her voice again" (417). Boyd is correct that Hurston did resume writing in earnest after the completion of her *Courier* series. However, if writing about McCollum helped Hurston find her voice, she used it in her correspondence with Huie to speak primarily of acts of silence and exclusion that both she and McCollum faced as women of color—intensely personal musings that even a liberal northern newspaper like the *Courier* would have found too controversial for its readership.

If correspondence with Huie provided a much-needed outlet for Hurston's complicated psyche, Huie also owed Hurston a debt. It was Hurston who first piqued Huie's curiosity about the McCollum case when she enlisted his help in uncovering "the truth" in Live Oak. In fact, if Hurston had not contacted Huie during her research for the *Courier* series, Huie's best-selling *Ruby McCollum: Woman in the Suwannee Jail* would in all probability never have been written. In fairness to Huie, however, by the mid 1950s, he did not lack for accolades. A well-established writer of both fiction and nonfiction, Huie had no qualms about tackling controversial and often dangerous issues head-on and had made a name for himself during his coverage of the Emmett Till lynching for *Look* magazine. In fact, as late as 1967, after the publication of his explosive novel *The Klansman*, he defended himself with a shotgun as local Klan members burned a cross in the front yard of his Alabama home. Like Hurston, Huie had been born in the South and had firsthand knowledge of the region's racial violence and inequity. Rather than retreating into the relative safety of silence as did so many other native southerners in the 1950s, Huie chose to publish pieces that unabashedly tackled longtime silences in the South. Unlike Hurston, however, Huie had two advantages before he ever arrived in Live Oak to begin research on what would eventually become *Ruby McCollum*: he was a man, and he was white.

Long before McCollum began sending letters to Huie soliciting his help in making public the "true" story of Adams's murder, Hurston also tried to establish a connection with McCollum. At the time of the McCollum affair, Hurston was a well-known and celebrated writer in her own right, and logic dictates that as a black woman Hurston could perhaps better empathize with McCollum's plight. McCollum, however, did not write to Hurston even though she was well aware that the *Courier* journalist was eager to speak with her. For those schooled in the politics of southern silence, it is not difficult to surmise why. McCollum was savvy in the ways of race and gender politics in Live Oak and the South as a whole, and she knew that in spite of Hurston's fame and excellent reputation, she could escape neither her gender nor her skin color—both decisive handicaps in a place like Live Oak where white men occupied the top tier of local and regional power structures. In the final analysis, then, Hurston's position in Live Oak rendered her by default in many ways as mute as McCollum herself, and no amount of literary clout could negate silences over one hundred years in the making. Frustrated by her lack of progress, Hurston contacted Huie and asked his help in delving into McCollum's case. As a white man, Huie occupied a position of power and freedom in the South that Hurston never could, and thus began the complicated—and cautious—friendship between the two writers that is documented in Hurston's letters.

Huie's stature as a white man in the segregated South did not entirely remove him from danger and controversy during his research in Live Oak. He was suspect from the beginning, with his every move monitored by Live Oak citizens and law enforcement officials alike. The fact that immediately upon his arrival in Live Oak Huie contacted Judge Adams and asked to interview McCollum served to compound his position as an "outside agitator," and as the following excerpt from *Ruby McCollum* illustrates, even Huie's positioning as a native southerner did not exempt him from the impenetrable silences surrounding the prisoner held incommunicado in the Suwannee County Jail since 1952. Huie describes his first meeting with Judge Adams as follows:

"Judge," I said finally . . . "I'm interested in this Ruby McCollum case. . . . I understand you've never allowed a newspaperman to talk with her?"

"That's correct. When Guy Crews was her lawyer, he raised the question of letting some of the Negro reporters from Northern newspapers see her. But I didn't want her bothered by these strangers. They were a threat to a quiet, orderly manner of trial. So I entered an order that would prevent their seeing her."

"Well, Judge," I said, "I have driven four hundred miles down here, and I want to see her. I have a letter in which she states she'd like to talk to me. I have conferred with her attorneys and they want me to talk with her. I'm a reputable journalist, a writer of books, and I have reputable publishers. I'm not subversive. The woman's case is before the State Supreme Court. I think she has a right to see me, and that I have a right to see her."

The Judge paused and spat into the golden gobboon.

"Now, brother," he said, "I don't want to see anything go wrong in that case. We have gotten along very well. The press has cooperated in a most friendly manner. So I don't want to make any exceptions to my rulings."

"Do you mean, Judge," I said, "that you *actually* are going to try to keep me from talking with a Negro woman who has been in a jail cell in Live Oak for eighteen months?"

"I'm afraid so," he answered. "That's my ruling. . . . I've been very careful to try to protect this community from embarrassment. . . ."

"Judge . . ." I said, "What can a Negro woman named Ruby McCollum say to me that would *embarrass a community*?"

"That's not the point," he argued. "This case has proceeded in a dignified, orderly manner. I'm not going to have an outsider coming in here—"

I interrupted him. "Now wait a minute, sir. How can you call me an outsider? Nine generations of my folks are lying up there in a family cemetery in Georgia. I was bred on Pickett's charge. You came down here from Missouri in 1906. Compared to me, you're the outsider."

Hawkbill knives sometimes flash at this point in West Florida, but the Judge composed himself.

"The other white newspapermen who have covered this case have been friendly and cooperative," he said. "You appear to be unfriendly. You want to commercialize this story and embarrass this community. I won't make any exception for you." (14–17)

This passage illustrates the stubborn determination of Judge Adams to keep McCollum isolated from anyone who could draw attention to her and Suwannee County. What Huie didn't know at the time of his interview with Judge Adams, however, was that in a few short months Huie's relentless efforts to circumvent these silences would eventually land him in a cell in the Suwannee County Jail not far from the one McCollum herself had occupied. So if Huie initially underestimated the power Judge Adams had in Suwannee County and Florida, by the time McCollum was judged insane and transferred to Chattahoochee, he had changed his opinion. Suwannee County citizens were bemused by this battle of wills. With nine generations of southern pedigree to his credit, they reasoned, Huie's upbringing should have taught him when to leave well enough alone.

Hurston and Huie met with varying degrees of success in their efforts to uncover the "real" story of McCollum. Letters McCollum wrote to Huie occupy an important place in this effort. Hurston, too, wrote to Huie, and although her letters have been previously published, little has been done to contextualize them in terms of the South's complex social formations and how southern ideology manifests itself in Hurston's correspondence with Huie, a white man. In other words, although at the time of the McCollum affair both Hurston and Huie were accomplished and respected writers, Hurston's letters reveal that even though she and Huie had much in common, Hurston perhaps sensed that they were far from equal. No scholarship exists that focuses on this part of the Hurston letters and what I believe to be the most compelling aspect of them: Hurston's complex subject positioning and the ways in which her awareness of both her race and her gender are reflected in both the public texts she wrote about McCollum and, more important, the private letters she wrote to Huie that intimate that she herself often felt ensnared in many of the same ideological webs that bound McCollum and Live Oak.

As a white man in the South, Huie was exempt from many of the constraints that hampered Hurston during her stay in segregated Suwannee County, but in many ways he, too, was in a precarious position. By virtue of his race and gender, when Huie came to Live Oak he already had a large margin of respect by default. Yet despite the powerful privilege he enjoyed as a white man, Huie found he was essentially powerless to alter underlying ideological formations in the community that perpetuated the social divisions he criticized. Moreover, as much as he despised segregation and the acts of violence against minorities it endorsed, Huie needed the freedom his dominant gender and race made possible; without it he would have had no more leverage in Live Oak than Hurston, who during her stay was relegated to the segregated lodgings, washrooms, and "colored" gallery of the Suwannee County Courthouse. Like Hurston's *Courier* series, the texts Huie wrote in connection with *Ruby McCollum: Woman in the Suwannee Jail* called into question practices of inequity in the South in general and McCollum's treatment in particular. At the same time, however, neither Hurston nor Huie could escape their own race and gender positioning and what such positioning meant in terms of their interpolation by the ideological formations they sought to challenge. In other words, while Hurston and Huie were both tireless advocates of McCollum and fought through their respective texts to bring to light practices of racial inequity and violence in Suwannee County, the texts each wrote also say a great deal about the influences of race and gender on a writer's discursive positioning in the context of southern ideology.

While Hurston and Huie struggled against silences that enveloped McCollum and what these silences meant in terms of their own positioning as writers producing text in and about the South, McCollum continued to wage a daily fight against the effects of enforced solitude and the pressure of her impending execution. Although McCollum never did reach the electric chair, her reprieve proved to be a mixed blessing. The two years she spent in the Suwannee County Jail exacted a heavy toll, but the years following McCollum's diagnosis of "prison psychosis" and her ensuing hospitalization in Chattahoochee do not, as others have argued, mark the end of her story. Instead, her behavior during these twenty years—described by psychiatrists early on as paranoia and later as selective amnesia—is problematic. Perhaps McCollum's behavior offers compelling evidence of the devastating effects of enforced silence in the South and, more important, the determination of dominant power structures to ensure its perpetuation. It is also possible, however, that McCollum may have been sane all along and simply chose not to conform to what others considered to be conventional behavior. As previously argued, McCollum's diagnosis of insanity was advantageous to individuals in Suwannee County who wanted to avoid almost certain criticism from liberal presses like the *Pittsburgh Courier* if she were ever executed. These individuals knew that McCollum's execution would once again exacerbate uncomfortable speculations concerning the community of Live Oak that in some small measure had abated since the end of the first trial. Closeting McCollum away from the general population and, in particular, journalists like Hurston, Huie, and others who struggled to interview her, neatly solved two problems in terms of preserving southern ideological power formations in Live Oak. First, holding McCollum in enforced isolation ensured that she could never have the opportunity to tell her story, and, second, if she ever *did* have the opportunity to speak, what rational individual would give credence to a woman judged certifiably insane?

People in Live Oak who feared that McCollum might somehow break the silences surrounding her had, in actuality, little to fear. By the time she was transported to Chattahoochee from the Suwannee County Jail, for the most part McCollum seemed to remember very little about Adams's murder. And if she did, she was reluctant to communicate it. Michel Foucault writes in his introduction to *Madness and Civilization* that the modern world has clearly divided madness from reason; moreover, he argues that no common discourse exists with which to commune between the two realms:

> In the serene world of mental illness, modern man no longer communicates with the madman: on one hand, the man of reason delegates the physician to madness, thereby authorizing a relation only through the abstract universality of disease; on the other, the man of madness communicates with society only by the intermediary of an equally abstract reason which is order, physical and moral constraint, the anonymous pressure of the group, the requirements of conformity. As for a common language, there is no such thing. (x)

As we approach the conclusion of the story of Ruby McCollum, Foucault's distinction between reason and madness takes on special significance. I argue that McCollum's amnesia was not, as some have said, proof positive of her insanity; rather it is an extension of the South's invasive rhetoric of silence and the ways in which this particular rhetoric often equates acts of subversion with "mental instability." In McCollum's case, perhaps her inability to remember the murder (or her unwillingness to vocalize the memory to others) performs as a speech act in its own right. If so, then Foucault's notion that reason and madness have no common language may not hold true in the American South, where the rhetoric of silence dominates reason and madness alike. Complicating this contention is, of course, how to identify within the complex confines of southern ideology where reason ends and madness begins—an issue that in large measure depends on one's subject positioning in southern social formations privileging race and gender.

"An Almost Insane, Ignorant Negro Woman"

On January 15, 1953, P. Guy Crews's suspension ended, and he, Frank Cannon, and Releford McGriff filed an appeal in the Florida Supreme Court on behalf of Ruby McCollum. The sixty-seven-page document contends that Judge Adams erred on fifty-eight separate counts during McCollum's trial—the most pertinent ones being Judge Adams's denial for a change of venue, the inadmissibility of Loretta as evidence, McCollum's lack of an impartial jury, and the refusal to consider any verdict less than murder in the first degree. On at least three separate occasions, the document emphasizes McCollum's "ignorance" in the context of her race and gender. The section addressing Crews's suspension, for example, describes McCollum as an "almost insane, ignorant Negro woman." Later, the brief contends McCollum lacked an impartial jury during her trial and again notes her status as "an ignorant Negro woman." Less than one page later McCollum is once more called "a very ignorant colored or Negro woman who killed her paramour" (31–33). Interestingly enough, McCollum's "ignorance" is also frequently associated with her mental state (evidenced through repeated references to her as "crazy" or "insane") and alleged to be at least part of the reason for her inability—or unwillingness—to communicate. "The appellant," the brief reads at one point, "is crazy and cannot tell anything in an intelligent way except by continuous prodding" (42). To be sure, there were many reasons why McCollum had never felt completely free to communicate with her attorneys. Notes she wrote from Raiford and the Suwannee County Jail on multiple occasions show that she trusted none of the members of her defense team and felt threatened on all sides—even by people who claimed to be her advocates. In fact, McCollum fired all of her attorneys several times, but they chose to ignore what they considered to be the ravings of a mentally incompetent, "ignorant" woman. On April 17, 1953, for example, McCollum wrote the following letter to Crews: "Please resign from my case. You and Mr. Cannon are fired for good. I notified the governor, State Supreme Justice, Judge Adams, and the Sheriff of Suwannee County that you were fired over three months ago. I want a refund of my money" (McCollum, Notes). On May 16, 1953, the *Pittsburgh Courier* printed the following account of the firing incident:

> Mrs. Ruby McCollum, doomed to die in Florida's electric chair for the killing of Dr. C. LeRoy Adams . . . again verbally fired Frank T. Cannon of Jacksonville, chief defense counsel, and informed him that she had written letters of dismissal to P. Guy Crews and Releford McGriff, associate counselors, both of Jacksonville. . . .
>
> Mrs. McCollum, in March of this year, wrote Mr. Cannon a letter dismissing him as her attorney, which he ignored. . . .
>
> Mr. Cannon says that neither he nor his associates have any intention of resigning from the case, for if the pending appeal before the Supreme Court is not perfected, it will become Governor McCarty's duty to sign Mrs. McCollum's death warrant.
>
> Her attitude in the matter, Mr. Cannon contends, is the evidence of a deranged mind. (Levin)

If McCollum's attorneys attributed her reticence to "ignorance" or a "deranged mind," Zora Neale Hurston was of another opinion. On February 28, 1953, the first installment of Hurston's ten-part series in the *Pittsburgh Courier* appeared, and in it she contends that acts of silence like McCollum's are too often misinterpreted:

> Certainly there was nothing in the early life of Ruby Jackson, later to become Ruby McCollum, that made relatives and neighbors see anything that might hint of what was to later come to pass. That, probably, was because the average person takes it for granted that silence means a lack of thought and internal activity.
>
> It is rarely considered that thoughts too profound for words might be surging through an individual like a great underground river, unless and until it bursts forth like an awesome Niagara or Victoria Nyansa. That was undoubtedly the case with Ruby McCollum. ("Life Story," installment 1)

The following week, Hurston's second installment underscores McCollum's private nature. "She revealed little about herself," Hurston writes.

"Even when she made words with her mouth, she really said nothing about her inside feelings. She was extremely self-contained" ("Life Story," installment 2). Hurston also takes issue with McCollum's supposed "ignorance." In almost every column she wrote for the *Courier*, Hurston contends that McCollum had an extensive formal education and possessed a keen and innate intelligence. Even Releford McGriff, one of the defense attorneys who penned the appeal asserting McCollum's "ignorance," concedes as much in an interview conducted by William Bradford Huie and relayed in *Ruby McCollum*. "Ruby's tragedy," McGriff told Huie, "comes from her being a little too well educated, a little too proud for her own good. What's happened to her has happened to other Negro women—and other white women—but heretofore the Negro women have been simple enough, and uneducated, and helpless, so they have had to take it. Ruby couldn't take it" (132). Hurston speculated extensively on exactly *why* McCollum reached the point where she "couldn't take it," and her columns on the subject—although sometimes tending to err on the side of the sensational as craved by a portion of the *Courier*'s readers—stress that McCollum was a woman who simultaneously feared and revered Dr. Adams. "She saw the net closing around her," Hurston's seventh installment of McCollum's life story on April 11, 1953, reads: "Did she want to escape? Well, yes, and, then again, no. . . . My God, her mother and father, brothers and sisters would die of shame if they dreamed of it. And Sam, the community of Live Oak would explode like gasoline. Please God, help her! For she didn't see how she could help herself" ("Life Story," installment 7).

In spite of the fact that Hurston was very intrigued by McCollum, she knew at the outset of her involvement in the case that she faced limitations in uncovering the "real" McCollum. It seemed that no number of interviews with McCollum's friends and family could ever reconcile the quiet, obedient, well-schooled Ruby McCollum and the woman who shot Dr. Adams on August 3, 1952. Hurston admits as much in her first *Courier* installment: "The truth is that nobody, not even the closest blood relations, ever really knows anybody else," she writes. "The greatest human travail has been in the attempt at self-revelation, but never, since the world began, has any one individual completely succeeded" ("Life Story," installment 1). Carla Kaplan, however, argues that Hurston closely identified with McCollum's complex psyche and points to several places in Hurston's *Courier* columns that seem to collapse McCollum and Janie, Hurston's protagonist in *Their Eyes Were Watching God* and whom Kaplan dubs her "most celebrated and autobiographical character" (608). Kaplan, for example, points to the following excerpt from Hurston's novel:

> [Janie] saw her life like a great tree in leaf . . . from barren brown stems to glistening leaf-buds; from the leaf buds to snowy virginity of bloom. It stirred her tremendously. . . . She was stretched on her back beneath the pear tree soaking in the alto chant of the visiting bees, the gold of the sun and the panting breath of the breeze when the inaudible voice of it all came to her. She saw a dust-bearing bee sink into the sanctum of a bloom. (8, 10–11)

The third installment of Hurston's columns in the *Courier* contains a passage very much like the one above, and there are similarities between Hurston's novel and other pieces she wrote about McCollum for the *Courier* as well. Kaplan writes:

> In Hurston's account, McCollum "felt like a blossom on the bare limb of a pear tree in the spring . . . opening her gifts to the world, but where was the bee for her blossom?" Janie is described numerous times as setting out on "a journey to the horizons." According to Hurston, Ruby McCollum "was ready to set out on her journey to the big horizon." When Janie's second marriage fails, "something fell off the shelf inside her . . . it was her image of Jody tumbled down and shattered." Describing the failure of Ruby and Sam McCollum's marriage, Hurston writes that "an image—something sacred and precious—had fallen off the shelf in Ruby's heart." Only from a position of sympathy and identification could Ruby McCollum inhabit these thoughts and feelings of Hurston's much-loved Janie. (608–9)

Perhaps Hurston—badly in need of money and writing under pressure of an impending deadline—deliberately "borrowed" passages from *Their Eyes Were Watching God* and retooled them for her McCollum pieces in the *Courier*. The lines were, after all, hers to do with as she wished. Or perhaps something in Hurston's growing involvement with McCollum struck the recesses of her subconscious and manifested itself in the eerie echoes of Janie evident in the *Courier* columns. Lucinda MacKethan contends that *Their Eyes Were Watching God* "follow[s] the growth of Janie from a girlhood marked by the word 'Hush' to a womanhood celebrating a sexual, linguistic, and narrative empowerment" (364), and in terms of the Hurston canon as a whole, Henry Louis Gates Jr. and Sieglinde Lemke argue that Hurston's "great themes—obsessions, really—are love, betrayal, and death" (xxiii). Certainly these "obsessions" surface in Hurston's portrayal of the fictional Janie, her coverage of the Ruby McCollum case, and her accounts of the struggles both McCollum and Janie faced in trying to find—and keep—their voices. Parallels between Janie and McCollum are, in fact, so numerous that a full analysis of them is beyond the necessarily limited confines of this chapter. If, however, Janie functions as arguably the most autobiographical of Hurston's characters, and if Hurston consciously or unconsciously collapsed McCollum with Janie in her *Courier* columns, then to some extent Hurston certainly empathized with McCollum on a level beyond that of "journalistic objectivity."

As Hurston grew to appreciate the complexity of McCollum's emotional state, she also connected with McCollum on the basis of their mutual race. Valerie Boyd writes, "Most of her articles focused on Ruby as a woman, rather than as a defendant" (416), and Kaplan contends that Hurston "certainly identified with the sexism and racism McCollum faced. Hurston's coverage of the trial makes frequent and pointed reminders that although she was a 'Famous Novelist, Author, and Lecturer' (as stated in her *Courier* byline), she was still relegated to the upstairs gallery, with every other black spectator at the trial" (608). The *Courier* used Hurston's ties to Florida to its advantage in the byline that accompanied her November 4, 1952, description of McCollum's first day in court. "Native to Florida," the description of Hurston reads, "Mrs. Hurston is a recognized authority on the manners and mores of the people about whom she is writing. She knows the people who live on the banks of the Suwannee River. She knows places like Live Oak, Florida." Certainly Hurston's many anthropological ventures in the Deep South did make her somewhat of an expert in the complexities of southern culture. But if Hurston knew places like Live Oak, Live Oak lost no time in making it clear to Hurston that it certainly had never known anything like *her*. As a writer—much less a *black woman* writer—Hurston was at first viewed as something of an amusing curiosity in Live Oak, but her persistent questions about sensitive issues surrounding McCollum raised the suspicions of black and white citizens alike. The fact that Hurston was a member of the black race and a Florida native did not go nearly far enough with Live Oak's tight-lipped citizens, who were less than eager to discuss Adams's murder with anyone outside of "their own." Consequently, the people Hurston interviewed during the time she spent in Live Oak researching her *Courier* series are almost exclusively limited to McCollum's friends and family members, both of whom were careful to say nothing about McCollum's relationship with Adams and, instead, limited their comments to McCollum's childhood, her marriage, and other "safe" nonracial topics.

Recall Hurston's "My Impressions of the Trial" and the group of Live Oak natives she describes overhearing in a diner. "If Ruby comes clear of this," one member of the group says, "I aim to buy her a brand new gun." But in much the same way that animals intuit the presence of danger, alarm ripples through the group when it senses Hurston's status as an "outsider," an interloper not yet to be trusted. "Then somebody became conscious of my presence," Hurston writes, "and the talk was turned off like a faucet." Although Hurston wrote in her October 18, 1952, *Courier* column, "people talk freely to me" in Live Oak, it should be evident by now that her assertion may have been more wishful thinking than fact. In actuality, Hurston gained many of her most valuable insights regarding the McCollum case from *not* asking questions and, instead, quietly listening to conversations among Live Oak residents such as the one that took place in the Suwannee County diner. Before Hurston became involved in the McCollum case, A. M. Rivera Jr., another reporter for the *Pittsburgh Courier*, described Live Oak on October 4, 1952, as "the Old South in microcosm . . . an entire section sacrificing its economic progress and its political freedom to the fetish of race supremacy." Regarding the atmosphere in the town two months after Adams's murder, Rivera wrote: "To the unsuspecting visitor, Live Oak appears to be calm, settled, and back to normal; and it might be, but those who know its personality best likened this ominous quiet to a coiled cobra" (Rivera, "Chill"). Immersed in such a volatile atmosphere infused with silence, Hurston realized that her keen ability to listen, observe, and remember would better serve her purpose than asking direct questions. In this way, she hoped to avoid what she calls in *Mules and Men* the "feather-bed resistance" inherent in any comments she managed to elicit from Live Oak residents—that is, if anybody were willing to talk to her at all. Hurston's anthropology work taught her a great deal about community cohesiveness, acts of evasion, and the reluctance of people "to reveal that which the soul lives by" (18). She writes, for example, in *Mules and Men*:

> The Negro, in spite of his open-faced laughter, his seeming acquiescence, is particularly evasive. You see we are a polite people and we do not say to our questioner, "Get out of here!" We smile and tell him or her something that satisfies the white person because, know-

ing so little about us, he doesn't know what he is missing. The Indian resists curiosity by a stony silence. The Negro offers a feather-bed resistance. That is, we let the probe enter, but it never comes out. It gets smothered under a lot of laughter and pleasantries.

The theory behind our tactics: "The white man is always trying to know somebody else's business. All right, I'll set something outside the door of my mind for him to play with and handle. He can read my writing but he sho' can't read my mind. I'll put this play toy in his hand, and he will seize it and go away. Then I'll say my say and sing my song." (18–19)

Barbara Johnson writes that this passage and others like it reflect Hurston's emphasis on "inside" versus "outside" and how these polarities inform both the object of Hurston's inquiry and her position in the production of text. Johnson locates Hurston's work outside the literary mainstream, yet at the same time she argues that Hurston's discourse is "constantly dramatizing and undercutting just such inside/outside oppositions, transforming the plane geometry of physical space into the complex transactions of discursive exchange. In other words, Hurston could be read not just as an *example* of the 'noncanonical' writer but as a commentator on the dynamics of any encounter between an inside and an outside, any attempt to make a statement about difference" (279). Hurston's texts about the McCollum case are particularly intriguing because whereas in *Mules and Men* she describes the evasiveness of blacks in response to inquiries from white anthropologists, during her stay in Live Oak she found herself on the receiving end of "feather-bed resistance" from members of her own race.

In much the same way that Johnson came to realize the implications of her status as "an institutional 'insider'" (279) during her research into Hurston's structures of address, Hurston realized during her research in Live Oak that her status as a reporter and a non-native of Suwannee County placed her irrevocably "outside" the discursive communities she needed most to access. As a result, residents in Live Oak were happy to tell Hurston about Ruby's shiny new Chrysler, the great care she took of her children, and even what games she most enjoyed a child. They even shared their prophetic dreams about McCollum. "Several claim to have already seen her spirit in one form or another," Hurston wrote in a *Courier* column on November 22, 1952. "She had appeared in the bedroom of a couple one night in the form of a cat-like animal and was crying piteously. To another she appeared as a woman with the head of an eagle with a flaming sword in her hand in flowing robes, circling their house for three nights running and crying out in defiance" ("McCollum Fights"). These same Live Oak citizens, however, would tell Hurston virtually nothing about what she really wanted to hear—details of McCollum's relationship with Adams.

Several columns written prior to Hurston's arrival in Live Oak describe the magnitude of resistance she was bound to face during her research. On September 20, 1952, for example, the *Courier* printed a column coauthored by Revella Clay and A. M. Rivera Jr. The piece nicely captures the fear that infused Live Oak after Adams's murder and the very different public and private faces donned by the community. "Live Oak, we found, is a deadpan town on the surface," they wrote, "but underneath it's a whispering town, afraid that something violent and terrible may yet happen. It's a town rife with rumors! Not one of those rumors puts any credence in the story Mrs. Ruby McCollum allegedly told authorities when arrested on August 3—that she shot Dr. Adams over a Medical bill (Clay and Rivera, "Will Ruby Talk"). On September 27, 1952, Rivera and several other members of the press traveled to Live Oak in an attempt to interview McCollum, but the interview they hoped for (predictably) did not materialize. Rivera writes:

> On Sunday morning, Attorney P. Guy Crews . . . assured us that he could perfect an audience with Mrs. McCollum and rode with us to the jail here in Live Oak. The jailer refused us admittance and stated it was the judge's orders. On Monday the judge notified the defense attorneys that he would see us in his chambers at 2 P.M.
>
> In the conference with Judge Adams, which was recorded, the judge . . . concluded with a denial of our request to see Mrs. McCollum. He lauded a *Courier* editorial which had praised him and the law enforcement officers for their alertness and precaution which averted a possible lynching.
>
> The judge managed to get into the record repeatedly his determination to see to it that Ruby McCollum gets "a fair and square trial." He stated that the Associated Press reports were in error and that he had decided that this case will not be tried in the press.
>
> The sixty-eight-year-old pompous jurist told the defense attorneys, who contended in a motion that the denial to let us talk with Mrs. McCollum was an abridgement of the right of free speech and

the right of free press, that no reporters would see Mrs. McCollum prior to the trial. He stated further that even at the trial the press would not be recognized. . . .

At the conclusion of the recorded interview, the judge admitted that this was the first time in the history of the county that such a conference had been recorded. When asked why he took such unusual precaution, he stated, "I just don't know what might come out of this conference." (Rivera, "Judge Won't Let")

If Hurston was somewhat anxious during her time in Live Oak, she clearly had good reason to be. On October 4, 1952, Rivera again emphasizes the pervasive fear in Live Oak. "People of both races here," he writes, "virtually tip-toe on a knife edge of suspense. . . . An assortment of fears has enveloped the entire community, all sorts of fears. The attention of the nation on the impending trial has irritated the leaders here who fear that the story of an illicit interracial love affair will wound the inflexible sensibilities of this typical plantation community. Negroes whisper the fear that if the story, which is circulated as gospel, is substantially supported at the trial, usual reprisals will result. One person after another reminded the team of *Courier* reporters . . . 'After all, we've got to live here'" (Rivera, "Chill"). Hurston's status as "outsider" in Live Oak's black community put her in a precarious position that intensified the longer she stayed. A less experienced and intuitive writer would no doubt have given up the *Courier* assignment in frustration, but perhaps due to her need for money or her inherent stubbornness, Hurston persevered and learned to use silence to her advantage.

Hurston was ambivalent in her opinion of her race even before she ever arrived in Live Oak, and the time she spent there exacerbated her growing stance that "My People," as she wrote in a letter to Huie, "are definitely a bunch of stinkers" (Kaplan 708). Simultaneously sympathetic to Live Oak's black citizens and angered by her inability to elicit meaningful commentary from them regarding McCollum and Adams, Hurston found herself in the position of being branded an "outsider" by individuals of her own color. Her ambivalence and her acknowledgment of this positioning surface, for example, on November 4, 1952, when in a *Courier* article she describes the bovine vulnerability of blacks who came to observe McCollum's first day in court. "The Negro spectators," Hurston writes, "all seated in the gallery, leaned forward and all looked in the same direction like cows in a pasture." In the same column, however, Hurston also notes the following exchange and implicit in it the general sense of frustration in the segregated gallery in the face of McCollum's imposed silence: "'That lawyer is no good,' a man in the second row murmured in deep disappointment. 'Why don't he let her talk?' 'That's what I say,' a woman's voice grumbled. 'He ain't let her say a word since the mess started'" ("Zora's Revealing"). Although she was a respected member of the press—or perhaps because of it—Hurston's columns in the *Courier* are evidence of her dual role as both an observer of these acts of silence and her own victimization by them. In a June 10, 1954, letter to Huie, for example, she rails that after the time she spent in Live Oak she became "completely anti-Negro as is possible for a human being to be. I washed my hands and turned my back on everything that pertained to A'nt Hagar's chillun. . . . I ought to know when I have been sufficiently lynched" (Kaplan 711). Hurston, however, also wrote to Huie of her efforts to remain objective in the columns she wrote for the *Courier* and her attempts to portray the McCollum case as a human drama as opposed to a racial one. "I would have no interest in defending Ruby because she is a Negro," she wrote on May 14, 1954. "My interest arose out of the dramatics of the case and the varied play of human emotions. I repeatedly resisted the urgings of the *Courier* to 'angle' the stories. I have no interest in skin colors at all, but people, individuals as they show themselves" (Kaplan 710). Hurston, however, discovered that in spite of her best efforts to remain neutral in terms of race, skin color was *the* deciding factor in Live Oak in terms of who had the power to speak and who was forced to remain silent. Although there were multiple acts of silence surrounding McCollum, with both whites and blacks alike essentially held hostage by secrecy and fear, the black community in particular held fast to what had long been a successful survival strategy: no matter what a person's skin color, trust no one from the "outside." In Live Oak, Hurston encountered the same cohesiveness in its black community that she had seen many times during her anthropological fact-finding trips across the state. There was, however, one important difference; in this particular community, her skin color did not necessarily guarantee her unqualified inclusion. *She* was now relegated to the "outside," and Hurston found it both an uncomfortable and unfamiliar place to be.

The columns Hurston wrote for the *Courier* are much more than an account of Ruby McCollum. If read carefully, they also offer clues regarding how Hurston dealt with her exclusion from the racially divided community steeped in silence that she fought so hard to enter. As both a presumed "insider" by virtue of her skin color and an "outsider" due to her fame and occupation, Hurston faced irreconcilable and multidimensional silences in her interactions with the Negro community during her coverage of the McCollum case, and although these acts of silence were imposed on her and virtually impossible to overcome, Hurston managed to reach an uneasy reconciliation with her own silencing during her stay in Live Oak. The result is a striking depiction in Hurston's *Courier* columns of a writer generating text both within and against silences that encompassed her, her subject matter, and the larger (and very different) discourse communities that informed both. Toni Morrison writes that many writers producing text about slavery "pull the narrative up short with a phrase such as, 'But let us drop a veil over these proceedings too terrible to relate.' In shaping the experience to make it palatable to those who were in a position to alleviate it, they were silent about many things, and they 'forgot' many things" (190–91).

I contend that finding herself faced with the magnitude of the story that is Ruby McCollum, Hurston, like Morrison, knew all too well that her task in Live Oak was, as Morrison writes, "to rip that veil drawn over 'proceedings too terrible to relate.'" Like Morrison, Hurston also knew that "the exercise is also critical for any person who is black, or who belongs to any marginalized category, for, historically, we were seldom invited to participate in the discourse even when we were its topic" (191). Hurston had no desire to make McCollum "palatable" to her readers, and if one believes Hurston's assertion that she cared little about the case's "race angle," she also dismissed notions that skin color (hers or anyone else's) would be a factor in her reporting of the case. Hurston's goal, then, was to depict McCollum in the most "objective" way possible, and as a black woman native to the South, Hurston came to Live Oak with the presumption that her unique anthropological background would enable her to do just that. Hurston may also have believed that if McCollum were being mistreated, columns in the *Courier* might perhaps provide a discursive space leading to change in Live Oak and its handling of the McCollum affair. But if Hurston arrived in Live Oak with either of these rather lofty presumptions, she left with the realization that she had radically underestimated the magnitude of acts of silences in Suwannee County. In fact, by the time she left Live Oak, Hurston more than likely knew that the text she produced about McCollum for the *Courier* would probably not even be read by members of either Live Oak's black or white communities. Written for a newspaper with a primarily black readership, Hurston's columns in the *Courier* were unlikely to fall into the hands of anyone in Live Oak's white community in a "position to alleviate" McCollum's suffering. The black community, driven by minimal incomes and fear, was also not likely to have access to the *Courier*. In a community as tightly under surveillance as Live Oak, a subscription to a northern, liberal newspaper with a high African-American readership would at the very least draw unwanted attention to its recipient, either black or white, and such excessive caution should not be dismissed as undue "paranoia." Consider, for example, the fact that in the Huie archives there is tucked amid his research notes on the McCollum case a typed index card apparently sent to him by a Live Oak informant. The card reads, in part: "Mail all your correspondence to me in a PLAIN envelope, too. Those postal people in Live Oak don't miss anything. They'd wonder why I would be getting mail from YOU!" (Anonymous). In other words, by the time Hurston left Live Oak she almost certainly knew that in spite of her best efforts she had been silenced on two levels. First, she had been explicitly excluded from the black community during her research on McCollum, and, second, the hard-wrung words about McCollum and Live Oak she did manage to produce for the *Courier* were destined to remain inaccessible to those whose silence she had tried so hard to break in the first place.

Morrison writes that rending the veil of silence that separates a writer from traumatic subject matter such as slavery—and I argue the abuse of Ruby McCollum both before and after her imprisonment—can only be accomplished by trusting one's own memories and the memories of others. Hurston, Morrison contends, captured this importance of memory when she wrote, "Like the dead-seeming cold rocks, I have memories within that came out of the material that went to make me" (qtd. in Morrison 192). Morrison adds, however, that "memories and recollections won't give me total access to the unwritten interior life of these people. Only the act of the imagination can help me" (192). Hurston, too, learned from the community of Live Oak and its pervasive acts of silence that if she were ever to construct a cohesive narrative about a subject as complex as McCollum, she would have to rely to a large extent on acts of imagination. Yet while Hurston struggled to relay to her readers the silences that choked Live Oak's black and white communities, she could not help but feel the stir of her own "memories within" and with them the exclusion and silencing implicit in a black woman's lived experience in the mid-1950s South. In writing about the McCollum case, Hurston struggled with silences and issues of race that had preoccupied her for most of her career, and it is fitting that her columns about McCollum in the *Courier*—among some of the last texts she produced in the difficult latter years of her life—are the result of her immersion in the same kind of silences that plagued her subject matter.

"A 'Writing Man'"

Martha Hunt Huie, the widow and second wife of William Bradford Huie, is her late husband's most energetic and tireless advocate. Framed by a cloud of white hair, her blue eyes twinkle when she speaks of him, and it is easy to imagine that when Huie met her several years after the death of Ruth, his wife of over forty years, he instantly must have been drawn to both her keen intelligence and quick wit. Yet I am also certain that if Bill Huie were a man habitually accustomed to getting his way, he soon discovered that he had met his match in Martha. On a bright summer day in June 2005, Martha Huie and I met for the first time. In the early stages of our conversation, she shared the following memory with me:

> I always thought he would have made a hell of a courtroom lawyer. He was gorgeous. He would undo his jacket and hook his thumb in his trousers. He could almost have been on screen. I have a memory burned into my head of one event. I was sitting on an ottoman and he was berating me about something, and I screamed at him, "I did not come this far by God. . . . My people came to this country before yours did. We've fought in every war this country ever fought in. I did not come down to this day to be conquered and dominated by you!" I looked up and he was smiling in spite of himself. He admired me at the same time that he could hardly put up with me.

Of course, I liked her instantly.

Mrs. Huie and I spent two days ensconced in the Ohio State University Archives, where we discussed the life and work of her late husband. It was her first and only trip to Ohio State since donating the William Bradford Huie Papers to the university soon after his death in 1986. The collection is extensive and reflects the multifaceted career of a complicated, driven writer. "He called himself a 'writing man,'" Mrs. Huie told me. "He didn't say, 'I'm a journalist.' He would say: 'That's just what I do. It's all I've ever done, and I don't know how to do anything else.'" But in spite of her willingness to discuss the life and work of her late husband, Mrs. Huie readily acknowledges the transitory nature of any act of memory. She is, refreshingly, a rhetorician at heart. "I'll be as factual as I can be," she cautioned, "but everybody is colored with subjectivity." On one point, however, she is certain. Even late in life, William Bradford Huie could not escape the desire—the *need*—to write about issues that were important to him. "I just wanted Bill to stop fighting and have a little joy and peace and serenity in his late days and to just give it up," she said. "But he could never do that. He never gave up. He never stopped."

Perhaps part of the reason Huie was habitually mired in controversy is because, as Mrs. Huie recalls, some facet of the general public viewed him as a "crusader" of sorts. "Bill would get letters from people about things that needed to be dealt with in this world," she recalled, "and of course he couldn't do that. But that is what people out there thought. They would say, 'This is a wrong that needs righting, and I'll bet William Bradford Huie could do that.'" "Righting wrongs," however, was only one aspect of Huie's career, and few people recognize what Mrs. Huie describes as the "spherical" quality of him and his texts. "It is like the story of the blind man and the elephant," she told me. "Bill Huie is not 'categorizable.' This, I believe, is what has stopped or interfered with a lot of academic people recognizing or using his work. They can't pigeonhole him, and it's very disturbing to them. His work contains fiction, nonfiction, and journalism. His was a multifaceted, varied career of national and international importance. Few people have a complete sense of who he was and what he has done; few people are capable of seeing 'the whole elephant.'"

It is without exception with "the whole elephant" that Mrs. Huie concerns herself. "Almost everybody who knew Bill and/or his work was either very pro–Bill Huie or very anti–Bill Huie," she told me, "and usually with no better reason for being one than the other. But I have always noticed and filed away people who could be comprehensive and knowledgeable about him and not be influenced one way or another by him as a person." One such individual, she told me, is David Halberstam, author of *The Fifties*. "The best description of Bill Huie is in that book," she told me. "It's not all positive, and it's not all complimentary, but it's right on target. The fact that David Halberstam had never met Bill impressed me because what Halberstam writes comes out of knowing Bill's *work* and not from knowing *him*. I like that because that's what's left of Bill Huie—his work." Following is an excerpt from Halberstam's text, taken in the context of Huie's investigation into the murder of Emmett Till:

Huie, who was considered more talented than respectable by many of his peers (whom he regularly scooped), represented *Look* magazine. And for the sum of about four thousand dollars, the two men, who had never taken the stand at their own trial, told the inside story of what had happened that fateful night.

Huie, who specialized in such eccentric journalism, was from Alabama. Shrewd, iconoclastic, he was proud of the fact that he was not, as he liked to point out, a liberal. He was looking for a story, not a cause. He had gone to Sumner after the trial, hoping to speak to a few of the defense attorneys and thereby piece together what had actually happened. He and the white Mississippi defense team had played cat and mouse for a while and shared more than a few drinks. One of the defense attorneys, John Witten, said that he didn't know if the two men committed the crime. His partner, J. J. Breland, was more outspoken. . . . The lawyers had cooperated, Breland told Huie, because they wanted the rest of the country to know that integration was not going to work: "The whites own all the property in Tallahatchie County. We don't need the niggers no more. And there ain't gonna be no integration. There ain't gonna be no nigger votin'. *And the sooner everybody in this country realizes it, the better.*"

With that, the lawyers gave Huie access to the two men and told Milam and Bryant to tell Huie what happened. Huie explained to them that because they had been acquitted, they could never be tried again. They were free men and his project would in no way change that. Then he suggested that he write an article based on their version of the events. Because the article would surely libel them—it would portray them as murderers—Huie said he would agree to make them a libel settlement in advance of four thousand dollars. This was not a payoff for their story, he emphasized. But just in case a film was made and the film libeled them as well, he made sure that they signed away the rights for would-be film libel, too. This was one of the most intriguing examples of checkbook journalism on record, and many people were appalled. "Others," Huie noted, "find this sort of thing distasteful and I have not found it particularly pleasing." Nevertheless, Huie hung around and talked with the two men over four nights, boasting to his editors, "I am capable of drinking out of the same jug as Milam and letting him drink first." Almost a decade later he would use the same method to get the cooperation of the two men who killed three young civil rights workers in Philadelphia, Mississippi. (434–35)

Clearly, Huie was a proud, even arrogant, man who was used to getting what he wanted, so when at Zora Neale Hurston's request he traveled to Live Oak to interview Ruby McCollum—and was promptly denied access to her—he was outraged. "Ruth and Bill were on vacation headed somewhere else," Martha Huie recalled. "Zora Neale had plagued him so much about this case, and I believe he thought that he could just walk in there and get to see Ruby. Then he'd turn it over to Zora and that would be that. Bill Huie had a terrible temper, and I can see how that would have really burnt him. If they had let him go in there and interview Ruby, it would have all been over. Tell them that. If they were stupid enough to oppose him, then they got what they deserved."

Hurston and Huie met when they both worked for the *Mercury*, and Mrs. Huie describes their friendship as "a solid, significant relationship of a certain kind. Very human and very respectable. Zora idolized him because he was a successful writer and because he had been helpful and paid attention to her. He had never pushed her away or denigrated her in any way or ever taken advantage of her." When I asked Mrs. Huie if she sensed from Hurston's letters, as I did, that Hurston seemed afraid of offending him, she replied: "I don't think she was *afraid* of it, but I do think she was careful. I think she wanted to get as close to him as she could because he was fascinating to her and she really liked and admired him. Fascinated as in snake and mongoose; that's a good way of putting it. But I also think that he liked and appreciated her and admired many things about her. In fact, I wouldn't be surprised if his relationship with Zora wasn't the genesis of his noticing civil rights and women's issues."

Eight letters that Hurston wrote to William Bradford Huie about the McCollum case survive, and they are written from Eau Gallie, Florida, where Hurston lived in a small house while trying to finish a book she was writing on Herod the Great. Hurston was in dire need of money, and as she writes in her first letter to Huie on March 28, 1954, her misfortunes began when the *Courier* failed to pay her the agreed-upon fee for her series of McCollum articles:

> Things happened to me that just about rotted the marrow in my bones, so that by the time that your letter arrived I was possibly at life's lowest point. And foolishly my pride restrained me from making explanations as I should have done. And strangely, my misfortunes came to me out of the Ruby McCollum case.

Briefly, I had paid down on an eight acre tract here with the notes at $50 per month. I also owed on my car. When the *Pittsburgh Courier* both wired and wrote me urging me to report the case for them, I told them my fee would be $1,000. They put up a poor mouth, but finally agreed to pay it in installments. In the end and after many agonizing delays, I have received in small sums a little over $200. I lost out on both my land and my car. As Mr. Cannon could tell you, they even left me stranded in hostile Live Oak for two days before the money was sent to enable me to get back to Eau Gallie. . . . The money I did get from the *Courier* was used up in the several trips that I made to Live Oak, and by the dishonorable behavior of that Pittsburgh gang, I was sunk. (Kaplan 704–5)

The letter Hurston refers to receiving from Huie is apparently his response to her request that he look into the McCollum affair. Frustrated by her own lack of progress in Live Oak, Hurston thought that as a white man—and a native southerner—Huie might meet with more success. At first, Huie had little interest in the case. He had recently published a very successful book, *The Execution of Private Slovik*, and was less than eager to begin a new project. "The Negro author, Zora Neale Hurston," Huie writes of his initial involvement the McCollum case in his introduction to *Ruby McCollum: Woman in the Suwannee Jail*, "had asked me to help establish the truth. . . . I didn't intend to write a story. I went only to ask questions about Ruby and the doctor, then give the answers to Miss Hurston and the *Courier*" (7–8). Huie, however, soon found himself intrigued by McCollum and the silences surrounding her. Like Hurston, he knew that making inquiries about a racially charged case such as McCollum's could be dangerous in the Deep South. After all, some argued that Live Oak was a Ku Klux Klan stronghold. But as a white man, Huie would be less likely to arouse suspicion than Hurston, who knew all too well the limitations and risks that came with her skin color even though in her first letter to Huie she appears unfazed. "A local man came to me," she writes, "to warn me that I would get into trouble with the KKK if I dared to aid you in any way. . . . Then I knew that I must rise out of my melancholy fog and give you whatever aid I could on your book. I am not one bit intimidated by the threat" (Kaplan 705). As proof of her willingness to help Huie, she writes, "I have some notes which I took as I watched the thing go on [McCollum's trial] which would not be in the stenographic records—impressions and significant little observations. You can have my notes" (Kaplan 705). Hurston was true to her word, and among Huie's research papers regarding McCollum are both Hurston's outline titled "Ruby McCollum: Impressions Gained As I Watched and Listened at Her Trials" and her unpublished essay "My Impressions of the Trial." Both end with "Respectfully submitted" and are signed with a flourish.

Hurston ends her March 28, 1954, letter to Huie as follows: "Please understand that I am not trying to horn in on your book. You are doing all the work and spending all the money on research, etc. I am merely offering you any little help that I can. If you think that I might have any information that you could use, call on me for it. Nobody is going to try to scare me and get away with it" (Kaplan 707). Hurston was a savvy reporter, and in this first letter she lists eight points to guide Huie's research that include concerns she had about the impartiality of McCollum's jury, rumors that Dr. Adams had been providing McCollum with narcotics, and the fact that "Judge Adams follow[ed] the jury into the jury-room and [was] conferring with them for several minutes before they were locked up" (Kaplan 706). Hurston also wondered about the "medical bill" that the prosecution contended had sparked Adams's murder, writing: "See about that letter to Sam McCollum from Dr. Adams on Saturday, the day before the murder. That was what provoked Ruby to shoot. I have my own idea of what was in it" (Kaplan 706). The notes that Hurston took during the McCollum trial and that she forwarded to Huie provide more details concerning this letter and Hurston's speculations regarding it. "That letter," she writes, "which was supposed to contain merely a bill for medical services had something so searing to Ruby's self love that she could not bear it. Since it was addressed to Sam McCollum and only came into her hands by accident, it is possible to deduce that Adams besought Sam to have Ruby leave him alone in his exasperation at her refusal to step aside" ("Impressions Gained"). *Ruby McCollum* addresses each of Hurston's eight points, and regarding the content of the "medical bill," Huie writes: "My own information, gathered in a manner which must not be discussed, is that the note read, 'Sam, you keep this Goddamn woman out of my office from now on. She's gone crazy as a bat.'" (189). Although the prosecution built its case against McCollum around the "murder-over-a-medical-bill" supposition, the transcripts of McCollum's trial are strangely silent in terms of providing actual proof that this bill ever existed. No medical bill was ever introduced into evidence, and Kaplan's collection of Hurston's

103
. . .

Punctuating
McCollum's
Sentence(s)
of Silence

correspondence includes an explanatory note with Hurston's first letter to Huie that reads as follows: "This letter disappeared and was never recovered" (706 n. 9).

Hurston writes to Huie again on May 14, 1954, and in this letter she praises Huie's new book, *The Execution of Private Slovik*. "I . . . was deeply moved," she writes. "Your mingling of words was superb" (Kaplan 708). She also apologizes for her delay in forwarding her material on Ruby McCollum. "I was bogged down in rewriting passages in *Herod the Great*," she writes, "and not too happy about it fearing that I was not making it sufficiently lucid, and came to that place where you loathe the sight of paper and the very touch of a typewriter. I know that you must be familiar with that feeling" (Kaplan 708). This letter has particular bearing on Hurston's coverage of the McCollum affair because in it she discusses at length her frustration with the black race. The following excerpt is evidence that, according to Kaplan, "Hurston could not get the Live Oak African-American community to speak to her about the McCollum case" (708 n. 3), and it seems that Huie had his share of difficulties as well. Hurston writes:

> But YES!! "My People" are definitely a bunch of stinkers. I take it that you are familiar with that folk tale where the monkey beside the road shakes his head at some capers that Negroes are cutting and sighs, "my people, my people." But another story, a sort of a sequel, has the monkey withdrawing from among us and sighing just as sadly, "Those people, those people." In spite of his long connection with the NAACP, James Weldon Johnson once complained to me sadly, "We are such a race of loud-mouthed cowards, such a collection of lying sycophants, such destroyers of each other and haters of superiority, such bullies among the weak, that I despair of the future. The white man does not need to keep us down as we untruthfully complain in public, for we will do that ourselves effectively. In fact, if it were not for the deterrent pull of the white man, even in the Deep South, no Negro would ever get a chance to show ability. Certainly Negroes are not going to make opportunities for other Negroes, for fear of being surpassed. I confess that I feel that a great part of my life and a great part of my abilities have been wasted, and if I had it all over again, I would take a different course. You are young . . . and obviously talented. I beg of you not to waste time on this so-called Race Problem. You will find it a thankless task." I have found

this only too true. Not my supposed "white enemies," but *Negroes*, have played every vile trick upon me that can be imagined, without rhyme or reason except hating to see me reap any benefit from hard work. While they lounge around the bars of New York, I am out in the unglamorous places gathering material, and when it bursts on the world, "Zora Neale Hurston has been lucky again, and the white people have piled more honors upon her which she does not deserve." You guessed it. I want no part of them, and if somebody were to set up a nation of American Negroes, I would be the very first person NOT to go there. I have found that ambition without talent is a terrible combination. It makes natural-born enemies of progress. Negro newspapers are loaded with would-be writers and naturally bloated with envy. They are the most brazen frauds on the American continent. Screaming about "Rights for Negroes" and lynching every Negro who shows any marked ability.

I am very glad for you to have had this experience among us on the Ruby McCollum case so that you can see us from the inside. Knocking around Live Oak, you must have learned a great deal about our great "courage" and truthfulness. (Kaplan 709)

Hurston's monkey story and its sequel ("my people" versus "those people") reflect Hurston's own shift during her time in Live Oak and her movement at the outset of her stay from a presumed "insider" due to the color of her skin to that of an "outsider" who, in spite of being an African-American herself, is relegated to the position of an observer—not a participant—in the larger group to which she fully expected to belong. Clearly frustrated that in spite of her hard work she was unable to elicit meaningful commentary from Live Oak's black community, she viewed this reticence as an act of betrayal by members of her own race who lacked the courage to help her publicize McCollum's situation. She was also angry at the *Courier* and its less than timely financial support of her research efforts in Live Oak. Since she lacked the assistance of Live Oak's black community and the *Courier*, Hurston had ample reason to believe, like Johnson, that addressing "this Race Problem" was indeed "a thankless task."

Later in this second letter, Hurston refers to Huie's invitation for her to join him in Live Oak and to her pointed exclusion from the Florida Folk Festival, an annual gathering of folklorists that met near Live Oak and to which in the past she had regularly been invited. The following

105
. . .
Punctuating
McCollum's
Sentence(s)
of Silence

excerpt echoes Hurston's vacillation between "insider" and "outsider" on two counts: her uncertainty regarding Huie's invitation to Live Oak and, as a result of her reporting the McCollum affair, her exclusion from the festival: "Thanks for your kindness to me, and if there is anything further that I can do for you, you must let me know. I was, and am not afraid to appear in Live Oak, but wondered if you really wanted me there, or just was being nice and polite. I was not invited to participate in the Florida Folk Festival because of my reporting this case, but my reputation, national and international as a folklorist will not suffer because of that. I should worry" (Kaplan 710).

However, according to Kaplan, Hurston *did* worry. "Throughout the fifties—though there had been glimmers of this earlier—Hurston became increasingly paranoid," Kaplan writes. "She feared other writers, publishers, the government, journalists, and especially communists" (608). In Hurston's first letters to Huie, she seems genuinely trusting and pleased to call him her friend. She makes reference to her respect for his work and expresses an eagerness to help him with his upcoming book on Ruby McCollum. Since both Hurston and Huie were established writers and shared a passionate interest in the McCollum case, the two already had much in common, yet at times in Hurston's letters she seems almost *too* deferential. For example, between the next two letters Hurston wrote to Huie a marked shift in tone occurs that hints at the possibility that she was not entirely sure of—or comfortable with—her role as Huie's sometime cocollaborator. Hurston's June 10, 1954, letter to Huie has a conversational tone, the mode of address common between two friendly equals. In the following excerpt, for example, Hurston draws connections between them by mentioning her family's ties to Alabama, Huie's home state:

> You don't know it, but there is a kind of kinship between us. Both of my parents were born in southern Alabama, Notasulga, Macon County, sort of straight west of Columbus, Georgia. If you shake the bushes in that vicinity, Hurstons and Potts (my mother's family) will fall out by the hundreds. There is a white woman here who is from around Columbus, Georgia, and when we meet, we call each other "cousin," she being of the Hurston clan, though she advises me that the real spelling is Hairston, and it has been handed down to her about the branch which moved west into Alabama a little more than a generation before the Civil War. My father was a mulatto, but

the Potts were all very dark. I am doing the old southern thing of "scraping up kin" by common statehood through my parents. (Kaplan 711–12)

Hurston also praises Huie's new book, promises to help him in any capacity with his McCollum pursuits, and closes with the hope that the two would work together in the future. "Two days ago I also received your autographed copy of *The Execution of Private Slovik*, and did not put it down until it was finished," she writes. "I found it surpassingly fine. It is, and should be acclaimed an American classic" (Kaplan 712). Her words concerning McCollum are also warm, and she promises: "I will get the material to you on time regardless of the money. I wish I had the cash to contribute to Ruby's new defense move. Though abhorring what she did, I was and am sorry for the poor thing" (Kaplan 713). It is unclear from the archives if Huie paid Hurston for her contribution to his research efforts and for the account of McCollum's trial Huie included in *Ruby McCollum*. As a man accustomed to paying for information—and often criticized for it—it is doubtful that Huie did not pay Hurston at least a nominal fee for her efforts. The fact that Hurston includes the qualifier "regardless of the money" in her letter indicates that there was more than likely some form of compensation involved in their partnership. Hurston, however, was an extremely proud and independent woman, and it is doubtful that she would have pressed Huie for payment regardless of how badly she needed it. In fact, in a later letter she writes that she hopes "to make a piece of change so that I can work on my book without worrying about money to live on" and in the next sentence professes, "Please, please bear in mind that you owe me nothing in the world" (Kaplan 722).

Hurston ends her June 10, 1954, letter to Huie with the pledge, "Here's to our partnership for the future, and I solemnly swear to do anything I am able towards your career and be utterly faithful to this vow" (Kaplan 714). Hurston's next letter, written on July 1, 1954, however, begins in a radically different tone than that of its predecessor. Whereas her June 10 letter is conversational and speculates about possible future collaborative efforts, Hurston's July 1 text begins abruptly, and she appears particularly concerned that she may have offended Huie by her prior remark about their being "cousins" via Alabama. "Herod the Great" was not progressing well, and Hurston knew that Huie was a powerful white man who, if she were lucky, could provide future collaborative opportunities and much-

107
. . .
Punctuating
McCollum's
Sentence(s)
of Silence

needed income. McCollum's second trial was approaching, and Hurston was eager to attend. However, as the following excerpt illustrates, funding continued to be a problem:

> First let me set you straight about this "cousin" business. Don't think that I was really trying to scrape up kin. With my tongue in my cheek I was merely poking fun at an old southern custom to make you laugh in spite of tussling with Judge Adams.
>
> And please do not conclude that I am seeking to muscle in as a collaborator on your book. That would neither be honest nor right. It is your book, but I stand ready to do any bits that you feel you want me to do. I predict that you are going past the million mark on it. The Negro population is going for it in a big way.
>
> I will be there at the trial. I know that it is going to be thrilling to see Adams upset. Honestly, I was filled with horror when I came to realize that they meant to kill this woman, and hustle her off without allowing her to tell the real story. At the time I almost puked when I saw Judge Adams put on that hypocritical act of sniffling when he got ready to sentence Ruby to the chair. . . .
>
> Frankly, which is the only sensible course, I am not sure that I can get up there to the trial unless you send me at least transportation. I expect to have my book in by then, but not enough time for Burroughs Mitchell to read it, I'm afraid. So there is the situation. (Kaplan 714)

Hurston was never particularly sympathetic to McCollum, at first because she tried very hard to maintain her objective approach to the case, and later because—her objectivity long gone—she sensed in McCollum a selfish control that in Hurston's opinion contributed to the shooting. The fact that Hurston did not particularly *like* McCollum, however, did not in any way mean that she was willing to stand idly by and watch McCollum be executed without consideration of her rights. Kaplan describes this shift in Hurston's viewpoint when she writes: "Her attitude toward McCollum evolved over time. At first, she was critical of the woman and bent over backward to maintain her own journalistic objectivity, even according the clearly prejudicial judge every possible benefit of the doubt. Eventually, Hurston's view began to shift. While she never excused the murder, she began to sympathize with McCollum's position. She was especially taken with McCollum's stoicism, her refusal to let the courtroom turn her into a spectacle or stereotype of black womanhood" (607).

Huie and Hurston were apparently of the same opinion, as can be seen in the following excerpt from the last page of *Ruby McCollum*: "Ruby was, after all, partially responsible for her tragedy," Huie writes. "In her best days I don't believe I would have liked her much" (249). In much the same vein, Hurston wrote to Huie: "But I hold Ruby to be chuckle-headed, too. The dumbest thing a woman can do is to refuse to fade out of the picture when the man is through with her. Certainly accounts for a lot of murders. I sensed this stubbornness in her by little things" (Kaplan 715). Hurston's July 28, 1954, letter to Huie supports her previous contention that McCollum was determined to have control at any cost:

> I sensed a cold control in the woman, also a determination to keep control. Her brother, the barber, told me that she was engaged to another fellow before Sam McCollum, but jilted him because, "He was not getting ahead fast enough." Then she told her lawyer, "I pick from the top. I had the top Negro man in the County and then won the top white one." The killing came because Ruby was not going to be outdone. Granting that Adams had jilted her, and that she was on bad terms with her husband, what was to prevent her from taking several thousand dollars and going north until the stink died down? Or even permanently? I am certain that is the course I would have followed. She could have easily laid her hands on $50,000, took her small children, and disappeared from Live Oak and had her second child by Adams in peace and safety and let the whole affair be forgotten. (Kaplan 716)

By September 6, 1954, however, Hurston turns her attention away from McCollum and writes of her growing concern for Huie and his efforts to raise money for McCollum's defense efforts. "I am indeed on the anxious seat," she writes, "but not because of me, but for your sake, and I will keep on wringing and twisting until I know that you have the money pledged by the *Courier* and the Elks in hand. Anybody who has had any dealings with the *Courier* will tell you how trifling they are about keeping promises about cash. . . . Lord knows I have had my lumps" (Kaplan 718–19). This letter is her most lengthy, and in part because of its length it provides one of the most complete (and complex) accounts of Hurston's views regarding relations between the black and white races. Her shift in her opinion of McCollum's actions is better understood after a reading of this letter, as is her anger at Live Oak's black community for their lack of cooperation during her investigation into the murder. Although Hurston was unwilling to either outright condemn McCollum for what she did or exalt her as a hero in her *Courier* columns, in this particular letter to Huie she states bluntly that McCollum "stinks like a million mules on a mile of manure" (Kaplan 719). Other *Courier* reporters had resisted condemning McCollum and argued that the shooting occurred in self-defense. These reporters also made much of the sexual relationship between McCollum and Adams. Hurston, however, could not bring herself to completely forgive McCollum and writes to Huie that McCollum is a woman who, in her opinion, was "possessed of the poverty of soul to kill a man when she found that she was not wanted":

> I am certain that you are telling the truth about Ruby's guilt. The *Courier* and I had some words on that point. I stood out for factual reporting while Nunn [editor of the *Pittsburgh Courier*] argued that I would leave her no reputation for them to fight on to save her life.
>
> But that is not the real story and they know it and they know that I know it. No matter what the Emancipation Proclamation says, we are still slaves in spirit, lousy with inferiority complexes, and no matter how degrading the circumstances, see glory in the white-pulling-sheets-with-black. The success of *Strange Fruit* by Lillian Smith, *Native Son* by Richard Wright, *Mulatto* by Langston Hughes, and *Deep Are the Roots*, authors names forgotten, was due to this angle. No matter how trashy the writing, if you get that part in you are sure of a large Negro sale, and most especially IF THE HERO OR HEROINE KILLS A WHITE PERSON. In vain do you search for dignity and self-respect. No, the folklore prevails that all white people secretly yearn for Negro lovers (men in particular) and off they go on a wild spree of gloating. The communists have discovered this, and their drive to gain the American Negro has been based on it. They offer to throw in a white wife or husband to Negro party members. I have witnessed some very stinky business in New York along that line. . . . On the occasions when I was solicited to join up, with the usual bonus, I went right to the heart of the matter without beating around the bush and told them that I could get all the white men I wanted without any help from them and pick from a higher bush for a sweeter berry. Ruby would be lionized for what she has done if she were free and arrived in places like New York, Chicago, Washington or Detroit, etc. So far as I am concerned, she stinks like

a million mules on a mile of manure. Not so much that she crossed the line, as the circumstances surrounding her act and because she is possessed of the poverty of soul to kill a man when she found that she was not wanted. Never do I read of an individual who claims to have killed for love but I am revolted, knowing so well that it does not happen. They are just mean-spirited individuals who can't stand to lose. (Kaplan 719–20)

Hurston's assertion that she "told them that I could get all the white men I wanted without any help from them and pick from a higher bush for a sweeter berry" is eerie in its similarity to a line she attributes to Ruby McCollum in her July 28, 1954, letter: "I pick from the top," Hurston quotes McCollum. "I had the top Negro man in the county and then won the top white one" (Kaplan 716). Kaplan and Boyd agree that Hurston and McCollum have much more in common than appears at first glance. For example, Hurston's involvement in the McCollum case came about during a vulnerable period in her own life, and Kaplan writes that Hurston identified on some level with McCollum because Hurston, like McCollum, knew firsthand the frustration of imposed silence. "Hurston had just completed *The Golden Bench of God*," Kaplan writes, "a novel she felt was one of her best . . . and it had been summarily rejected. She had been the victim of a court case in which her own voice was either silenced or not taken seriously, as if whatever a black woman might say in her own defense was of no consequence" (607–8). Hurston argues, however that whites alone are not responsible for the suppression of black women. Black men, too, Hurston writes, "will double-team a Negro woman who surpasses them in achievement with utmost skullduggery and think nothing of it. IT IS SAFE. Anyway, you can hear a Negro man say, 'I don't allow no *woman* to cuss me.' A man can cuss him because he has a harder fist" (Kaplan 721). Hurston writes that these same black men, however, secretly found satisfaction in the fact that Adams desired McCollum; moreover, they were pleased that a powerful white individual like Adams was killed by a Negro. She writes: "So you see, in Ruby McCollum's case and others similar, they *want* to believe that she was irresistible to Dr. Adams, and they are secretly glorying in the fact that a Negro killed a white man, something none of them have the courage to do themselves. They love to read about it, even in fiction such as in the stories I mentioned. You remember Paul Robeson's long run in *Othello*. An educated Negro man in New York gloated to me, 'I have been to see it four times. I love to see Paul Robeson choking that

111

. . .

Punctuating
McCollum's
Sentence(s)
of Silence

white woman to death. White folks have killed enough Negroes.' Hence the rush at the box office" (Kaplan 721).

If Hurston's September 6, 1954, letter to Huie is largely devoted to a discussion of race, in a handwritten postscript she shifts to more inclusive considerations, what she describes in a prior letter as "the dramatics of the case and the varied play of human emotions" (Kaplan 710). Human motivation and interaction consistently provided the focus of Hurston's *Courier* columns about the McCollum affair, and in this postscript to Huie she is still clearly drawn to the story's universal themes rather than its potential to serve as any sort of "lesson" for either blacks or whites. "My interest in the case," she writes, "has never been that Ruby was a heroine that should be saved at all costs, but that of a writer in that it is a good story by the time you analyze all the characters concerned, and as you point out, the reactions of the community to the scandal. I see Ruby and Dr. Adams of the same essential human type—success had persuaded both that they were above and beyond the laws that govern ordinary mortals" (Kaplan 723).

Hurston discovered that in spite of her desire to transcend hotly contested race issues during her coverage of McCollum, achieving such transcendence proved problematic. In Hurston's contribution to Huie's *Ruby McCollum*, for example, the original manuscript written for inclusion in his text describes how drinking water was available to those seated in the white section of the courtroom, but Hurston makes no reference to any such provision in the segregated gallery. In correspondence to Huie sometime in late 1954 or early 1955, Hurston refers to this manuscript: "I point out the lack of drinking water in the courthouse for Negroes. You can make the change or not as you see fit" (Kaplan 723). Huie did change Hurston's original text, and the edited passage as it appears in *Ruby McCollum*, with Huie's addition appearing in italics, reads as follows: "The janitor passed the bucket and the dipper around to the jury, and also to court officers, but white spectators could go up and get a drink. *Under the separate-but-equal doctrine there was a similar bucket for the Negro galleries*" (96). Perhaps Huie feared further antagonizing an already angry Judge Adams by publicizing the fact that his courtroom did not follow the laws of separate-but-equal doctrine, but considering the overall inflammatory nature of *Ruby McCollum* it seems unlikely that such a small point would have had much impact. For this reason, Huie's addition to Hurston's text is puzzling, yet the alteration of her manuscript did not appear to disturb Hurston. She continued to be complimentary of Huie's work: "You are a great artist. As your sentences flow past my inner mind, I am impressed by both the happy choice of words and the rhythm of sentence-passage.... If you do not get the Nobel literary award on this work, I shall be surprised" (Kaplan 724). Hurston ends this particular letter by again mentioning the Florida Folk Festival and silences that I contend are strikingly similar to Huie's apparent anticipation of a potential backlash in Live Oak in response to racial inequities described in Hurston's unedited manuscript:

> You see, I *know* my west Florida. There is eternal conflict between that backward area and peninsular Florida. Those crackers up there are "agin" *everything* that smells like progress. You have seen their unreasonable attitudes, their stubborn bitterness when opposed. Because I wrote you about this case, the prominent ladies who run the Foster Memorial and state folk festival bar *me*—held to be if not the #1 folklorist of America, among the highest bracket, certainly #1 in Florida—from the festival *and* the dear lady feels justified in not returning my only copy of *Mules and Men*. They would certainly have accused us of not flying right if I had shown up. (Kaplan 724)

If Huie thought neutralizing Hurston's portrayal of Judge Adams's inequitable courtroom accommodations would indicate his own efforts to "fly right" in Suwannee County, he was mistaken. Ever since his confrontation with Huie over access to McCollum, Judge Adams had been patiently waiting for the opportunity to squelch the author's unwelcome interference in affairs that Adams considered strictly the concern of Live Oak's judicial system. And since it was well within Huie's legal rights to ask questions, Judge Adams had no recourse but to allow him to proceed about his business undisturbed—that is, of course, unless Huie made a mistake. And during McCollum's second trial, Huie did just that. The fact that the judge's subsequent actions against Huie brought even *more* bad publicity to Live Oak seemed of little consequence to Adams. He had already weathered the worst public storm of his long career, and no amount of unfavorable press could lessen his eagerness to lock Huie in the same jail that for two years had housed Ruby McCollum, the woman he directly held responsible for the turmoil in his town and an upcoming book that was almost certain to bring more.

"Fear of the Unknown"

On May 2, 1953, well before her second sanity hearing, the *Pittsburgh Courier* reported that McCollum's mental state was deteriorating and questioned whether she would be competent to stand trial a second time. The column reads as follows:

> A reliable source told the *Courier* this week that Mrs. Ruby McCollum may be on the verge of losing her mind through "fear of the unknown."
>
> The source fears that the subterranean recesses of Mrs. McCollum's subconscious mind are being closed against reality. The *Courier* was told that Mrs. McCollum had been found by visitors to her cell, wrapped up in a blanket or sheet and huddled in a pitiful mound upon her cell bunk.
>
> Ruby, the *Courier* was told, has repeatedly expressed the fear that she may be "killed" or "poisoned."
>
> The source of this "fear" is locked within the recesses of Ruby's mind, giving cause for observers to think that she may be on the actual brink of becoming mentally unbalanced.
>
> Subjected to the constant probing of public curiosity since she shot white Dr. LeRoy Adams, newly elected Florida solon, in his Live Oak office in 1952, Mrs. McCollum has been under a severe mental strain.
>
> Since the fatal shots rang out and Ruby was taken into custody, the story of her clandestine relationship with Dr. Adams, which has been largely ignored by the white press, has become common knowledge to readers in the Negro press. . . . Whether or not Ruby can continue to retain her sanity with a death sentence staring her in the face is something that only her own mind can answer. ("Living")

The following week, the *Courier* called for a full medical examination of McCollum and describes her life since August 3, 1952, as "a continuous Hell on Earth" ("Is Ruby Sane?"); however, McCollum did not receive any examination or medical attention until 1954, when her defense attorneys raised the question of her competency to stand trial. When the request for a mental evaluation was granted, Frank Cannon asked if McCollum might be examined at the Florida Hospital for the Insane, but Judge Adams denied the request. Instead, Adams appointed two psychiatrists, William McCullagh of Jacksonville—who determined McCollum's competency for her first trial—and Frank Fernay of Lake City, and ordered that the examination be held in the Suwannee County Jail. The *Suwannee Democrat* reported on September 3, 1954, that Cannon was convinced of Mc-

Collum's insanity and that "his client's mental condition had deteriorated to such an extent that she refused to use the mattress provided for her and lies on the bare springs of the prison cot with a blanket wrapped around her from head to foot" ("McCollum Trial"). The *Democrat* also addressed the issue of outside access to McCollum, which is unusual considering the newspaper's previous silence on the matter, and for the first time the *Democrat* mentions Huie's involvement in the case. The column reports that the defense was unsuccessful in convincing Sheriff Hugh Lewis to permit the press access to McCollum and that "Author William Bradford Huie, who says he is writing a book on Dr. Adams, was a spectator in the courtroom. He has been trying to interview her but was denied permission by an earlier order of Judge Adams which permits no one but members of her family and her attorneys to see her" ("McCollum Trial").

Although McCollum had written Huie several letters and knew about his fight to save her life, the two had never met prior to McCollum's competency hearing. Huie describes his initial impressions in the following excerpt from *Ruby McCollum*:

> Ruby had once weighed one hundred and forty-five pounds, which made her fat for her height. Now she weighed eighty-seven pounds. She wore a yellow bandana about her head like a turban. Her brown dress hung loosely. Her cheeks and eyes were sunken.
>
> Three years ago she had been in the high cotton, possessed by the two Big Men in the community. Now the two Big Men were decomposed in their graves, and Ruby was the shabby remnant which survived. She had endured emotional tumult, hypochondria, despair; had been capable of murder; and for two years she had lain in a cell on an iron cot.
>
> Because I had studied her life, I could think of Ruby as a human being; perhaps McGriff and Cannon could, too; but to everyone else in the courtroom Ruby McCollum was a corpse which long ago should have been buried, but which, because of "outside interference," had persisted above ground, a community disposal problem. (207)

The problem of how to "dispose" of McCollum was not a difficult one. Having already tried her once, publicly pronounced her guilty, and broken any remaining resistance she may have had left by housing her in solitary confinement for almost two years, the safest way to avoid a new trial and the possibility that McCollum might somehow manage to break her si-

x

x

115

. . .

Punctuating
McCollum's
Sentence(s)
of Silence

lence would be to have her pronounced incompetent to participate in her own defense. In other words, if the Florida Supreme Court would not allow Judge Adams to execute McCollum, then Adams would have to settle for the next best thing—placing McCollum in institutional isolation for the rest of her life.

In spite of what many considered McCollum's "irrational" behavior while housed in the Suwannee County Jail, her symptoms are actually quite consistent with those of other individuals who have suffered from emotional or physical trauma. Because McCollum was unable to verbalize and thereby assimilate into her current reality the source of her trauma—a key step in the recovery process—she, like other trauma victims in similar situations, appeared to withdraw from reality altogether. Susan Brison, herself a trauma victim, defines a traumatic event as "one in which a person feels utterly helpless in the face of a force that is perceived to be life-threatening" and writes that, according to the *Diagnostic and Statistical Manual of Mental Disorders IV*, reactions to traumatic experience include "the physiological responses of hypervigilance, heightened startle response, sleep disorders, and the more psychological, yet still involuntary, responses of depression, inability to concentrate, lack of interest in activities that used to give life meaning, and a sense of a foreshortened future" (40). Brison argues that recovery from traumatic experience depends on the degree an individual is able to verbalize the initial traumatic experience and, as a result, become "whole" again. Breaking the silence of trauma suffered in isolation through communion with others is, Brison argues, a crucial step in resolving trauma's "radical disruption of memory, a severing of past from present and, typically, an inability to envision a future." However, the effectiveness of these trauma testimonies, what Brison calls "speech acts of memory" (39), is dependent in large measure on the willingness of the trauma victim's surrounding culture to hear and empathize with the disturbing narratives. Brison writes:

116
. . .
The
Silencing
of Ruby
McCollum

> All memory of (human-inflicted) trauma . . . is cultural memory in at least two respects. First, traumatic events are initially experienced in a cultural context (even when endured alone) and are taken in under certain descriptions and other (for example, sensory) representations and not others. What is happening/what happened can be understood only in terms of the meanings of the traumatizing actions and accompanying words. . . . Second, how (and even whether) traumatic events are remembered depends on not only how they

are initially experienced but also how (whether) they are perceived by others, directly or indirectly, and the extent to which others are able to listen empathetically to the survivor's testimony. The traumatic event is experienced as culturally embedded (or framed), is remembered as such (in both traumatic and narrative memory), and is shaped and reshaped in memory over time according, at least in part, to how others in the survivor's culture respond. (41–42)

McCollum's chances to overcome her past traumatic experiences and, as a result, her mental and physical "wholeness," were radically reduced because, first, she feared that she could not speak freely with anyone about the murder and the traumatic months leading up to it, and, second, the surrounding culture of Live Oak was not at all supportive of her doing so.

In 1980, six years after her release from the Florida Hospital for the Insane, the *Ocala Sun-Banner* columnist Al Lee wrote that McCollum remembered little of the Adams shooting or her trial. "I don't remember what I was in there for," she replied when asked to recall the courtroom drama. "They asked a lot of questions and there was objections and sustainings. I forgot all that" (Lee, "Memory"). Lee's column alleges that during her incarceration and after her release McCollum suffered from Ganser's Syndrome: "Dr. George Bernard, a University of Florida psychiatrist, said Ganser's Syndrome often acts as a barrier, 'and is a hysterical type of neurosis and unconscious screening out of a highly unpleasant experience.' Said the psychiatrist. 'Loss of memory is one of the main characteristics.' Mrs. McCollum has her own perspective. 'The Lord helps me not to cry, not to think about it. I help myself, praying'" ("Memory"). Marita Sturken argues that the act of forgetting (and the recollection of repressed memories) can tell us much about both a given individual and, more important, the culture that informs him or her. For example, in the context of the recent rise in instances of recovered memory, Sturken writes:

> Perhaps the most powerful cultural defense that has stymied the recovered memory debate is the prevalent notion of forgetting as a form of illness, a loss of self, and a threat to subjectivity. Indeed, one way to understand recovered memory syndrome as a cultural and national phenomenon is not to see it simply as memory, but rather as a form of cultural forgetting. It is important to examine the ways in which a sense of memory as production and forgetting as negation has limited this debate. A central element that binds these sto-

ries together is not their remembering but the fact that these memories were forgotten. How, one wants to ask, have so many people repressed these memories? And, why are people so easily convinced that they (and, by extension, the nation) have forgotten? Perhaps we should be asking, What does the act of forgetting produce? What lack is it contingent upon? (243)

McCollum never did recover her memory, or if she did, she never admitted to it. On the one hand, McCollum's amnesia may have been very real, rendering her truly unable to recall the traumatic experiences of the shooting and her solitary confinement. On the other hand, she may have never lost her memory at all and simply discovered that feigning amnesia discouraged prying questions. Huie writes in *Ruby McCollum* that McCollum's jailer accused her of "only 'acting crazy'" in the days immediately prior to her second competency hearing. The jailer's wife concurred and "insisted that the prisoner was not mentally ill, and she pointed out that when Ruby wanted to write her son in the Army she could remember the long address, with many digits in the numbers, and that Ruby had an excellent memory for telephone numbers" (218). Yet during her trial McCollum asserted on multiple occasions that she could not remember significant details related to the shooting. If McCollum's amnesia was exclusive to events related to Adams's murder and is indicative of trauma brought on by the murder and Adams's treatment of her beforehand, and if, as Brison contends, recovery from traumatic experience is contingent on the subject's ability to verbalize the traumatic experience itself, McCollum's condition appears to have been irreversible.

Ernst van Alphen, however, writes that trauma and memory are inextricably linked to discursivity. In terms of van Alphen's theoretical framework, McCollum's inability (or unwillingness) to verbalize her trauma may have been due to the limitations of language and not, as some argued, her own self-imposed reticence. Van Alphen writes: "People often speak of 'traumatic experiences' or 'traumatic memories'; I, however . . . argue that the cause of trauma is precisely the impossibility of experiencing, and subsequently memorizing, an event. From this perspective it is contradictory to speak of traumatic experience or memory. If we assume that experience is somehow discursive, 'failed experience' becomes a good case for laying bare the function of discourse in experience: it is in failed experience that the close interconnectedness of discourse and experience is disrupted. This disruption enables us to see exactly what is discursive about experience" (26).

Van Alphen's contention that trauma cannot be assimilated because there exists no discourse with which to represent it is based on his study of Holocaust survivors. "The remembrance of Holocaust events," he writes, "is, then, technically impossible; this problem is fundamentally semiotic in nature" (26). McCollum's silence and forgetting, like the "failed experience" of van Alphen's Holocaust survivors, may have been neither symptomatic of a serious "mental illness" nor a crafty conscious choice on her part. She may have found the initial trauma so great that there simply existed no language with which to adequately express it. Given the fact that McCollum was encouraged to remain silent through intimidation and isolation, it is not difficult to see why "forgetting" the past might have brought her some tenuous measure of control and safety—especially since she was held hostage by a town and a culture that valued silence over all else.

Andrea Nicki writes that any woman who does not conform to gender-specific modes of behavior in our society runs the very real risk of being labeled "crazy." Certainly McCollum's behavior during her incarceration in the Suwannee County Jail does indicate that she was laboring under severe emotional strain, but even before the murder she had been hospitalized several times at Dr. Adams's request. In these crucial months before the shooting, McCollum's growing unwillingness to conform to the mandates of southern silence by submitting unconditionally to Adams marked her as "irrational," in Adams's mind, and the shooting itself only served to confirm to the citizens of Live Oak that she was, as the prosecution alleged, insane. For a woman—and particularly a black woman—to act in such a manner went against the grain of long-held southern ideologies. For example, the fact that McCollum managed her husband's finances and had an open affair with a white man indicated that she cared little about southern "rules" regarding gender and race. After the murder, Live Oak searched for a rational explanation for McCollum's behavior—a way to assimilate her actions into the broader social fabric—and finding none, contended that she must be insane. Nicki writes that women who exhibit a desire for control are often labeled as "crazy" by larger society, and I argue that this contention holds especially true in the South. She writes: "Conventional feminine behavior involves quietness, self-effacement, and cautiousness that does not give rise to manic, risky involvement in plea-

Punctuating
McCollum's
Sentence(s)
of Silence

surable activities like sexual affairs or financial investments, activities that are condoned, even applauded, in men. Women who display mania are doubly deviant, defying norms of femininity and challenging an Aristotelian paradigm of humanity as self-controlled and moderate, occupying a mean between extremes. Women who exhibit levels of self-confidence and initiation that would be seen as normal or average in men risk being labeled "mentally ill" (88). Considering the fact that McCollum craved control—a characteristic of her personality repeatedly cited by both Hurston and Huie—then perhaps Adams's murder was this desire for control taken to the extreme. However, many sources confirm that Adams was physically abusive, so McCollum may have felt that murder was the only way to escape a life-threatening situation. In any event, control played a crucial role in the sexual relationship between McCollum and Adams as well as the murder itself. Control, however, was also of paramount importance to white power formations in Live Oak, and silence was the most effective way to ensure that these formations emerged unscathed after McCollum was either executed or safely locked away for good. A new trial threatened the foundation of silence upon which Live Oak rested—silences that had been severely damaged during McCollum's first trial but, as a result of McCollum being out of the public eye for two years, were strong once again.

"In a Calm and Reasonable Manner"

Both Zora Neale Hurston and William Bradford Huie were present during McCollum's second sanity hearing. However, Huie's presence in the courtroom would ultimately prove to be his undoing. It was well known in Live Oak that Huie was working on a book about McCollum; it was also well known that he had close ties with the *Pittsburgh Courier*, one of the most liberal black newspapers in America. Judge Adams was also not pleased that Huie continued to threaten him with legal action if Adams did not allow the press to have access to McCollum. All of these factors combined to make Huie a less-than-welcome presence in Live Oak and guaranteed him an especially cold reception in Judge Adams's courtroom. Nonetheless, Huie was in attendance on August 30, 1954, when Drs. Frank Fernay and William McCullagh were appointed to examine McCollum and report their findings regarding her mental state.

After Judge Adams ruled that court would resume on September 23 pending McCollum's competency evaluation, Frank Cannon and Huie left Live Oak. The men stopped for a quick bourbon in a bar on the outskirts of Lake City and decided to seek out Dr. Fernay, who lived in the area. Huie contends in *Ruby McCollum* that his decision to speak with Dr. Fernay was based strictly on the supposition that while Dr. McCullagh was thoroughly acquainted with sensitive nature of the McCollum case, Dr. Fernay might not be so well informed. "When he goes up there to the jail," Huie recalls Cannon musing during their trip, "Ruby may not talk to him; she may refuse to cooperate with him in any way, and all he'll hear will be what those folks around the jail tell him. If there was some way that he could be told the whole story, he might be helpful to us" (214). Huie and Cannon located Dr. Fernay, and Huie spoke briefly with him as Fernay fished from a lake near his home in Lake City. Huie's account of the meeting given in *Ruby McCollum* is rather vague and confined to a single paragraph. It reads as follows:

> I told him that Judge Adams had handicapped the defense by order-ing that Ruby could be examined "only by psychiatrists licensed to practice in the State of Florida"; that this was a handicap because the psychiatrists I hoped to interest in the case were in other states. I told him something about LeRoy Adams; something about the bolita racket; something about the sexual relationship between the doctor and Ruby; and I tried to describe the type of psychiatric treatment which Ruby had undergone in the months prior to the murder. I told him that Judge Adams had denied Ruby the right to talk with me, or with any other reporter, but that we expected to win this right, and I told him that, in the interest of my own investigation, I'd appreciate the opportunity of talking with him after he had ex-amined Ruby. (216)

On September 17, however, the *Democrat* reported that Dr. Fernay had officially withdrawn from the case after he "informed Judge Hal W. Adams that 'he was not situated so that he could handle the assignment'" ("Ruby McCollum Murder"). Instead, Dr. William Ingram Jr., an associate of Dr. McCullagh, took over.

On September 21, the two psychiatrists filed their report detailing Mc-Collum's inability to rationally participate in her own defense. The report reads in part as follows: "History and examinations indicate that Ruby McCollum is psychotic (insane), suffering from a Prison Psychosis. Due to this mental condition, it is our opinion that she is not in condition to con-duct a rational defense. It is recommended that she be transferred to the Florida State Hospital, Chattahoochee, Florida, to the Criminal Insane Section, for further observation and treatment" (Report of Committee).

121
. . .
Punctuating
McCollum's
Sentence(s)
of Silence

A psychiatric evaluation conducted by a Dr. M. C. Moore and dated September 21, 1954, however, provides more detail concerning McCollum's condition:

> On the day of my examination, I found her in a filthy, foul-smelling jail cell, lying on a cot without mattress with her entire body, including her head, covered with an old Army blanket. Scattered around the bed were many cans of food, also refuse. Most of the odor was due to her own physical uncleanliness. With her brother present, many attempts were made to converse with her but failed to elicit any response other than peeking from under the blanket on two occasions. The more she became aware of someone present, the more she continued a constant agitation-like attempt to pull the blanket tighter and more securely around her body. At no time did she lie perfectly still. After some time, the blanket was forcibly removed from her head and she struck at the examining physician. . . .
>
> A physical and neurological examination was impossible because of the patient's resistance and combativeness.
>
> From the results of my examination and review of other information that I was able to gather concerning this patient, it is my opinion that this patient is delusional. This means, of course, that she has certain phantasies [*sic*] which are not true. For example, she has a false idea that people are trying to poison her with her food or by means of some harmful gas. Her refusal to talk and converse with those trying to help her is also evidence of her inability to reason sanely. For these reasons, I believe that she is unable to carry on a rational defense due to her present mental condition, which is definitely abnormal. ("Psychiatric Evaluation")

Huie and Cannon were present on September 24, when Drs. McCullagh and Ingram reported their findings to Judge Adams. Since both physicians agreed that McCollum was incompetent to stand trial, Judge Adams had no choice but to commit her to the state mental hospital. McCollum was transported there immediately.

If McCollum's removal to the Florida Mental Hospital in Chattahoochee was a letdown for those individuals wishing to see her sentenced to death for the murder of Dr. Adams, another extraordinary event occurred that day that more than made up for the McCollum saga's rather anticlimactic ending. Immediately after committing McCollum, Judge

122
. . .
The
Silencing
of Ruby
McCollum

Adams dropped a bombshell that astonished everyone—but no one more so than Huie, who without warning found himself the object of Judge Adams's wrath. Long frustrated by Huie's meddling in affairs that Judge Adams considered none of his business, Adams shocked the courtroom when, in the words of the October 1 *Democrat*, he cited Huie for "contempt of court because of statements he has made in connection with the Ruby McCollum case. . . . In the petition it is contended that Huie 'did represent to the said Dr. Frank A. Fernay that the said Hal W. Adams, circuit judge aforesaid, was prejudiced and against the said Ruby McCollum and that the said Hal W. Adams was bias [*sic*] in the matter of the State of Florida versus Ruby McCollum'" ("Writer"). The subpoena gave Huie until October 9 to prove why he should not be charged with contempt, and Huie writes in *Ruby McCollum* that as he left the courtroom that day "one of the deputies said to me: 'The old man is going to get even with you now, Huie. You interfered with him. Now he's going to interfere with you. You sprung that nigger out of this jail. Now we're going to put you right in that cell that we let her out of'" (222).

Huie was ordered to pay a fine of $750 plus the cost of the court proceedings. If he refused, he would be confined in the Suwannee County Jail for six months. Huie contends in *Ruby McCollum* that his initial refusal to pay the fine was based on the fact that so many people had contributed to both his assistance of McCollum and efforts to fight his own contempt charge. "I could no longer think of myself," he writes. "Other men had contributed their energies. I had no right to pay the fine" (242). Therefore, Huie was arrested and spent sixty-three hours in the Suwannee County Jail before Huie's attorneys appeared before the Florida Supreme Court and managed to have him released on a writ of habeas corpus and posting a $2,500 bond. Huie eventually decided to pay the original fine, but when he attempted to do so, he discovered that Judge Adams had ordered the sheriff of Suwannee County to refuse to accept it on the grounds that Huie's previous choice to be jailed in order to preserve his right to appeal forfeited his ability to satisfy the judgment by paying in arrears. On August 7, 1955, Judge Adams issued an order for Huie's arrest, and it was delivered to New York, where police refused to act on it without order from the governor of Florida. At the time of *Ruby McCollum*'s publishing, the matter had still not been settled, and the afterword of the 1964 second edition of Huie's book mentions the incident only briefly. "At the Suwannee County courthouse," he writes, "I looked for my old antagonist, Sheriff Hugh Lewis. . . . I remembered our conversations, in his office, and

123
. . .
Punctuating
McCollum's
Sentence(s)
of Silence

while I was in jail. My last evidence of him had been his endorsement on my check for $750, on October 16, 1957" (185). Clearly Huie had been allowed to pay the original fine levied in his contempt-of-court charge, yet the text is silent on precisely how this turn of events took place. Located in the William Bradford Huie Papers, however, is compelling evidence of why silence permeates this particular aspect of Huie's involvement with McCollum. An undated Western Union telegram to Huie reads as follows:

> Have just returned to office and your letter of October 9th awaited me. Florida cabinet meets tomorrow and while consideration of Pardon Board matters is not on agenda it would be possible to discuss your request at this time. However I am reluctant to do this without making the personal suggestion which I sincerely believe to be in the best interest of all concerned that you think further about the question of accepting the condition attached by the Board to your pardon. I assume you realize our decision was based on honest convictions and was not one made in the hope that it would be popular. It was our good faith belief that having once offered to pay the fine you would not now refuse to do so. Reconsideration by the Pardon Board would seem to me to invite only a prolongation of the controversy to the benefit of no one and I certainly would not make this suggestion if I felt you were placed in an unreasonable position by the action of the Board. Bear in mind that based upon the advice of the Attorney General we have no lawful authority to rebate or refund any of the bond which was entreated. I am grateful to you for your comments about my efforts to approach the problem facing the South today in a calm and reasonable manner. (Collins, Telegram)

The telegram is signed by LeRoy Collins, governor of Florida. Along with this telegram is another short letter to Huie from Governor Collins. Written on official State of Florida letterhead and dated October 22, 1957, it reads as follows: "I have received and forwarded your check to the sheriff of Suwannee County. It is a relief to know that this controversy has at long last been laid to rest. I would like to express my sincere thanks to you for your understanding and acceptance of my suggestion." Clearly Huie found himself under pressure to quietly settle the contempt matter from forces much more powerful and far-reaching than either Judge Adams or Suwannee County. Perhaps in the interest of self-preservation or perhaps

124
. . .
The
Silencing
of Ruby
McCollum

due to dwindling funds and energy, Huie surrendered the battle he knew he could not win, paid the fine levied by Judge Adams, and was finally able to disentangle himself from Live Oak and the McCollum affair.

Some may view Huie's decision to pay the fine levied against him as cowardly. After devoting such time and energy to breaking the silence of southern ideologies, they reason, how could he—a man of such supposed high principles—give up so easily? This question can only be answered by reminding the reader of the pervasive nature of silence in the South and the single-minded sense of purpose with which southern ideology weaves its web. This perpetuation of southern ideological formations is a complicated process—as has been illustrated throughout this text—and in the final analysis I doubt that few people finding themselves in Huie's situation would not have chosen his same course of action. In fact, I contend that it was Huie's intimate knowledge of the very nature of silence in the South that in the end convinced him to follow Governor Collins's suggestion. Those less familiar with Huie's adversaries would have perhaps fought on to the detriment of their personal safety. For me to make such a statement about silence in the South in the late 1950s is not alarmist; it is, in fact, realistic. Consider, for example, Huie's assertion in the second edition of *Ruby McCollum*:

> Then I found proof of what I always suspected: that Hugh Lewis had been a member of the Ku Klux Klan; that, like some of the sheriffs in Mississippi in 1964, he had tried to serve both the cause of justice and the cause of the Invisible Empire.
>
> On June 28, 1958, the Florida Legislative Investigating Committee cited Hugh Lewis for contempt because of "his refusal to answer questions about Ku Klux Klan activity." Before the Committee Lewis admitted under oath that from 1950 to 1955 he was an active member of the Klan. He admitted that in 1955 Klansmen brutally flogged a Negro in Suwannee County. He admitted he had made no arrests although he knew the identity of the floggers. But to the Committee he refused to identify the floggers, contending that to do so might result in "killing or serious injury to one or more persons."
>
> In that he was correct. Had he identified the floggers, his fellow Klansmen might have murdered him or a member of his family. . . . A measure of the voting majority in Suwannee County is Hugh Lewis'

reelection as sheriff in 1960 . . . after the pubic disclosure that he was under Klan discipline and therefore unable to arrest or identify Klansmen guilty of racial crimes. (185–86)

Huie's decision to end his connection with Ruby McCollum and all that her case entailed was wise. To continue to fight was not only futile but also extremely risky business indeed.

If Huie's wranglings with the legal system in Florida ended in 1957, his association with McCollum lasted for many more years. The William Bradford Huie Papers contain several short letters McCollum wrote to Huie during her confinement in the Florida State Mental Hospital in Chattahoochee. In a letter dated July 11, 1966, for example, McCollum writes simply: "Please help me. I want to go back home." Then, on December 16, 1971, she writes: "I have been here since 1954, September 16. This is December 16, 1971. I have been up here seventeen years. I want to go back to my own home now in Suwannee County. Please help me." She ends the note with a heart-wrenching postscript, "P.S. All my four kids are married." On May 22, 1973, she writes: "How are you today? I feel O.K. about as well as you could expect. I just want to go back to my Sam Jr., Kay, Sonja, and Loretta. I want you to please help me."

It is, however, McCollum's last letter to Huie that is her most poignant. In a wild scrawl that disregards the regimented lines of her Florida State Hospital stationery, she writes: "Just to say Merry Christmas and Happy New Year. Peace on earth good will to men. I hope to see you soon." Yet even the passage of time is not enough to heal some wounds. Prison authorities continued to bar Huie's every attempt to meet with McCollum—and the peace on earth and goodwill to men that McCollum envisioned has yet to materialize in the silent South.

Conclusion

. . . .

Chaos staggered up the hill
and got the daisies dirty
that were pretty along the road:
messy chaos I said
but then in cooler mind saw
incipient eyes revolving in it
with possibly incipient sorrow
and had to admire how
it got along at all
in its kind of weather:
passing, it engulfed me
and I couldn't know dissolving
it had rhizobia with it
to make us green some other place.

A. R. Ammons, "Chaos Staggered Up the Hill"

AFTER BEING RULED mentally incompetent in 1954, Ruby McCollum spent the next twenty years in the Florida State Mental Hospital in Chattahoochee. Arthur Ellis, author of *The Trial of Ruby McCollum*, writes that during the 1950s the place was an "infamous chamber of horrors" where doctors routinely treated residents with Thorazine and electro-convulsive shock therapy (515). Fortunately for McCollum and many others like her, however, the Baker Act passed in 1972, which entitled any person involuntarily committed to a mental institution the right to review every six months. After the passage of the Baker Act, Frank Cannon, one of the attorneys who had previously defended McCollum, began work to gain her release. "I just said to myself," Cannon told reporter Al Lee in January of 1980, "'Hell, I'll get ole Ruby out,' and I did—got her out of jail to Chattahoochee and from Chattahoochee to home" (Lee, "Memory"). On October 26, 1973, Lee reported the following concerning McCollum's final hearing before her release: "A psychiatrist who examined her with two colleagues prior to the hearing said she is 'quite incompetent,' although reported as harmless. State law permits release of incompetents if it is determined they would do no harm to themselves or others. Alone, Mrs. McCollum would be as 'helpless as a new baby in the snow,' the psychiatrist said" (Lee, "Lawyer").

After her release in 1974, McCollum spent several years in a foster home near Silver Springs, Florida, under the watchful eye of landlady Ella Gaskin. William Bradford Huie paid McCollum $40,000 for the rights to her life's story, and these funds—along with a spending allowance of $1.15 a day—provided for her minimal needs. When her health began to fail in the early 1980s, McCollum entered a nursing home in Ocala. A former schoolmate of McCollum's from Fessenden Academy visited McCollum several times during her confinement, and she told me that McCollum appeared to be lucid and articulate. "They like to say she was crazy," the woman said, "but she weren't no more crazy than I am. Wouldn't you act crazy too if they was trying to put you in the electric chair?" Then she laughed, "Ruby always was a smart one," she said. "She had a reason to blow Adams away, and she had a reason for acting like she did after she done it."

According to Lee, tragic events during and after McCollum's release from Chattahoochee had by 1980 rendered her an old woman who "fondly, and with nostalgia . . . turns to the past" (Lee, "No Animosity"). That year, for example, McCollum's daughter, Sonja, died of a heart attack. Kay Hope, another of McCollum's daughters, died in an automobile accident in 1978. In a cruel twist of fate, Kay was killed on her way to pick up Sam Jr., who had been released from prison after serving a three-year prison sentence for ten counts of illegal gambling activities. Ellis writes that Loretta, the alleged biracial daughter of McCollum and Adams, "lives quietly in New Jersey with her husband and four children, and resists the attempts of anyone to pry into her family history" (517). All of my efforts to locate Loretta failed, so if Ellis is correct and she does reside in New Jersey, Loretta has succeeded in remaining anonymous.

One reason that Huie had more luck than I did in persuading people familiar with the McCollum case to break their silence is because early on he was fortunate enough to uncover what is now known as the "Blue Will" affair. While researching what would eventually become *Ruby McCollum*, Huie resided at the Blue Lodge, a series of small stone cottages on the outskirts of Live Oak and owned by a man named LaVergne Blue. It was there, according to Huie, that Blue told him a startling tale. The following excerpt from Blue's story is taken from Huie's text:

> Three or four weeks after the funeral, Jeff Elliott [a close friend of Adams] came in the office and asked me if the doc had been my heir—if I had made a will leaving all my property to Dr. Adams.
>
> "Why, of course not," I said. "I intend for my property to go to my cousin in Illinois."
>
> "That's funny," Elliott said, "because in the doc's files, just as plain as day, is the last will and testament of LaVergne Blue, leaving everything you've got to the doc. The will even gives the doc complete authority over the disposition of your body. . . ."
>
> I am now certain that he had planned to kill me and take my property. I owe my life to Ruby. . . . She was the first one to discover that he was a monster, and she killed him, and she rendered us all a service. (113)

Blue gave Huie a copy of the will, complete with Blue's signature forged by Adams, and Huie circulated it liberally in Suwannee County. That copy now resides in the Huie archives, and across its face is written the following statement signed by LaVergne Blue: "I hereby declare this document to be fraudulent and a forgery, and to be null and void, and to be of no effect." The "Blue Will" scandal successfully broke Adams's credibility with many Live Oak citizens by proving beyond the shadow of any doubt that he was not the honorable man many previously had supposed. Unlike Huie, however, during the course of my research into the Ruby McCollum affair

129
· · ·
Conclusion

I had no such silver bullet. Beyond my Live Oak pedigree and southern accent, I had nothing to engender trust in those individuals I managed to persuade to speak with me about McCollum. Moreover, I had nothing to add to the McCollum story—no new information that after fifty years would finally close a painful chapter in the community's past. All I had to offer were questions, and in Live Oak those are still in no small supply.

Huie and I do, however, have our similarities. In 1964, Huie attempted to interview Sam Jr. for the upcoming second edition of *Ruby McCollum*. Sam refused to speak with him, so Huie arranged for an outside party, Bob Delaney, a Tallahassee reporter, to conduct the interview. Delaney's memo regarding the meeting appears at the end of Huie's 1964 text and is predictable. The memo reads in part as follows: "Sam has a confident way about him. He smiles easily, is a nice-looking, extremely husky young man. But his whole attitude is that of wanting to be left alone. In response to several questions, he said: 'I don't want to seem difficult but I had just rather not go into it'" (187). I also attempted to contact Sam Jr. and met with no success. I wrote to him early in this project and explained that I wanted to give him an opportunity to comment on his mother and verify the accuracy of my research. He never replied.

Zora Neale Hurston died in poverty in 1960, and at the age of seventy-six, Huie followed her in 1986. Many of Hurston's papers, including the unfinished text of "Herod the Great"—whose lack of progress had so tortured her during the McCollum years—were partially or completely destroyed after her death. As workers were sifting through her personal effects, Hurston's manuscripts were mistakenly identified as trash and set ablaze in her backyard. At the time of Huie's death, many of his books—including *Ruby McCollum: Woman in the Suwannee Jail*—were out of print, yet for several years Martha Hunt Huie presided over "William Bradford Huie Week" at Snead State Community College in Alabama, where she served as chair of the art department in the 1970s.

The end of my own entanglement in the saga of Ruby McCollum, although certainly not as grand as the Hurston or Huie legacies, is perhaps in its own way a fitting conclusion. Typical of the maddening contradictions that had dogged my progress throughout this project, my final tasks—verifying McCollum's death and her place of burial—were plagued with uncertainty. A search of the State of Florida Office of Vital Statistics resulted in no record of McCollum's death, although people in Live Oak and Ocala who had known her told me they were certain that she had died "about ten years ago." Ellis, however, writes in the concluding pages of his text that McCollum "passed away on May 23, 1992, at the age of 82, less than a year after her closest brother, Matt, died. She now lies by his side, surrounded by a grove of Live Oak trees, in the cemetery behind the Hopewell Baptist Church north of Live Oak" (516). I contacted Dr. Ellis and requested specific directions to McCollum's grave. He complied, and with little trouble I located the small, white country church referenced in his text. In the burial ground directly behind it, I did indeed find a nondescript concrete slab and accompanying marker that bears McCollum's name, her birth date, and a death date of May 23, 1992.

Considering the lack of a valid certificate of death for McCollum, I was curious to know how Ellis had discovered her final resting place. I wrote to him, and he responded with the following information regarding what he considers to be McCollum's grave site: "I knew Ruby's family," he wrote, "so I knew where she was buried at the 'secret' family service held for her when she passed away." But in spite of this new information regarding McCollum's grave and Ellis's certainty concerning its validity, I remained unable to dismiss the nagging fact that I could locate no certificate of death for McCollum on file with the State of Florida Office of Vital Statistics. Finally, after much additional searching, I did discover a certificate of death for a "Ruby McCollum*n*." The dates of birth and death correspond to the ones inscribed on the headstone behind Hopewell Baptist Church near Live Oak, and the place of death is listed as New Horizon Rehabilitation Center in Florida, McCollum's last place of residence. Furthermore, Samuel McCollum*n* Jr. of Live Oak, Florida, is listed as the informant of death. The name and address of the facility that oversaw the disposal of the deceased are listed as "Charles T. Hall Funeral Home" in Live Oak—the same Charles Hall who allegedly worked closely with Sam McCollum Sr. during his reign as the "Bolita King" in Suwannee County.

Typographical errors do occur, so it is not inconceivable that a clerical mistake caused the misspelling of McCollum's name on her certificate of death. There is, however, no chance of a clerical mistake occurring in the case of her final resting place; it is clearly listed as "rural cemetery" in "Ocala, Florida."

Determined to resolve the contradiction concerning the location of McCollum's burial site, I again traveled to Ocala, to the place that in the 1950s was called Zuber and that McCollum called home during her childhood. There I met Alvis Summers, an affable man and proprietor of the largest African-American funeral home in the area. Summers expressed surprise that "rural cemetery" was listed as McCollum's final resting place.

Such a vague listing, he said, was not permitted under state guidelines. But it was something mentioned by another woman present during our conversation that caught my attention the most. "I believe," the woman mused, "that Ruby's buried not far from here with the rest of the Jacksons." Summers nodded his agreement. "And I'll tell you something else," he added; "I'll bet if you go up there to Live Oak and dig under that slab, all you'll find is dirt."

McCollum's maiden name had been Jackson, and as was (and is) customary in the South, private cemeteries often held the remains of several families. According to Summers and the woman I spoke with, the Jackson family dead were located in an isolated rural cemetery near Ocala. "You'll never find it," they told me. "The road leading to it is locked up, and you don't have a key." At my insistence, however, Summers provided directions that ended with the directive: ". . . then you'll see a clump of houses. Just pull in up in the yard of any one of them and ask where the Jacksons are buried."

Through equal portions of determination and luck, I located the small community Summers referenced. After parking my car in the dirt front yard of a dilapidated wooden house, I saw an old woman sitting on the front steps shelling peas. "Yeah, I know where it's at," she told me when I—with a firm handshake and brandishing the name of Alvis Summers like a shield—asked the location of the Jackson plot. "It's right up the road. But you'll never find it, and you ain't got the key. They lock it up now, you know. Vandals and such was going back in there up to no good." She stopped and took a sip of coffee from a cup at her elbow that was missing its handle. "But you look like a nice woman," she said after sizing me up. "Go on up to the church and tell 'em you need the key."

"The plot is behind the church?" I asked, and she laughed. "Lord, no, honey. But the man who's got the key lives *beside* the church," she said. "Tell him you know Alvis, and he won't give you no trouble."

The woman was correct. The man I took to be the caretaker of the cemetery brightened somewhat when I mentioned Summers's name. Still, I had interrupted his dinner, and he was impatient. "What's your business up in there?" he asked as I stood awkwardly on his porch. "I'm writing a book," I answered, "a book about Ruby McCollum." After a long minute of silence, he finally stood aside and said: "Well, come on in. I'll get the key." I stepped inside, where an old man sat intent on a bowl of soup. I was clearly not welcome and was glad when the caretaker returned. "Go west a piece," he said, pressing a ring of keys into my palm. "The gate's just up the main road, but I doubt you'll find it. Dark's coming on, and I ain't been up there in a while." Then he turned and walked to the table where his dinner was growing cold.

I scanned the overgrown roadside for the gate the man referenced for a full twenty minutes, but night was indeed fast approaching, and I almost despaired of finding it. Finally, I approached a farmhouse where a man was busy feeding his horses. "Yeah, I know where it's at," the man said. "I'm not surprised you couldn't find it. What are you driving?" he asked, and I pointed to my car. "Tell you what," he said, wiping his face, "The wife said supper's in a couple of minutes, but I've got time to take you back there. I'll go in my truck, and you follow. Most times there are limbs and trees in the road. If so, I'll move 'em for you."

Not quite believing my luck, I followed the man as he drove his pickup truck out to the main road. There he stopped and got out.

"Anything wrong?" I asked.

"No, ma'am," he said. "Here's the gate you was looking for."

"Where?" I asked, seeing only a seemingly impermeable wall of vines and brambles.

"Right here," he laughed, and reached out to push away what seemed to be years of growth that completely concealed an iron gate secured with a padlock. "Not surprised you couldn't find it," he said and winked.

We unlocked the gate, and we slowly made our way down a very narrow dirt road—barely a trail—bordered on both sides by trees and vines. Then the trees ended, and we skirted the edge of a large open field. The grass was tall, and it brushed the undercarriage of my car as we approached another dark green tunnel of trees. Then the man stopped, rolled down his window, and pointed. "Straight ahead there," he called. "That's where the cemetery's at. I got to get on back home, but you'll be all right. Looks like the road's clear."

The only indication that I was near the Jackson family burial ground were two ancient tombstones stacked one on top of the other to the left of an opening in the trees. They bore no names or dates—time and weather had removed those long ago—but the function of the stones was unmistakable. However humble, they served as the entrance to a tiny cemetery that appeared as I drove through an enclave of oaks.

Even though it was well past dusk, I did find the Jackson family plot. There lay Sonja's grave, marked only with a tin plate that bore her name and her birth and death dates. And directly next to Sonja was a gentle swell in the grassy earth that could very well be Ruby McCollum's unmarked final resting place. Of course, I cannot be certain. I continue to question Ocala natives when I can, but so far I have been unsuccessful in finding anyone who remembers exactly where McCollum is buried. Very few people are left, in fact, who remember her at all.

If McCollum is buried in that tiny rural cemetery in Ocala, someone—most likely Sam Jr.—went to a great deal of time and effort to conceal her grave. And even though I have no proof of this supposition except for a misspelled name on a certificate of death—a misspelling I believe to be intentional—and the speculation of a few Ocala natives, I somehow sense that she *is* there. Perhaps it is because I believe the secluded spot, so isolated from the outside world and its prying eyes, to be a fitting place for her remains. Or perhaps it is because I have become so acutely aware of the silence and secrecy that enveloped McCollum during her lifetime that I cannot imagine her without them even in death. Whatever the reason, and in spite of my continued uncertainty about the matter, I am profoundly grateful for the few minutes I stood alone in that quiet graveyard in the gathering gloom and surrounded by the Jackson family dead. There, for the first time since my immersion in this project, I heard echoes of redemption in what until then had been only endless southern silences filled with suffering.

Implications

Throughout this book I have emphasized the dynamic presence of silences in the South evidenced in the 1950s in Suwannee County, Florida, and how issues of race and gender informed them. These kinds of silences, however, are neither exclusive to the case of Ruby McCollum nor the small town of Live Oak. Instead, they still very much infuse the larger South over fifty years after "that McCollum mess" shook Live Oak and Suwannee County to their core.

Consider, for example, Ellis's *The Trial of Ruby McCollum*, published in 2003. "I had a book signing set up," Ellis wrote to me, "in . . . the only store in Lake City that handles book-signing events since there are currently no bookstores in the area. When I called to confirm the date, the manager asked for more information on the book, and when he reviewed it, he cancelled the event, stating, 'That topic is still too sensitive in this area.'" And in the summer of 2001, Alice Randall, author of *The Wind Done Gone*—a scathing parody of the revered *Gone with the Wind*—found herself, like Ellis, battling the powerful southern ideological forces. Prior to the release of her book, Randall and Houghton Mifflin fought a very public battle against the Mitchell Trust when it claimed $10 million in damages and attempted to block the publication of her text—a book that, in the words of the complaint, would cause "irreparable harm and damage to their business reputation and goodwill, as well as the artistic reputation and goodwill of the novel *Gone with the Wind*" (*Suntrust Bank v. Houghton Mifflin* 16–17). Cynthia Tucker of the *Atlanta Journal-Constitution*, however, astutely contends that the Mitchell Trust's attempt to block the publication of Randall's book was much less about protecting the revenue that *Gone with the Wind* continues to generate than it was about preserving the much more valuable iconic myth of the Old South and the silences it perpetuates:

> The broad acceptance of Mitchell's novel has lent her story the aura of actual social history. That means millions of readers take as realistic her superficial portrayals of steely Southern belles, dashing suitors/husbands, and, most of all, stupid but devoted slaves. . . .
>
> No, this fight is over something far more precious to defenders of the Confederacy: preserving the Old South mythology that Mitchell creates. This mythology, so distant from actual history, cannot countenance the tortured South that William Faulkner so artfully and accurately portrays in his works. And it cannot tolerate Randall's parody, with its bitter, scheming slaves, homosexual planters, and, most of all, miscegenation between masters and slaves.
>
> In Mitchell's *Gone with the Wind*, sexual liaisons between planters and their slave-mistresses do not exist. And the Mitchell Trust means to keep it that way.

Although the suit against Houghton Mifflin was eventually overturned, the fact that it occurred at all is indicative of the fact that acts of silence continue to dominate the southern ideological landscape and that racial and gender equity in the region is still far from a reality.

So in spite of significant progress the South has made in addressing issues of subjugation, silence today remains a prominent component of the region's ideology. Theorizing why these acts of silence occur and how they continue to replicate themselves over time (as I have attempted to do in the context of the Ruby McCollum murder saga) is important scholarly work, yet much remains to be done. The stakes are high because efforts to understand acts of southern silence have the potential to help us address other silence-based ideologies beyond the geographic borders of the American South.

It is an all-too-simple task to identify contemporary acts of silencing that have occurred outside the confines of the southern states. Daniel Wilkinson, for example, recounts in his *Silence on the Mountain* horrific acts resulting from the short-lived Law of Agrarian Reform that redistributed rich coffee-growing land to the working class. Wilkinson, a young civil-rights worker, traveled to Guatemala in 1993 to investigate the deaths of more than two hundred thousand people in the region, most of whom died—or, in the Guatemalan vernacular, "were disappeared"—at the hands of the U.S.-backed military government. One particularly poignant point in Wilkinson's text details how the entire town of Sacuchum described for him the rape, torture, and massacre of members of the community, a story that had never before been told to the outside world for fear of retaliation.

Another contemporary example of the oppressive power of silence is the massacre that occurred in Quebec in 1989 at the École Polytechnique. There, Marc Lepine entered a classroom, ordered men and women into opposite corners of the room, and stated, "I hate feminists." He then opened fire, killing a total of fourteen women and eventually himself. Wendy Hui Kyong Chun writes that silence characterized the reaction of the school in terms of Lepine's having targeted "feminists":

> On the first anniversary of the massacre, the school's director, André Bazergui, sent letters to several news outlets asking them to use restraint in their coverage: "Let's forget about this guy. This guy was completely crazy. By talking about him . . . you are just encouraging more crazy people to act like him" (Lalonde "Students' Silence"). This "you" is not only aimed at the media, who played an active role in the propagation and resolution of the massacre; it is also aimed at the feminists, who were perceived as needlessly propagating the massacre for their own purposes. Although Bazergui phrases his comment as a call for restraint for their own safety, he positions feminists as aggressors whose talk *encourages* massacres. (123–24)

Chun points to the fact that women and others who chose to discuss the larger implications of the École Polytechnique massacre—and in the process drew attention to larger issues of violence that routinely occur against many women—were either condemned for using the victims to advance a single political platform or accused of inciting more violence by repeatedly "reminding" the public at large of the event. Clearly the implication in Bazergui's call for silence is damaging on two levels. First, encouraging women to remain silent about acts of violence committed against them does not allow their testimonies, which have been proven to be a vital part of the trauma victim's recovery process. Second, alleging that women's acts of testimony promote *more* violence implies that safety can only be found in silence. To speak, then, becomes an act that is dangerously subversive to women everywhere and one that runs the all-too-real risk of ending in tragedy.

One should not forget, however, that Ruby McCollum may have *chosen* to remain silent during her imprisonment in the Suwannee County Jail and that her refusal to speak contributed in large margin to her being labeled mentally incompetent. What may have been McCollum's self-selected silence, then, in the end probably saved her life, but the cost was high—twenty years of institutionalization and isolation. A question that continues to haunt Live Oak and Ocala natives is whether or not Mc-Collum was truly driven mad by the two years she spent in solitary confinement in the Suwannee County Jail or if she feigned mental illness to escape the electric chair. This question is not an easy one to answer, but it is important in terms of what I consider to be an undertheorized effect of acts of silence in the context of women who exhibit unconventional behavior and, consequently, have been deemed incompetent. Andrea Nicki writes:

> In ethical discourse (and philosophical discourse in general) there needs to be less talk of failures to realize ideals of rationality and autonomy and human paradigms of normalcy and intelligibility. Rather, there should be more emphasis on the achievements both of those challenging oppressive social systems who are typically seen as "crazy radicals" and those with abuse-related psychiatric disabilities who have been told far too many times through actions, words, or silence that they are worthless. (99)

Nicki is correct in her assertion that silence can be a powerful form of oppression. Yet if silence has been proven an effective way to police those individuals who fail to conform to dominant social formations and the ideologies they embrace, then I contend that silence in the hands of the disenfranchised serves a similar function. McCollum's silence, then, is perhaps both evidence and validation of the profundity of her trauma. Moreover, her refusal to speak may have been anything but proof positive of her incompetence. Like a woman under attack who manages to wrest the weapon from the hands of her attacker, McCollum during her two years in the Suwannee County Jail may have appropriated silence in her own defense against those individuals and ideologies that for so long had held her under siege. Far from proving that McCollum was "crazy," her silence may well have been a conscious tactical maneuver—and one that she knew all too well from her own experience to be highly effective.

McCollum, however, may *not* have chosen to remain silent, and the fact that she did so may have been entirely out of her control. Recall, for example, Ernst van Alphen's contention that trauma victims often fail to speak because no discursive vehicle exists with which to convey the depth of their suffering. They remain silent, then, because conventional language cannot capture the horror of their lived experience. Van Alphen argues in the context of his study of the Holocaust that "the problem of Holocaust survivors is precisely that the lived events could not be experienced because language did not provide the terms and positions in which to experience them; thus they are defined as *traumatic*. . . . In this view, experience is the result or product of a discursive process" (27). In other words, it is possible that McCollum—like the trauma victims studied by van Alphen—simply could not articulate through the only linguistic framework available to her the magnitude of what she had experienced before Adams's murder and after her arrest even if she had wanted to do so.

An event in the context of our own lived experience—September 11, 2001—illustrates the very real difficulties of assimilating into language experiences that are beyond the representational power of speech. On October 3, 2001, for example, Julia Angwin of the *Wall Street Journal* wrote: "Everybody knows what happened September 11, but nobody knows what to call it. It is without precedent and is proving difficult to capture in a single phrase. So in daily conversations, many people are resorting to an assortment of vague monikers to describe the events: 'the terrorist attacks,' 'the events of Sept. 11,' 'the bombing,' 'the tragedy,' or simply 'it.'" Whether McCollum's reticence was due to her inability to assimilate into the confines of language the suffering she allegedly endured at the hands of Dr. LeRoy Adams or she self-selected silence of her own volition, theorizing the multidimensional dynamics of acts of silence that surrounded her has clear repercussions for advancing our understanding of current trauma victims and, more important, linking these specific traumas to larger ideological concerns.

It is precisely because acts of silence are confined neither to Live Oak nor the larger southern United States that a greater theoretical understanding of them—how they proliferate and the specific race and gender ideologies they advance—is of crucial importance. A failure to acknowledge the wider implications of the oppressive and often violent silences that characterize the story of Ruby McCollum and the rhetorical power of them is to miss what I consider to be an important component of any cultural studies-based analysis: raising awareness and, ideally, affecting change. Patrick Brantlinger argues that any discussion of the juncture of society and language must have as its impetus an awareness of the inextricable bonds that link theory, discourse, and culture. "Theory begins," he writes, "precisely with the recognition of the socially situated and constructed nature of all discourse. . . . The sea of everyday life in which everyone swims consists of either rhetoric, or ideology, or both; if theory means anything (if it has any consequences), it means alertness to this condition, the human condition. But insofar as understanding anything is the necessary first step toward fixing it or letting it alone, theory also proffers the hope, at least, of opting for social change. Literary theory paradoxically becomes social theory via the linguistic turn" (304). I would add, however, that silence is an integral component of any ideology, and as such, it is by definition a powerful rhetorical strategy in its own right. Conceptualizing silence as a discursive, and consequently *cultural*, act is important because in doing so we take the first step in establishing what Raymie McKerrow calls "critical rhetoric," a practice that aims to expose the characteristics of domination while advancing the practice of continual self-reflection. "A critical rhetoric," McKerrow writes, "seeks to unmask or demystify the discourse of power. The aim is to understand the integration of power/knowledge in society—what possibilities for change the integration invites or inhabits and what intervention strategies might be considered appropriate to effect social change" (441–42). I would add that these intervention strategies should include a three-part awareness of the dynamics of silence in discursive formations: the actions, reactions, or *lack* of actions particular silences evoke; a keen awareness of the dominant ideologies that contextualize these silences; and, of critical importance to rhetorical and cultural studies scholars, the identification of particular discourses that enforce or perpetuate them.

Although acts of silence continue to dominate our cultural and rhetorical landscapes, certain destructive silences are, thankfully, in the process of being broken. In terms of the Quebec École Polytechnique 1989 massacre, for example, Chun argues that the public discussion launched by Lepine's antifeminist sentiments ultimately proved to be a productive and necessary part of the healing process:

Their interpretation of the event thus moved from "ideology" to victim testimony. Because they linked this event to other acts of violence endemic to a patriarchal society, the public outpouring of testimony by women who had been abused by men—or who felt vulnerable to male violence—became essential to establishing the historical and national significance of the massacre. In essence, validating Lepine turned feminist testimony from a misfired or failed testimony—testimony that does not register as producing the truth—to a successful one. . . . Two years after the massacre, under the pressure of these witnesses and their supporters, the Canadian government would declare December 6th an official day of commemoration for female victims of male violence and would launch a Royal Commission to investigate violence against women. (118)

In 1991, the United States government, under the order of then Secretary of Defense Richard Cheney and continued by the Clinton and Bush administrations, censored media coverage of the rising number of U.S. casualties in the conflict in Iraq. In October 2003, Dana Milbank of the *New York Times* reported:

Since the end of the Vietnam War, presidents have worried that their military actions would lose support once the public glimpsed the remains of U.S. soldiers arriving at air bases in flag-draped caskets.

To this problem, the Bush administration has found a simple solution: it has ended the public dissemination of such images by banning news coverage and photography of dead soldiers' homecomings on all military bases.

In March, on the eve of the Iraq war, a directive arrived from the Pentagon at U.S. military bases. "There will be no arrival ceremonies for, or media coverage of, deceased military personnel returning to or departing from Ramstein airbase or Dover base, to include interim stops," the Defense Department said, referring to the major ports for the returning remains.

The prohibition of images of American soldiers killed in Iraq and the coffins that contain them (metal boxes euphemistically dubbed "transport cases" by the military, according to *USA Today*'s Gregg Zoroya) sent an unspoken but very clear message that acts of silence can advance specific ideologies in profound and disturbing ways. On October 4, 2004, however, Ralph Begleiter, a University of Delaware professor, successfully sued the United States government for the release of these military images of honor guard arrival and transfer ceremonies at Dover Air Force Base. "Images of body bags," an editorial in *USA Today* on October 23 argued, "don't cause the public to question military campaigns. Rather, questions about the rightness of the missions feed doubts. A clear-eyed assessment of the nation's involvement has a better chance of garnering public support than efforts to squash legitimate news coverage." Finally, three long-cold civil rights murders have again returned to the forefront. In December 2004, Florida Attorney General Charlie Crist announced the reopening of investigations into the bombing deaths of Harry T. and Harriette Moore. "The FBI's inability to bring anyone to justice, despite a full-blown investigation," reported the *St. Petersburg Times* on December 26, 2004, "has prompted cries of a cover-up for decades." Investigation into the murder of Emmett Till, too, has been resumed after many years, and the conviction of Edgar Ray Killen in June 2005 for the killings of three civil-rights workers brings with it hope that the current trend toward breaking these and other destructive silences will continue.

If many individuals in north Florida have forgotten Ruby McCollum, the legal field at large has not. Her case has been cited, discussed, or mentioned more than forty times in subsequent cases since she was granted a new trial in 1954. This continued awareness is cause for optimism, and it is one of two reasons that I present this book. First, I hope to generate a larger awareness of the issues implicit in acts of silence informing one woman and the society in which she lived. Moreover, however, I hope to preserve the story of Ruby McCollum and present it as indicative of what can happen when silences and the ideologies that inform them go unchecked—no matter where or when they occur.

Not long ago, I visited Louise Perry, an African-American woman who was instrumental in my choosing to investigate acts of silence in the South. The last time I had visited Louise was in March, and the countryside near Live Oak had been painted with the untamed lushness I remember so well from my childhood. Bright wildflowers and graceful lilies grew in great pre-Easter nosegays along the highway, and the dogwood trees were in full bloom. Now, however, it was late December, and a hard freeze the night before testified that spring was still far away. As my sister, her husband, and I stood in Louise's front yard and said our good-byes before beginning the long trip home, I pointed to a rail fence that during my previous visit had been resplendent with white roses. Now, however, the blooms were gone.

"Looks like the frost killed your roses," I sighed.

"Lord, no, baby girl," she laughed. "That rose ain't dead. It always comes back. It was here before I came, and it'll probably be here long after I'm gone." Then, typical of Louise, she rounded up a shovel, and proceeded to retrieve a cutting for me to take home.

"Does it like sun or shade?" I asked.

"Oh, probably don't make no difference," she said. "We don't pay it no mind, and it just keeps on growing. The only thing you got to know about this rose is that it likes to climb. It's a climbing rose."

"It's a *mean* rose," my brother-in-law retorted as he tried to wrestle my sample into submission for transport home. He was right. All of us were in various stages of entanglement or nursing our wounds.

"Yeah," Louise nodded, "it's got lots of thorns, but it's sure pretty come springtime."

I planted that cutting in my backyard, and I hope that one day it will drape my arbor with festoons of snow-white blossoms. But I cannot be sure. Far from its home near Live Oak, it may not tolerate the sandy soil and heat of tropical Florida. Yet I take encouragement in the fact that it is from hardy stock. Since its transplant, it has put out new green shoots; like the silences that continue to infuse Live Oak, it is clearly a survivor. Like Ruby McCollum, it knows how to endure.

.   .   .   .

Many years ago I was a faculty member in an English department at a
large university that had for most of the years of my tenure there tried
unsuccessfully to hire an African-American woman scholar to fill a position in African-American women's literature. During one year's effort, the
department met to discuss and rank three candidates who had recently
visited campus for the traditional round of interviews. Each of the three
candidates had impeccable academic credentials as well as an established
reputation as a superb scholar and teacher; our discussion therefore focused almost entirely on the issue of which candidate offered a "better
fit" for our department—that is, which candidate would make a "better
colleague." I remember the meeting quite vividly, though not because it
was unusually contentious. Most of our department meetings were lively
and spirited when they were not contentious and embattled. I remember
this meeting because at an especially embattled point in the discussion of
one particular candidate our "senior feminist theorist" announced that the
faculty would never be able to agree to offer the position to the candidate
because, as she put it, "no one likes an angry black woman." As I remember
the moment, her comment was dropped into the discussion and imme-

diately disappeared from it like a heavy stone dropped into roiling dark water. Her prediction was accurate: we didn't offer the position to that candidate; neither did we succeed in filling the position that year.

My feminist colleague might have said "no one likes an angry *woman*"; she certainly would have been correct. Feminism's long duré has done little to change the gender ideologies that code anger—especially when it takes the form of loud, angry speech—as entirely unattractive, irrational (if not hysterical or crazy), and unacceptable when enacted by women and girls. As Tammy Evans observes in her fascinating study of the rhetoric of silence, the South does not have exclusive rights to "better seen than heard" or its twin sister, "pretty is as pretty does." If feminism has done little to dislodge the gendered (and racialized) view that "no one likes an angry woman," it has ironically provided the occasion for an extension or refinement of that view: "no one likes an angry feminist." What's perhaps even more ironic is that this viewpoint is sometimes held, though often left unspoken, by feminists themselves. When my feminist colleague made the statement "no one likes an angry black woman," I don't know whether she was voicing her own view—she certainly may have been since she said nothing further to press her point—or if she was attempting to name and expose a situation in the department (and, I would add, in white America at large). In the speech act I heard that day, "no one likes an angry black woman," the emphasis in her voice quite clearly fell on "black," and thus I choose to believe her comment was meant to bring race (and racism) into a discussion held by a company composed entirely of white (mostly male) academics empowered at that time to decide the immediate professional fate of an African-American woman scholar. Our refusal to hear this speech act (whether or not it was the one intended), our refusal to confront and honestly examine the racialized (and racist) underbelly of the case that was made that day against hiring a candidate who, when standing before that company of white (mostly male) academics, arguably presented herself quite professionally (that is, with unshakable confidence, keen intelligence, and true passion)—in a word, our silence that day—lingers in my memory as unspoken testimony to the racism (and sexism) that continue to orchestrate the fateful interplay of silence and speech, language and agency. It would appear that not enough has changed since 1952.

In 1952 in Live Oak, Florida (the synecdochic representative of "the South" and, indeed, America itself in Evans's compelling treatment), Ruby McCollum must have been one angry black woman when she shot LeRoy Adams. How could she not have been angry, even dangerously angry (*en-*

raged might be a more accurate term)? Ruby was a woman, a black woman, born in the era of Jim Crow and the land of lynchings, where she lived her entire life. She was a black woman at a time when white men could still assume with impunity the right to appropriate the bodies and lives of African-American women and men, girls and boys. She was a southern black woman at a time when the field and the house just about exhausted her legitimate employment opportunities. Through a finely wrought reading of texts by and about McCollum, Evans shows that it mattered little that Ruby was wealthy, that she lived in one of the finest houses in the area, that she wore expensive clothes, that she and her husband, Sam, could more than adequately provide for their children's every need through the proceeds of their illegal gambling enterprise. Her wealth and success could not protect her from Adams's abuse, if her allegations of abuse are true. (And why, from the vantage point of 2005, would one not believe at least some version of those allegations? Who benefits from the belief that Ruby was entirely unprovoked, was simply "crazy"?) Her wealth and the self-interest of law enforcement officials who likely received money in exchange for their silence about Ruby and Sam's illegal livelihood could not protect her once she crossed the line that hot summer day in 1952. If "no one likes an angry black woman," "no one" presumably refers to those who benefit the most from strictly enforced dichotomies between white and black, male and female, rich and poor. In Live Oak, LeRoy Adams was representative of the prosperous white patriarch who, like generations of white men before him, had the temerity to enforce those dichotomies and at the same time cross the line.

As many feminists before me have argued, anger should be understood in a social and political context—that is, as a response to a sense of violation. Those who are routinely violated by, for example, prevailing ideologies of race and gender must be actively silencing a tremendous amount of anger if they are not routinely expressing it. The story of Ruby McCollum serves as a representative anecdote (to use Kenneth Burke's term) for the history of race relations in this country and their terrible consequences. Ruby McCollum, I'll venture to say, was heir to generations of righteous anger, and on that fateful day acted not only as an individual but also as a representative of those generations. In my view, there is no mystery remaining to be solved as to why Ruby shot Adams. (Receiving a bill from a man who routinely abused her and used her body as white men had used generations of African-American women before her surely might have been the last straw. The second speech act contained in that act—"I'll use

145

· · ·

Afterword

and abuse you and then bill you for my services, and you'll pay, silently and in full"—might have been the last straw for me as well.) The reason Ruby shot Adams remains the nation's "family secret"—something most of us know at some level but are unwilling to admit into public discussion. The true mystery, it seems to me, lies in why we, as a nation, remain unwilling to confront our history of racism (and misogyny). Yet, it's a mystery that Evans has, in these pages, already solved.

The story of Ruby McCollum, however it is "fictionalized" (as Evans so insightfully puts it), is as compelling and tragic as it is too familiar in the history of race relations in the South and in this culture at large. In her examination of this chapter of public memory, Evans gives her subject some measure of posthumous dignity, justice, and mercy while recognizing her own complex positioning as a southern white woman working through the various strands of "that McCollum mess." Also compelling is the insight that Evans brings to the complexity of the phenomenon of silence. Certainly, the liberation movements of the 1960s politicized silence—in effect, gave voice to it—and thereby clarified the sense in which silence is a condition of the existence of oppressed and subjugated peoples. Evans refines this understanding even further by bringing to the study of silence a rhetorical perspective. Not only are there rhetorical occasions in which silence becomes the only speech act available, but there also are highly charged political forces at work that actively silence individuals and groups. In Evans's treatment, silence becomes an action rather than simply a passive condition or a failure to speak and therefore act. Understanding silence as a performative speech act shifts attention to silence as a fullness rather than an empty absence, as an act to be interpreted and interrogated. This understanding makes silence loud, as it were, makes it clamor for further study.

Lynn Worsham
Illinois State University
September 2005

. . .
Afterword

Appendix

. . . .

Zora Neale Hurston's
"My Impressions of the Trial"

My comprehensive impression of the trial of Mrs. Ruby McCollum for the murder of Dr. C. LeRoy Adams was one of a smothering blanket of silence. I gained other vivid and momentary impacts, but they were subsidiary and grew out of the first. It was as if one listened to a debate in which everything which might lead to and justify the resolution had been waived. Under varied faces, one was confronted with the personality of silence. Some conformed by a murmuration of evasions, some by a frontal attack that this was something which it would not be decent to allow the outside world to know about, and others by wary wordlessness.

It amounted to a mass delusion of mass illusion. A point of approach to the motive for the slaying of the popular medico and politician had been agreed upon, and however bizarre and unlikely it might appear to the outside public, it was going to be maintained and fought for. Anything which might tend to destroy this illusion must be done away with. Presto! It just did not exist.

I found myself moving about in this foggy atmosphere even before the first sanity hearing. Fearing to be quoted, many in the Negro neighborhood of Live Oak avoided even the suspicion of having told anything to a newspaper representative by fleeing my very presence. Others loudly denounced Ruby McCollum for having slain Dr. Adams to make sure that if "the white folks" heard anything that they said about the case at all, it would be pleasing to them.

"Ruby" (before August 3, they would have not have dared to speak of her by her first name) "had done killed the good-heartedest and the best white man in Suwannee County, if not in the whole State of Florida. They won't be doing her right unlessen they give her the chair."

"Ruby McCollum knowed better than to go messing around with that white man in the first place. She didn't have no business with him. She knowed so well that she was a nigger. How come she couldn't stay among her own race?"

"I hope and pray that there ain't no salvation for Ruby at all. Killing up that nice Dr. Adams. You could always go to him when you was in a tight for money and he sure would help you out. And if you didn't have the change to pay him when he waited on you, he would scold at you and say, 'Did I ask you for any money? I'm trying to get you well.' And Ruby had to go and kill a nice man like that."

"No, Doc Adams never dunned nobody for money at all. You could pay him when you was able to do so. Never heard of him bearing down on nobody because they owed him money."

"But Sam and Ruby McCollum wasn't no bad pay neither. That's how come I can't see to my rest how come they got to fussing over her doctor's bill and ended up in this killing-scrape. Everybody knows that them Mc-Collums paid what they owed on the dot. They had it to pay with and they sure Lord paid. Everybody in Live Oak and Suwannee County will give 'em that. They never owed nobody."

Hints like that now and then gave away the code. Let you understand that they were play-acting in their savage denunciation of Ruby McCollum. The sprig of hyssop was in their hands and they were sprinkling the blood of the pascal lamb around their doorway so that the angel of death would pass over them. This was West Florida, and somehow the Negro population of Live Oak felt apprehensive.

And inside the courthouse on this December day of the trial, a man and a woman came up the stairs to the galleries reserved for Negro spectators and took seat next to me. The woman murmured for my benefit, "Don't be surprised what might come off here." They looked down the row of seats and the man said, "I hope no fool don't go and block up that aisle."

"But you wouldn't run off and leave me, honey, if something was to take place, would you?"

"Not if you can keep up, baby."

The local white people felt no such timidity about physical violence. But fear was there. It stemmed from what the outside world would say about the trial, and hence the banning of the press.

"Ruby has killed a white man, and not only that, the most prominent white man in Suwannee County. She ought to die for that, and she's going to die. You can't let women go around killing up every man they take a notion to. We don't want these newspaper men coming in here and printing lies about us. Ruby was just full of meanness, shooting Dr. Adams to death rather than to pay her doctor's bill."

"We don't have to believe a word that a woman says who will murder a good man because he sent her a bill for waiting on her. That baby of Ruby's is not Dr. Adams' child. Oh, it might look sort of bright-colored like some say it does, but it could be Sam McCollum's like them other three. Sometimes babies are throw-backs, and take after their fore-parents, you know."

"Oh, we all recognize that Doc Adams got around right smart among the ladies, that woman in Lake City, this one and that one, was separated from his wife for years until he put in to run for the State Senate, but he never had nothing to do with Ruby like that. She's lying. She just hated to pay him that money she owed the man. A brutal murder without any excuse for it at all."

It was like a chant. The medical bill as motive for the slaying was ever insisted upon and stressed. It was freely admitted by all that the McCollums had always been good pay. Paid what they owed with promptness every time. Yet, there was this quick and stubborn insistence that the medical bill, and that alone, could have been the cause of the murder. It was obviously a posture, but a posture posed in granite. There existed no other, let alone extenuating circumstances. This was the story, however bizarre it might appear to outsiders, and the community was sticking to it. The press was discouraged from "confusing" the minds of the state and the nation by poking around Live Oak and coming up with some other loose and foolish notion.

I sought and had more than one interview with Judge Hal Adams. My impression of the Judge who was to preside over this trial was a man possessed of many substances marketable in the human bazaar. I found no fault with the broad black Stetson, the black string tie of the past century, his chewing tobacco, his witty turn of mind, nor yet his mouth full of colorful Southern idioms. To me, these were externals, and need not of necessity indicate his type of mind. How he conducted the trial was my yardstick. We got along very well indeed.

But naturally I was disappointed when he told me that he could not allow me to interview Ruby McCollum. I had been sent to Live Oak by the *Pittsburgh Courier* first and foremost to get an interview with the defendant in this case, and second, to report the case as it developed. But Judge Adams was not short and harsh with me in his refusal. He said that the very nature of the case made it advisable to deny access to Mrs. McCollum to the press. He did not want the case tried in the newspapers before it was presented in court. Justified or not, I gave house-room to the impression that if/when the court permitted Mrs. McCollum to be interviewed, that I was as likely as anyone else to get the scoop. Then seeking to coordinate my favorable impression of Judge Adams with the impression I had gained of an existing dogma of Ruby McCollum's motive for slaying Dr. Adams so widespread in the locality, I pondered as to whether the judge had lent his prestige to its acceptance. But if so, was it native to his spirit, or was he a captive of geographical emotions and tradition?

There was abundant precedent for this mental query, the case of General Robert E. Lee being the most notable. This truly great military genius and greater of soul than as a soldier, hated the institution of slavery, and had freed his own slaves. He believed devoutly in the Union and regarded secession as the ultimate death of the nation. Yet, when the struggle came, his decision was that he would go along with Virginia and his neighbors.

From the minute this matter occurred to me, Judge Hal Adams became the foremost figure of interest to me in this trial. The slaying had been admitted by the defendant, and the degree only of her guilt was left to be decided by the trial. To me, the real drama was inherent in the reactions to the evidence presented, or allowed to be admitted by Judge Adams. There is an old southern saying to the effect that a man ain't got no business pulling on britches unless or until he's got guts enough to hold 'em up. Another saying that considers the strength and caliber of a man says, "The time done come when big britches got to fit Little Willie." Could Big Britches fit Hal Adams, or to put it another way, could Hal Adams fit himself into big britches? Fate had issued the challenge to him. My mind was entirely open. I would let the Judge furnish the answer.

The confirmation for me that I was right in the impression that the Negroes of the locality were using protective coloration and concealing their own thought about the case lay in the fact that the closer the association had been with the McCollums, the more violent were their denunciations of Ruby. One example was furnished by Hall, the Negro undertaker. Rumor informed me that Sam McCollum's money had set Hall up in business, and though it was thoroughly established that Hall had also been on very intimate and confidential terms with the late Dr. Adams—often driving the Doctor at night to his amorous rendezvous—he could scarcely have felt as violent toward his benefactors, the McCollums, as he pretended. It was only natural for Hall to realize that he might be suspected of sympathy with Ruby because of past benefits, and thus he was giving himself a cat-bath to forestall possible retaliation from White Live Oak. That is, washing himself off with his tongue.

I had the same impression concerning the janitor of the County Courthouse. It was said that this Negro had been the McCollum yardman for twelve years. He had, during those years, enjoyed numerous favors from the McCollums. Yet, nobody could match his violent denunciation of Ruby nor his expressed hopes and prayers for her speedy execution. He was waiting for Judge Adams every morning when he arrived at the courthouse to carry in his briefcase or any other luggage that the Judge might have, and being most obsequious every moment, to the extent that the Judge publicly thanked him at the end of the trial. No one could blame him for looking after the comforts of the Judge, and certainly I do not, for Judge Adams appears to me to be a most kindly and considerate person, and easy to like. The motives of the janitor are under scrutiny here, and especially so when it is considered that this man had been an inmate of Raiford himself, so it is alleged, and it certainly would do him no harm to be on the good side of a County Judge when the police rapped on his door the next time. Rightly or wrongly, the janitor believed that the Judge wanted such an expression from the Colored folks, and he was moved to furnish it with great enthusiasm. Nor do I censure the man for his behavior. I merely examine it as part of a pattern which I found. A fleeing away from fear.

But in all fairness to this humble man, human nature cannot be ignored. The McCollums were wealthy and otherwise stood high in the community. These local Colored people were for the most part little people, the kind of people, irrespective of race, who have only the earth as their memorial. With death, they go back to the ground to rejoin the countless millions of other nameless creatures who are remembered only by the things which grow in soil. There is ever a residue of resentment against the successful of the world. It has nothing at all to do with race. Thus from the beginning of time the most popular story is one in which the poor triumph over the more fortunate. Heaven, where the humble will be equal or superior to the powerful on earth: Dives and Lazarus; the Cinderella story; the peasant boy who wins the Princess and with her, one half of the kingdom; Dick Whittington, Lord Mayor of London. So there was a certain amount of revengeful satisfaction in seeing Ruby, the high-cockalorum brought low. No longer could she stir their envy.

And there was bound to be a certain amount of grim satisfaction on the part of many Negro men when it was found that Ruby had gotten into "bad trouble" by giving herself to a White man. This complaint has come down from slavery days, the advantage that White men have over Negro men with women. In a café with the juke-box playing at the top of its voice, the case was mentioned, and a tall man pleasuring himself with breaded pork chops and side dishes of collard greens and fried sweet potatoes snarled, "I ain't got no sympathy for Ruby at all. All before, she wouldn't even wipe her feet on nobody like us. If she just had to have herself an outside man, she could of got any kind she wanted right inside of her own race. That's one thing about our race, we're just like a flower garden. You can get any color from coal-scuttle blonde to pink-toed white." (This is a very common boast made always when Negroes rail against miscegenation, not seeming to realize that by it they are endorsing the very thing which is being denounced. For obviously if there had been no miscegenation, there could be nothing but black individuals among us). "Naw, she had to go and have that White man, and when she knows so well how these White men don't allow us no chance at all with *their* women. Colored women ought to be proud to stick to their own men and leave these White men alone."

"And more 'specially when they ought to know that White men ain't no trouble at all. They can't do nothing in the bed but praise the Lord. Nothing to 'em at all."

A loud guffaw of gloating laughter from all the men at this. The thought sort of evened things up.

"We gets all we want for nothing, but they got to pay for it, and they had better, 'cause they sure can't bring nobody to testify and neither sinners to repentance. Shucks!"

Even louder laughter. But a tipsy woman (she would not have dared to speak had she been sober, or of a more discriminating type).

"Talk that you know and testify to that you done seen. Some of these here White men got lightning in their pants. In the 'Be' class, be there when you start and be there a long time after you done fell out."

In the shocked and enraged silence that followed this, the slattern must have been jolted to a soberer state, for she added sheepishly, "That is, it could be. I wouldn't know my own self."

"You better say 'Joe' 'cause you don't know" one man growled, giving expression to the emotions of his male hearers. "Tain't a thing to the bear but his curly hair. Don't you stand there and tell that lie that a White man can do with a woman what a Colored man can do. Oh, I reckon some of these trashy nigger women who is after their money will lay up under 'em, like Ruby McCollum done, and moan and squall and cry to make 'em think they're raising hell, but that's only because of the spending-change the White man puts out. But everybody knows that a White man ain't no trouble, not a damn bit, and any old nappy head that tells me they is in my hearing is going to get a righteous head-stomping."

No female picked up the challenge, naturally, so the men took the floor and the occasion to give the matter a vimful "reading." They poured out all the stored resentment of the centuries between 1619, when the first batch of Negro slaves were landed in the English colonies, to September 1952. This age-old hobby horse was flogged along from Ginny-Gall to Diddy-Wah-Diddy. (Mythical places of Negro folklore reputedly a long way off. Like Zar, which is on the other side of Far).

In a way, but a limited way, these men had a point. However, by the measuring-stick of history, which is the recording of human behavior, their contention had no standing for the simple reason that force was lacking to back it up. From the cave-man to the instant hour, usage has hallowed the rule that to the victor belongs the spoils, and the primest spoils are women. Perhaps when the millennium has arrived, and the lamb is sharing an apartment with the lion, some changes will be made. In fact, we will know that that blessed age has arrived when the males of every species relinquish the pick of the females to the weaker individuals. But it has not yet arrived, and the victor, whether the war be of a military or of an economic nature, takes his pick of the females, or to be more accurate, the females pick *him*.

The men felt that this angle figured in the case, and it did to an extent, but nobody at all even hinted that there was any exchange of monies between Ruby McCollum and Dr. Adams. It was not that kind of an affair. But anyway, the scab of the age-old sore was scraped off and it oozed blood afresh.

"I'm glad that Ruby killed him. He ought to of been satisfied with his own women. But he had to keep on messing around until he got killed. Good enough for him."

"Yep, Ruby shot him lightly and he died politely. If Ruby comes clear of this, I aim to buy her a brand new gun."

Then somebody became conscious of my presence in the place and the talk was turned off like a faucet. A voice demanded stewed new peanuts. This was a dish that I had never heard of, but found that it was well known fare in the area, fresh-dug peanuts shelled and cooked with side-meat or ham-hock like any other pea. The owner of the café snorted that he didn't bother with no trashy grub like that.

Then a woman moaned, "Poor Ruby is going to get the 'lectric chair. I seen it in a dream last night. I seen her with her head all shaved."

"Nobody didn't tell me, but I heard that Ruby meant to kill Sam before she died."

"But she never kilt him. Appears to me like Sam just naturally scared hisself to death. You know how scared Sam was of White folks. He figured they might lynch him for what Ruby had done."

"Well, anyhow it was told to me that that wasn't none of Sam's gun she killed Dr. Adams with at all, 'cause Sam had done carried his gun out of the house more'n a week before the killing."

"Oh, you can hear anything except sinners praying for repentance. Let's squat that rabbit and jump another one."

"I help you to say! Some folks around here must have been raised on mockingbird eggs." (There is a folk belief that if a person eats a mockingbird egg, they can no longer keep a secret).

Vainly did I seek the witnesses for the Defense. There were none. Even the closest friends of the McCollums must have been persuaded that the risk was too great. The names of eight Negroes were added to the jury panel, seven of whom disqualified themselves as being friends of Dr. Adams. The eighth somehow seemed to have been overlooked until the jury box was filled.

All this indicates the climate of the Ruby McCollum trial outside of the Courthouse, and had bearing upon the trying of the case, or so it seemed to me.

From my seat in the balcony on the east side of the building, I could get a good view of the courtroom. It was clean and comfortable enough as courtrooms go. Provisions had been made for custom and comfort. Tobacco-chewing and snuff-dipping are common enough in the area not to be apologized for, so spittoons were handy in the official section. The Judge and jury had been taken care of that way.

The substantial building had evidently been constructed before drinking fountains were common in public places, so the janitor presently came up the center aisle toting a bucket of ice water and balanced it on the corner of the railing enclosing the court officers. One glance told me that a man had bought the outfit, for the bucket was white enamel with a red rim around the top, and the dipper was white enamel, but with a dark blue handle. A woman would have seen to it that they matched. The janitor passed the bucket and dipper around to the jury when he thought that they wanted a drink, and also to court officers, but White spectators could go up and get a drink if they wanted it.

I was in my seat as soon as the door was opened to spectators, a good hour before court set at ten o'clock. The main floor of the room began to fill immediately. The first to enter was four matrons. They took seat on the very front row. One brought a son about two years old. Another had her knitting along. A few rows back, a young woman had an infant child in her arms. It got to fretting and crying during a tense period in the trial and many people frowned at her, wondering why she did not take that fretting child out of there so they could hear better. When Judge Adams looked pointedly in her direction, she reluctantly rose and went out.

But long before court set, eyes kept going to the door behind the railing through which both Judge Adams and Ruby McCollum must eventually enter. Bring her in and let them have their pleasure of her. It was plain that none doubted the conclusion of the trial. The uprising was going to be put down. The emotion rose like a fume from the lower floor.

As the hour drew near, Judge Adams passed through the room from his office at the front of the building and exchanged pleasantries with friends in the audience and behind the rail. I could see that his presence was tantalizing, for everybody, including myself, was anxious for the business to begin. Visiting lawyers, including ex-Governor Caldwell occupied seats on the right of the platform inside the railing and passed off the time with chat.

A side drama relieved the tedium somewhat. A. K. Black, State's Attorney for Suwannee County was already there with the Assistant State's Attorney, O. O. Edwards. Naturally they were attracting much interest on the occasion. Black is a short, plump man in a rumpled blue suit and with a bald spot on top of his head so perfectly round that it might be the tonsure of a monk. He is not impressive in appearance, but a Negro seated behind me murmured, "Don't let that sleepy look fool you. He's just playing possum. He's going to get Ruby unlessen her lawyer watches out right smart. That Black is a 'getting fool.' I done seen him at it."

O. O. Edwards did little greeting and mixing around. He appeared to be preoccupied, not to say dedicated, and his look was grim.

Into this scene and setting Frank T. Cannon made his entrance, and I mean entrance. You could hear people commoting around him as he came through the door. Cannon, Solicitor for the Court of Record of Duval County, (Jacksonville) was Ruby McCollum's new lawyer, replacing the recently disbarred P. Guy Crews. There were three more additions to this item. First, Frank Cannon had been born and raised in the vicinity of Live Oak. Therefore, he was being honored as a home boy who had matched his wits with the lawyers in the big city and made his mark. Then the looks of the man. Cannon is possessed of a challenging head of thick, wavy hair, an extra-handsome profile, becoming suntan, tall graceful body clothed in raiment of good taste and good quality. Then the man has what is known in the theatre as stage presence. Something exudes from him and grabs hold of the audience. So smiling voices called out to Cannon, and hands were extended. He was a one man procession down the aisle. He had stolen the scene from the prosecutor.

Perhaps in this commotion, I was the only one who looked to see what effect this had on his legal opposition. Edwards registered nothing, but I caught a brief look on the face of Black, that if that look had been a bullet, it would have worked Cannon three times before it killed him and five times afterwards. Nor, was I mistaken in my interpretation of it, for after the trial began, it came out that Black had not only attempted to have Cannon barred from the case, but Cannon publicly accused him of also trying to have him run out of town. A free translation of the reaction of Black to Cannon's sudden entrance into the case read that Cannon, being who he was, had probably had things pretty much his way around

Live Oak before he moved to Jacksonville to seize his share of success and glory there, and now, when this sensational case gave Black his chance at the center of the stage with national publicity, here comes that handsome, wavy-haired fool to hog the spotlight. Black had behaved little, but human. That is my impression of the incident.

Court set at last, and Ruby McCollum was led in by a State Trooper. Then the place came really alive. I could tell that she had been given the opportunity to groom herself with more care this time. Her hair was pressed and hung in a long bob to her shoulders, but confined loosely by a net. It was parted on the left side neatly, and being December, she had on a coat, a camelshair coat bright green in color over a pale yellow wool dress. Her small feet were encased in low-heeled black pumps. She is small, and looked almost childish in her seat.

She had walked in briskly with an expressionless face. She looked neither to right nor left as she moved to the Defense table and took her seat beside Cannon.

In the course of the two sanity hearings, the balked first trial, and the real trial, I have striven to enclose my impression of Ruby McCollum in a sentence, but failed. As to her physical appearance, I would say that she is attractive, but not beautiful. A sort of chestnut brown in color, with the breadth of face I think of as feline, though there was nothing sly or calculating in it that I could discern. Even under her terrible strain, she appeared to be possessed of dignity. As before, she seemed to set herself as she took her seat in a resolved position. Her right elbow rested on the arm of the chair, and her head resting on her hand, lightly inclined to the right. I did have the impression that every muscle of her body was consciously set and locked in place as she sat lest they betray her disturbed condition. The only sign of nervous strain that she exhibited was an occasional swinging of her crossed feet. Again, she would extend her right hand at full length and examine it in minute detail. Flex and extend the fingers and look at them very studiously; turn it and examine palm and back as if it were something new and interesting to her. Since it was the hand which had wielded the gun on Dr. Adams, I could fancy that she might be regarding it as having a separate existence, a life and will of its own and had acted without her knowledge or consent.

There was one poignant, one heart-rending scene while Ruby was on the stand. She maintained her shut-in, expressionless mask through the questioning by State and her own counsel until one could say that Ruby McCollum was a woman without nerves until that time, as Cannon led her through her story to the moment of the actual slaying. Ruby did not break down and weep piteously; she did not scream out in agony of memory with her voice, but there was an abrupt halt in her testimony and something rushed forth from the depths of her tortured soul and inhabited her face for a space. The quintessence of human agony was there. I witnessed momentarily the anguish of the hours, perhaps the days and weeks which preceded the slaying on August third, the indescribable emotions of the resolve to slay, to blot out from the world that which she had come to know and which tightened her hand upon the gun, and the memories of it all which lived down deep in the barred cavities in the cellar of her soul with an eternal life which she could bestow but could not take away. What I beheld in the eyes of Ruby McCollum in that instant when she balked into silence, when the agony of her memories robbed her of the power of speech for a time, may God be kind and never permit me to behold again. In a flash, I comprehended the spacial infinity of the human mind, that mother of monsters and angels, and the ineffable glory and unspeakable horror of its creations.

That illuminated minute was the hub and life of the trial for me. It gave sense and meaning to all that had gone before and everything that could possibly follow. Now, I could discern that what was going on the courtroom was nothing more than a mask, and that the real action existed on the other side of silence. The defendant had freely admitted the slaying of Dr. Adams. She was in the hands of the law, and therefore, there was no reason for the legal machinery of Suwannee County and the State of Florida to be operating here on the case except to fix the degree of the guilt of Ruby McCollum.

Yet, thirty-eight times Frank T. Cannon had attempted to create opportunity for the defendant to tell her story and thus throw light on her motives, and thirty-eight times the State had objected, and thirty-eight times Judge Adams had sustained these objections. My faith was in Judge Adams, and after that terrible minute, I looked at him confidently and said, almost audibly, no, Judge Adams will never allow this. He will never consent for any human being to be sent to their death without permitting the jury to hear their side of the story. He won't! Judge Adams won't! It was only when he exhibited anger and threatened Cannon with contempt of court if he persisted, that I wilted back, first in my soul and then in my seat. My disillusionment was terrible. My faith had been so strong. Cannon's words, uttered with tragic resignation, "May God forgive you

158
· · ·
Appendix

for robbing a human being of life in such a fashion. I would not want it on my conscience," screamed in my consciousness.

But race had nothing to do with me. Had Judge Adams been as black as Marcus Garvey, and Ruby McCollum as fair as the lily-maid of Astolat, still I would have felt the same. And my discomfort increased when I then recalled that A. K. Black and Dr. C. LeRoy Adams were on the most intimate terms, and so it was hardly possible that he did not know all that Ruby had to tell already. He made no denial when Cannon charged directly, "And nobody knows this any better than the State" (Black).

This impression was deepened when Thelma Curry, the late Dr. Adams' colored receptionist was called to the stand as a prosecution witness. Things went on very well until she tried to tell about a quarrel she overheard between Dr. Adams and Ruby a few days before the slaying. Immediately she was recalled from the stand by Edwards, and Adams added his bit by telling her, "Get down and go back where you came from!" Nor had she been allowed to tell what she knew about the letter.

That letter! It is still my impression and will ever be that the motive for the killing was in that letter. The State based its whole case on that letter, maintaining that it was nothing more than a monthly medical bill for $116 and that Ruby shot Dr. Adams four times rather than pay it. Still this letter was never introduced into evidence by the State. This added to my mounting feeling of horror. I could not avoid the conclusion that the omission had purpose, and that purpose was sinister. Therefore, I lacked the feel of solemnity I should have felt when Ruby stood and was sentenced to death by Judge Hal Adams. And her statement when she was asked if she had anything to say and she said simply, "I do not know whether I did right or not when I killed Dr. Adams" held a mountain of meaning for me.

I sum up my impressions of the trial of Ruby McCollum for the murder of C. LeRoy Adams in the clearest way I know how, now. It was as if I walked in a dream, somebody else's dream, of fog and mist with occasional heavy drops of cold rain. Somewhere beyond me, and hidden from me by the enshrouding mists, the tremendous action of this drama of Ruby McCollum and Dr. Adams, and the actors in the trial went on. It was behind a sort of curtain, on the other side of silence.

Works Cited

Adams, C. LeRoy. "To the Voters of the 17th Senatorial District." *Suwannee Democrat* (Live Oak), April 11, 1952.

———. "To the Voters of the 17th Senatorial District." *Suwannee Democrat* (Live Oak), April 18, 1952.

———. "To the Voters of the 17th Senatorial District." *Suwannee Democrat* (Live Oak), April 25, 1952.

Angwin, Julia. "After the Cataclysm, Americans Grope for the Words to Describe 'It.'" *Wall Street Journal*, October 3, 2001.

Anonymous note. Typescript. Box 31, folder 277. William Bradford Huie Papers, Ohio State University, Columbus.

"Attorney Asks Court to Not Try Ruby McCollum in County." *Suwannee Democrat* (Live Oak), August 22, 1952.

Berlin, James. "Revisionary History: The Dialectical Method." In *Rethinking the History of Rhetoric: Multidisciplinary Essays on the Rhetorical Tradition*, edited by Takis Poulakos, 134–51. Boulder: Westview Press, 1993.

Boyd, Valerie. *Wrapped in Rainbows: The Life of Zora Neale Hurston*. New York: Scribner, 2003.

Brantlinger, Patrick. "Antitheory and Its Antitheses: Rhetoric and Ideology." In *At the Intersection: Cultural Studies and Rhetorical Studies*, edited by Thomas Rosteck, 292–312. New York: Guilford Press, 1999.

Brison, Susan J. "Trauma Narratives and the Remaking of the Self." In *Acts of Memory: Cultural Recall in the Present*, edited by Mieke Bal, Jonathan Crewe, and Leo Spitzer, 39–54. Hanover: University Press of New England, 1999.

Bullard, Alice. "The Truth in Madness: Colonial Doctors and Insane Women in French North Africa." In *Being Global: From the Enlightenment to the Age of Information*, edited by Mita Choudbury, special issue, *South Atlantic Review* 66, no. 2 (2001): 114–32.

Burke, Kenneth. "The Five Key Terms of Dramatism." Introduction to *A Grammar of Motives*, by Burke. 1945. Berkeley and Los Angeles: University of California Press, 1969.

Carby, Hazel. "'On the Threshold of Woman's Era': Lynching, Empire, and Sexuality in Black Feminist Theory." In *"Race," Writing, and Difference*, edited by Henry Louis Gates Jr., 301–16. Chicago: University of Chicago Press, 1985.

Cash, W. F. *The Mind of the South*. New York: Alfred A. Knopf, 1941.

Chafin, Kenneth. Foreword to *In the Name of the Father: The Rhetoric of the New Southern Baptist Convention*, by Carl L. Kell and L. Raymond Camp, xi–xv. Carbondale: Southern Illinois University Press, 1999.

Chun, Wendy Hui Kyong. "Unbearable Witness: Toward a Politics of Listening." *Differences: A Journal of Feminist Cultural Studies* 11 (1999): 112–49.

Cixous, Hélène. "The Laugh of the Medusa." *Signs: Journal of Women in Culture and Society* 1 (1976): 875–93.

Clay, Revella, and A. M. Rivera Jr. "Will Ruby Talk at Trial?" *Pittsburgh Courier*, September 20, 1952.

Collins, LeRoy. Letter to William Bradford Huie. Box 31, folder 277. William Bradford Huie Papers, Ohio State University, Columbus.

———. Telegram to William Bradford Huie. Box 31, folder 277. William Bradford Huie Papers, Ohio State University, Columbus.

Condit, Celeste Michelle. "The Character of 'History' in Rhetoric and Cultural Studies: Recoding Genetics." In *At the Intersection: Cultural Studies and Rhetorical Studies*, edited by Thomas Rosteck, 168–85. New York: Guilford Press, 1999.

Crews, Harry. *A Childhood: The Biography of a Place*. 1978. In *Classic Crews: A Harry Crews Reader*, 17–170. New York: Simon and Schuster, 1995.

"Don't Believe Rumors Wait for Facts." *Suwannee Democrat* (Live Oak), August 8, 1952.

"Dr. Adams Slain by Negress." *Suwannee Democrat* (Live Oak), August 8, 1952.

Ellis, Arthur. E-mail to the author. December 24, 2003.

———. *The Trial of Ruby McCollum: The True-Crime Story That Shook the Foundations of the Segregationist South*. Bloomington: 1stBooks, 2003.

Felman, Shoshana, and Dori Laub. *Testimony: Crises of Witnesses in Literature, Psychoanalysis, and History*. New York: Routledge, 1992.

Foucault, Michel. *Discipline and Punish: The Birth of the Prison*. Translated by Alan M. Sheridan Smith. London: Lane, 1977.

———. Preface to *Madness and Civilization: A History of Insanity in the Age of Reason*, by Foucault, translated by Richard Howard, v–vii. New York: Vintage, 1965.

"A Friend, a Leader Is Lost in Dr. C. LeRoy Adams." Editorial. *Suwannee Democrat* (Live Oak), August 8, 1952.

Gates, Henry Louis, Jr., and Sieglinde Lemke. Introduction to *Zora Neale Hurston: The Complete Stories*, ix–xxiii. New York: Harper Perennial Publishers, 1995.

Gilbert, Sandra M., and Susan Gubar. *The Madwoman in the Attic: The Woman Writer and the Nineteenth-Century Literary Imagination*. New Haven: Yale University Press, 1979.

Ginzburg, Carlo. "Microhistory: Two or Three Things That I Know about It." *Critical Inquiry* 20 (1993): 10–35.

Glenn, Cheryl. Preface to *Unspoken: A Rhetoric of Silence*, by Glenn, xi–xiii. Carbondale: Southern Illinois University Press, 2004.

———. "Silence: A Rhetorical Art for Resisting Discipline(s)." *JAC* 22, no. 2 (2002): 261–91.

Goffard, Christopher. "53 Years Later, State Seeks Closure on Hero's Death." *St. Petersburg Times*, December 26, 2004.

Green, Ben. *Before His Time: The Untold Story of Harry T. Moore, America's First Civil Rights Martyr*. 1999. Gainesville: University Press of Florida, 2005.

Griffin, Larry. "Why Was the South a Problem to America?" In *The South as an American Problem*, edited by Larry J. Griffin and Don H. Doyle, 10–32. Athens: University of Georgia Press, 1995.

Halberstam, David. *The Fifties*. New York: Fawcett–Random House Publishing, 1993.

Harper, Jack. "News of Famous Killing First Heard from Pulpit." *Tallahassee Democrat*, November 28, 1973.

Hobson, Fred. *Tell about the South: The Southern Rage to Explain*. Baton Rouge: Louisiana State University Press, 1983.

Holland, Spessard. Letter to Thurgood Marshall. February 14, 1944. In *Papers of the NAACP*, edited by Martin Paul Schipper, part 7, reel 25 0501. Library of Congress, Washington, D.C.

Huie, Martha Hunt. Interview with the author. Ohio State University, Columbus. June 8–9, 2005.

Huie, William Bradford. Research. Typescript. Box 31, folder 276. William Bradford Huie Papers, Ohio State University, Columbus.

———. *Ruby McCollum: Woman in the Suwannee Jail*. New York: E. P. Dutton, 1956; rev. ed. New York: Signet, 1964.

———. "The Strange Case of Ruby McCollum." *Ebony*, November 1954, 16–28.

Hundley, Daniel R. *Social Relations in Our Southern States*. 1860. Baton Rouge: Louisiana State University Press, 1979.

Hurston, Zora Neale. "The Life Story of Mrs. Ruby J. McCollum." *Pittsburgh Courier*, installment 1, February 28, 1953.

———. "The Life Story of Mrs. Ruby J. McCollum." *Pittsburgh Courier*, installment 2, March 7 1953.

———. "The Life Story of Mrs. Ruby J. McCollum." *Pittsburgh Courier*, installment 7, April 11, 1953.

———. "My Impressions of the Trial." Typescript. Box 31, folder 281. William Bradford Huie Papers, Ohio State University, Columbus.

———. "Ruby McCollum: Impressions Gained As I Watched and Listened at Her Trial." Typescript. Box 31, folder 279. William Bradford Huie Papers, Ohio State University, Columbus.

———. *Mules and Men*. 1935. New York: Negro Universities Press, 1969.

———. "Ruby McCollum Fights for Life." *Pittsburgh Courier*, November 22, 1952.

———. "Ruby Sane!" *Pittsburgh Courier*, October 18, 1952.

———. *Their Eyes Were Watching God*. 1937. New York: Harper Perennial Publishers, 1990.

———. "Zora's Revealing Story of Ruby's First Day in Court." *Pittsburgh Courier*, November 4, 1952.

"Is Ruby Sane?" *Pittsburgh Courier*, May 9, 1953.

Jackson, Matt. Letters. Box 8, folder 64. William Bradford Huie Papers, Ohio State University, Columbus.

Johnson, Barbara. "Thresholds of Difference: Structures of Address in Zora Neale Hurston." *Critical Inquiry* 12, no. 1 (1985): 278–89.

Jones, Anne Goodwyn. "The Work of Gender in the Southern Renaissance." In *Southern Writers and Their Worlds*, edited by Christopher Morris and Steven G. Reinhardt, 41–56. College Station: Texas A&M University Press, 1996.

"Judge Hal Adams Is Guest Speaker at Meeting of Live Oak Woman's Club on Friday." *Suwannee Democrat* (Live Oak), January 14, 1944.

Kaplan, Carla, comp. and ed. *Zora Neale Hurston: A Life in Letters*. 2002. New York: Anchor Books, 2003.

Kell, Carl L., and L. Raymond Camp. *In the Name of the Father: The Rhetoric of the New Southern Baptist Convention*. Carbondale: Southern Illinois University Press, 1999.

Lalonde, Michelle. "Students' Silence Part of Debate over Killings." *Globe and Mail*, December 4, 1990.

Lee, Al. "Lawyer Tries to Free Woman from Institution after 20 Years." *Tampa Tribune*, October 26, 1973.

———. "Memory of Murder Fades After 28 Years." *Ocala Star-Banner*, January 13, 1980.

———. "No Animosity Against Ruby." *Ocala Star-Banner*, January 14, 1980.

Letter from Lake City Resident to Huie. April 15, 1970. Box 8, folder 64. William Bradford Huie Papers, Ohio State University, Columbus.

Levin, C. A. "Ruby Fires 3 Lawyers!" *Pittsburgh Courier*, May 16, 1953.

"Living in State of Fear." *Pittsburgh Courier*, May 2, 1953.

MacKethan, Lucinda H. "Hurston, Zora Neale." In *The Companion to Southern Literature: Themes, Genres, Places, People, Movements, and Motifs*, edited by Joseph M. Flora and Lucinda H. MacKethan, 363–64. Baton Rouge: Louisiana State University Press, 2002.

"McCollum Jury to Be Picked." *Suwannee Democrat* (Live Oak), December 12, 1952.

McCollum, Ruby. Letters to William Bradford Huie. Box 31, folder 277. William Bradford Huie Papers, Ohio State University, Columbus.

———. Notes to Attorneys and William Bradford Huie. Box 31, folder 274. William Bradford Huie Papers, Ohio State University, Columbus.

———. Recantation Letter. Box 31, folder 277. William Bradford Huie Papers, Ohio State University, Columbus.

"McCollum Trial Is Recessed." *Suwannee Democrat* (Live Oak), September 3, 1954.

McIver, Stewart B. "'Neath Swaying Palms." Introduction to *Murder in the Tropics*, by McIver, ix–xii. The Florida Chronicles, vol. 2. Sarasota: Pineapple Press, 1995.

McKerrow, Raymie. "Critical Rhetoric: Theory and Praxis." In *Contemporary Rhetorical Theory: A Reader*, edited by John Lucaites, Michelle Condit, and Sally Caudill, 441–63. New York: Guilford, 1999.

Milbank, Dana. "Curtains Ordered for Media Coverage of Returning Coffins." *Washington Post*, October 21, 2003.

Miller, J. Hillis. "Narrative." In *Critical Terms for Literary Study*, 2nd ed., edited by Frank Lentricchia and Thomas McLaughlin, 66–79. Chicago: University of Chicago Press, 1995.

Moore, Harry T. Letter to Roy Wilkins. March 25, 1944. In *Papers of the NAACP II*. A 408. Library of Congress, Washington, D.C.

———. Letter to Thurgood Marshall. June 30, 1944. In *Papers of the NAACP II*. A 408. Library of Congress, Washington, D.C.

Morrison, Toni. "The Site of Memory." In *Inventing the Truth: The Art and Craft of Memoir*, edited by William Zinsser, 183–200. Boston: Houghton Mifflin, 1998.

Nelson, Cary. "The Linguisticality of Cultural Studies: Rhetoric, Close Reading, and Contextualization." In *At the Intersection: Cultural Studies and Rhetorical Studies*, edited by Thomas Rosteck, 211–25. New York: Guilford Press, 1999.

Nicki, Andrea. "The Abused Mind: Feminist Theory, Psychiatric Disability, and Trauma." *Hypatia* 16, no. 4 (2001): 80–104.

Park, Edith. Letters to William Bradford Huie. Typescript. Box 31, folder 277. William Bradford Huie Papers, Ohio State University, Columbus.

———. Sworn Statement. Typescript. Box 31, folder 276. William Bradford Huie Papers, Ohio State University, Columbus.

Peckham, Joel. "Segregation/Integration: Race, History, and Theoretical Practice in the American South." *Southern Quarterly* 40, no. 1 (2001): 28–38.

Peter, Emmett, Jr. "Suwannee County in Grips of Bolita; Sheriff Says He Can't Act Against It." *Tampa Morning Tribune*, January 24, 1952.

"Psychiatric Evaluation." Typescript. Box 31, folder 284. William Bradford Huie Papers, Ohio State University, Columbus.

Report of Committee Finding Incompetency. January 11, 1955. Typescript. Box 31, folder 284. William Bradford Huie Papers, Ohio State University, Columbus.

Rich, Adrienne. *Blood, Bread, and Poetry: Selected Prose 1979–1985*. New York: W. W. Norton, 1986.

Rivera, A. M., Jr. "Chill Anxiety Grips Race Where Matron Shot Medic in Florida." *Pittsburgh Courier*, October 4, 1952.

————. "Judge Won't Let Ruby Talk." *Pittsburgh Courier*, September 27, 1952.

Romine, Scott. "Framing Southern Rhetoric: Lillian Smith's Narrative Persona in *Killers of the Dream.*" *South Atlantic Review* 59, no. 2 (1994): 95–111.

Royster, Jacqueline Jones. *Traces of a Stream: Literacy and Social Change among African American Women*. Pittsburgh: University of Pittsburgh Press, 2000.

"Ruby Found Guilty of Murder." *Suwannee Democrat* (Live Oak), December 19. 1952.

"Ruby McCollum Murder Trial Reconvenes Friday." *Suwannee Democrat* (Live Oak), September 17, 1954.

"Ruby McCollum to Be Tried in Suwannee September 29." *Suwannee Democrat* (Live Oak), September 5, 1952.

Ruby McCollum v. State of Florida. Typescript. Box 31, folder 283. William Bradford Huie Papers, Ohio State University, Columbus.

Searle, John R. "How Performatives Work." In *Essays in Speech Act Theory*, edited by Daniel Vanderveken and Susumu Kubo, 85–107. Amsterdam: Benjamins, 2002.

Sebring, Howard L. Supreme Court of Florida, *En Banc. McCollum v. State.* (Available at Westlaw 74 So. 2d 74.)

Signed Statement. Typescript. In *Papers of the NAACP*, edited by Martin Paul Schipper, part 7, reel 25 0479. Library of Congress, Washington, D.C.

"Slayer's Husband Dies in Ocala." *Suwannee Democrat* (Live Oak), August 8, 1952.

Smith, Lillian. *Killers of the Dream*. 1949. New York: W. W. Norton, 1994.

State of Florida v. Ruby McCollum. Typescript. Box 31, folder 282. William Bradford Huie Papers, Ohio State University, Columbus.

Sturken, Marita. "Narratives of Recovery: Repressed Memory as Cultural Memory." In *Acts of Memory: Cultural Recall in the Present*, edited by Mieke Bal, Jonathan Crewe, and Leo Spitzer, 231–48. Hanover: University Press of New England, 1999.

Summers, Alvis. Interview with the author. November 10, 2003.

Suntrust Bank v. Houghton Mifflin. No. 1:01 cv-701. District Court for the Northern District of Georgia. March 16, 2001.

"Suspension Blows Trial Sky High." *Suwannee Democrat* (Live Oak), November 21, 1952.

Suwannee Democrat editor. Letter to William Bradford Huie. Box 31 folder 277. William Bradford Huie Papers, Ohio State University, Columbus.

Thakur, Shivesh C. *Religion and Social Justice*. New York: St. Martin, 1996.

"Thousands at Beloved Doctor's Funeral Rites." *Suwannee Democrat* (Live Oak), August 8, 1952.

Trumbull, Stephen. "Live Oak Drama Like Fiction." *Miami Herald*, March 21, 1954.

"Truth about War Casualties." Editorial. *USA Today*, October 23, 2003.

Tucker, Cynthia. "GWTW Richly Deserves Parody by Black Writer." *Atlanta Journal-Constitution*, May 27, 2001.

Tucker, Susan. Preface to *Telling Memories among Southern Women: Domestic Workers and Their Employers in the Segregated South*, by Tucker, 1–12. Baton Rouge: Louisiana State University Press, 1988.

van Alphen, Ernst. "Symptoms of Discursivity: Experience, Memory, and Trauma." In *Acts of Memory: Cultural Recall in the Present*, edited by Mieke Bal, Jonathan Crewe, and Leo Spitzer, 24–38. Hanover: University Press of New England, 1999.

van Buren, Paul M. *The Edges of Language: An Essay in the Logic of a Religion*. New York: Macmillan, 1972.

White, Hayden. "The Poetics of History." Introduction to *Metahistory: The Historical Imagination in Nineteenth-Century Europe*, by White, 1–43. Baltimore: Johns Hopkins University Press, 1973.

Wilkinson, Daniel. *Silence on the Mountain: Stories of Terror, Betrayal, and Forgetting in Guatemala*. New York: Houghton Mifflin, 2002.

"Writer William Bradford Huie Subpoenaed for Court Contempt." *Suwannee Democrat* (Live Oak), October 1, 1954.

Yaeger, Patricia. *Dirt and Desire: Reconstructing Southern Women's Writing, 1930–1990*. Chicago: University of Chicago Press, 2000.

"Yes, Bolita Is Still Being Sold." *Suwannee Democrat* (Live Oak), April 18, 1952.

Zoroya, Gregg. "Return of U.S. War Dead Kept Solemn, Secret." *USA Today*, December 31, 2003.

Index

· ·

Tammy Evans is a part-time lecturer at the University of Miami at IMG Academies. Areas of special interest include southern studies, cultural studies, and rhetorical theory.